MW01622145

ART JOURNEY AMERICA ❧ LANDSCAPES

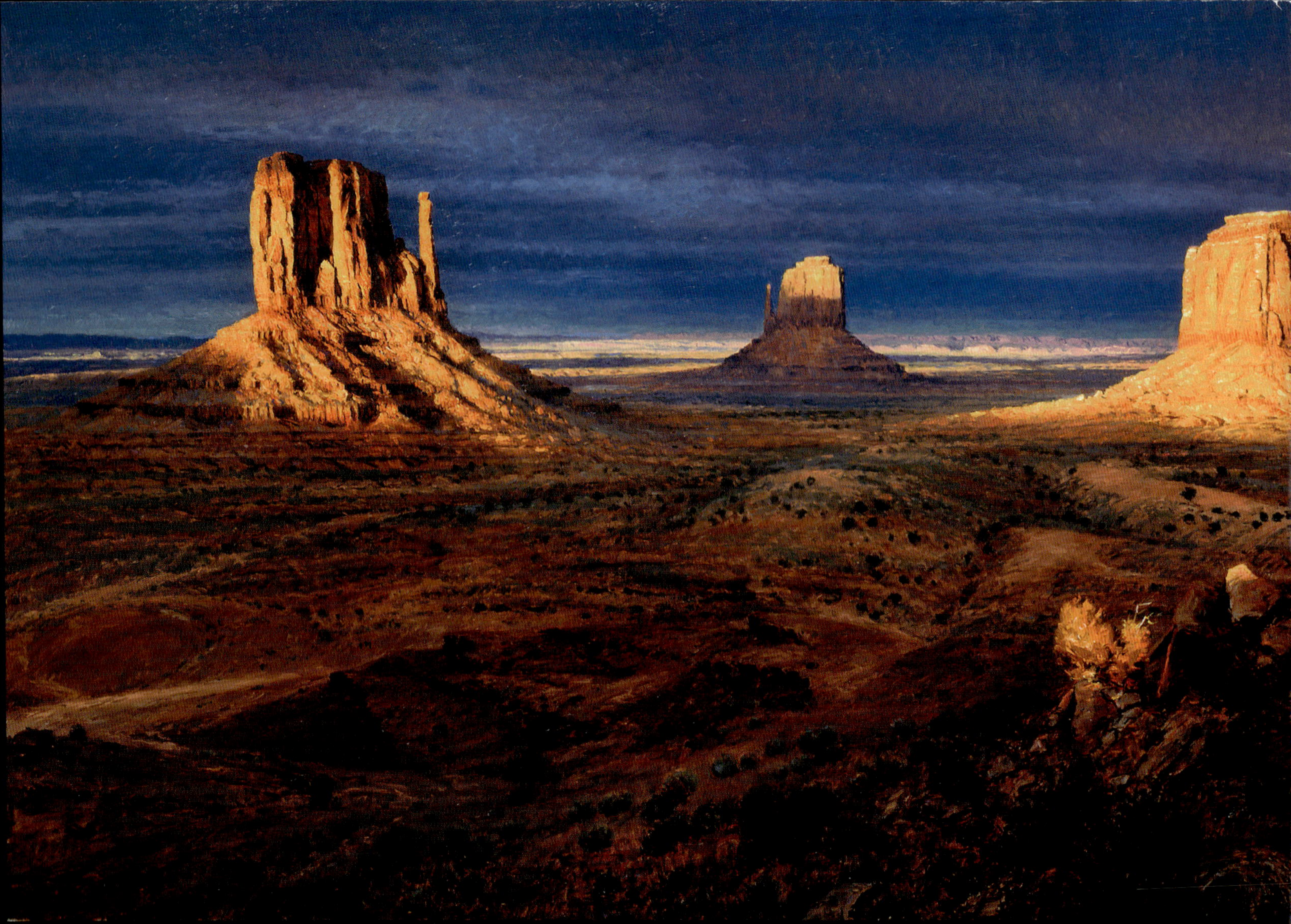

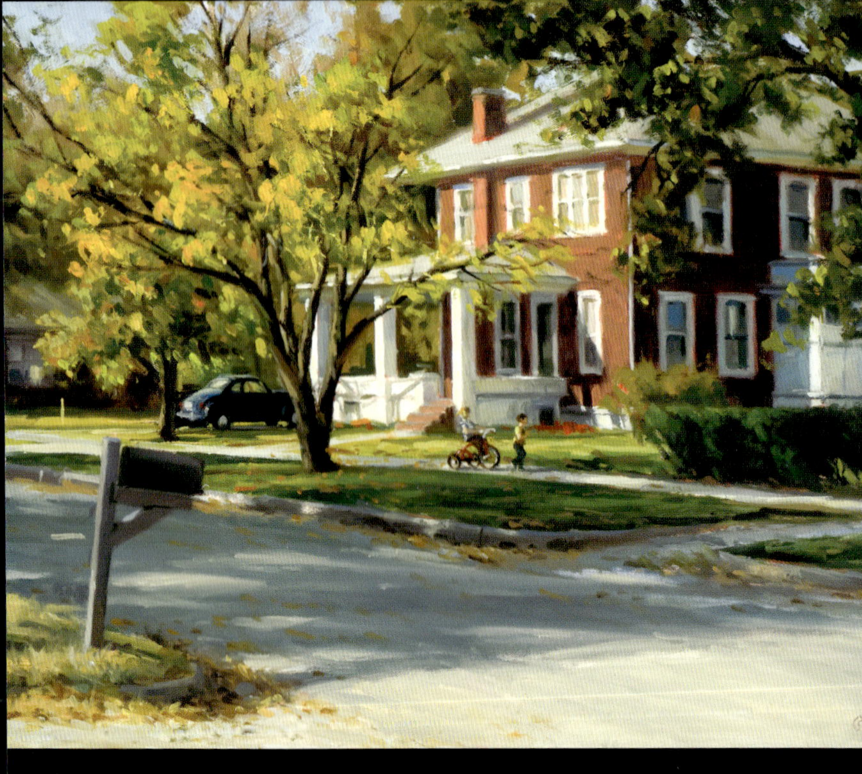
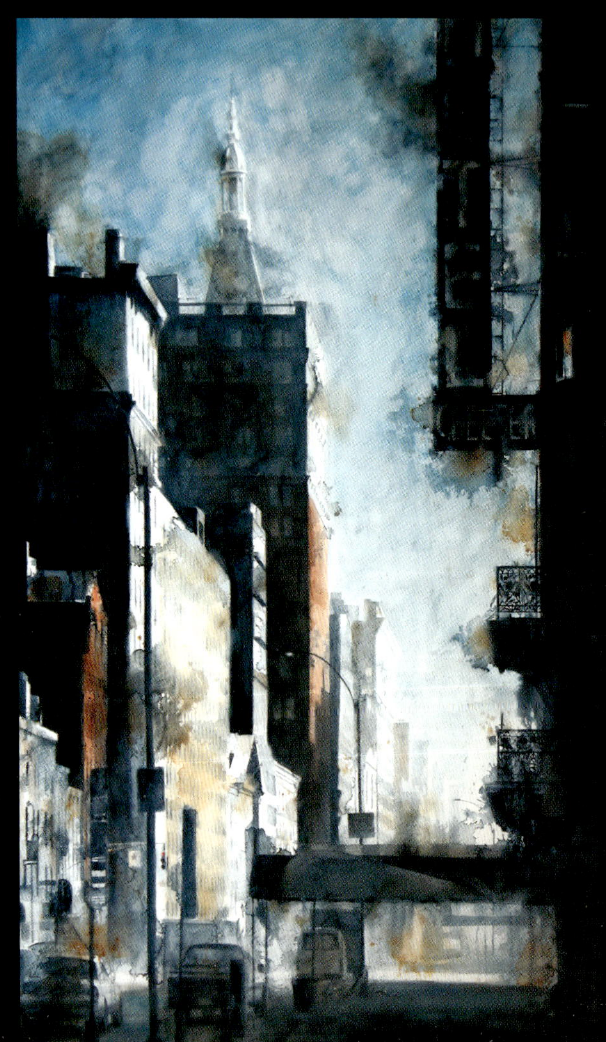
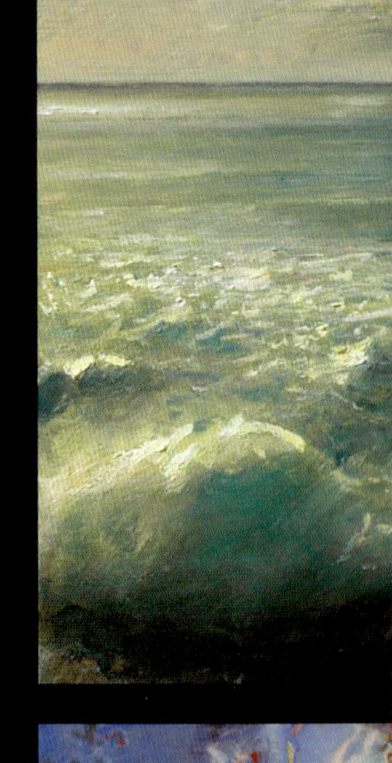
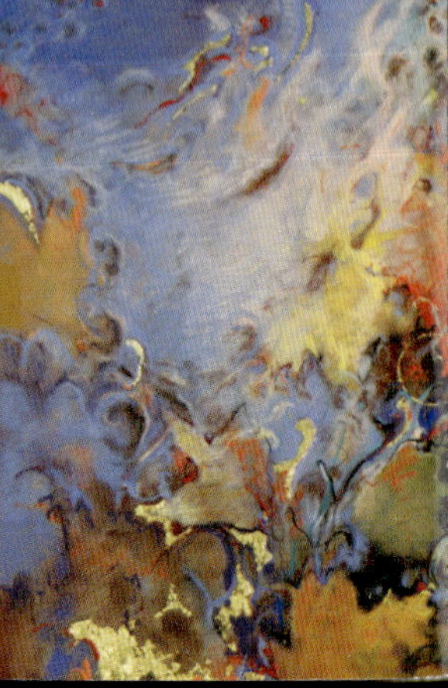

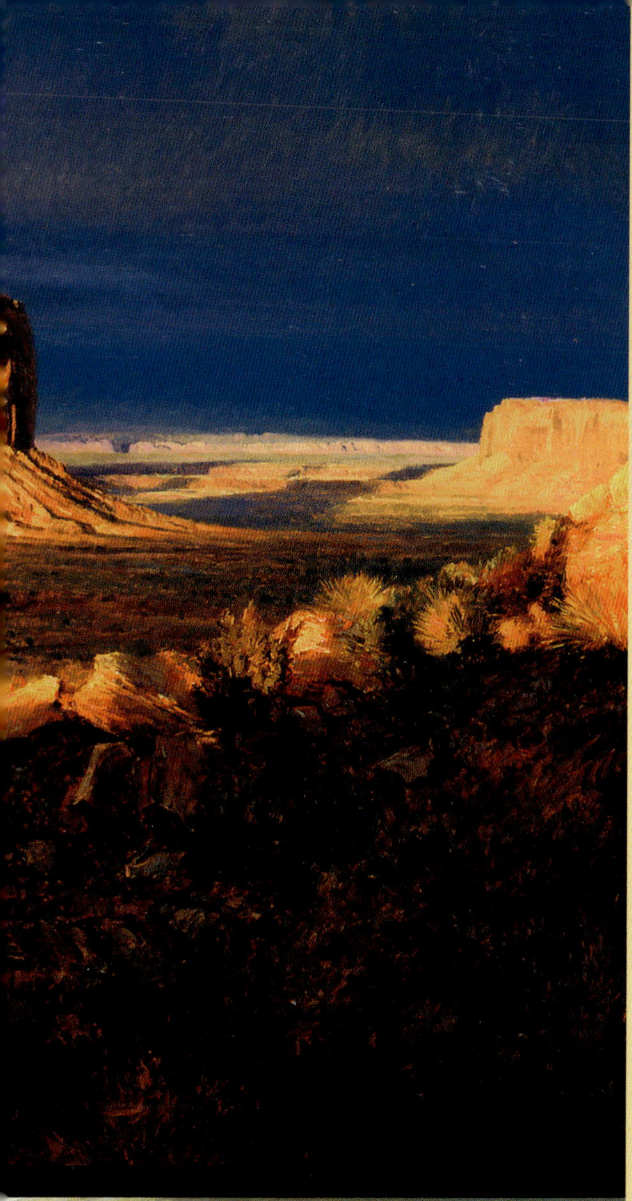

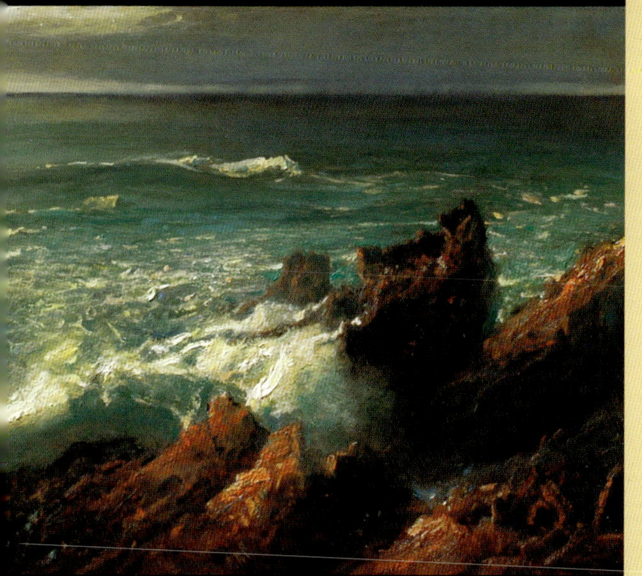

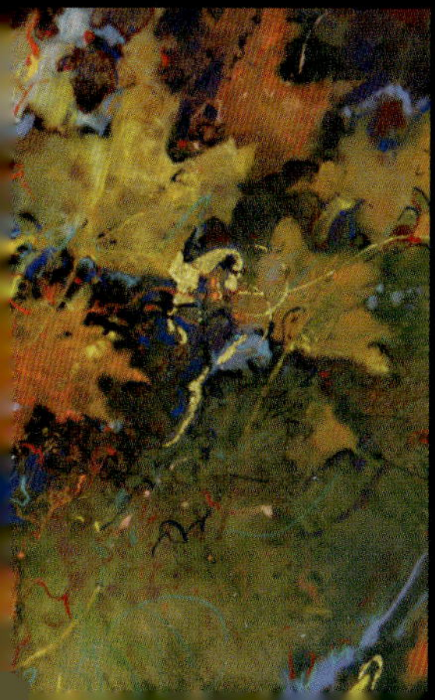

art journey america

LANDSCAPES

89 PAINTERS' PERSPECTIVES

Edited by *Kathryn Kipp*

NORTH LIGHT BOOKS
CINCINNATI, OHIO
www.artistsnetwork.com

CONTENTS

Foreword by Maureen Bloomfield, editor, *The Artist's Magazine* 6

THE ARTISTS

Scott Lloyd Anderson 8
Douglas Atwill 10
Robert L. Barnum 12
William Berra 14
Gordon Brown 16
Nancy Bush 18
Cole Carothers 20
Arthur Chartow 22
Arturo Chávez 24
Lorenzo Chavez 26
Len Chmiel 28
Brian Cobble 30
Gil Dellinger 32
Dennis Doheny 34
David Drummond 36
Joellyn Duesberry 38
Kathleen Dunphy 40
Sterling Edwards 42
Sy Ellens 44
Josh Elliott 46
Max Ferguson 48
Peter Fiore 50
Alan Flattmann 52
Terri Ford 54
Alyce Frank 56
Jonathan Frank 58
Guido Frick 60
Jon R. Friedman 62
Grant Fuller 64
Catherine Gill 66
Michael Godfrey 68
Walt Gonske 70
Mark Gould 72
Hugh Greer 74
Lisa Grossman 76
Albert Handell 78
Liz Haywood-Sullivan 80
Joyce Hicks 82
Robert Highsmith 84
William Hook 86
William Hosner 88
Cindy House 90
Colleen Howe 92
Rod S. Hubble 94
M. Katherine Hurley 96
Ann Huston 98
Margie Kuhn 100
Donna Levinstone 102
Dennis Liberty 104
Kim Lordier 106

Kevin Macpherson 108
Stanley Maltzman 110
Richard McDaniel 112
Richard McKinley 114
Mark Mehaffey 116
Jay Moore 118
Elizabeth Mowry 120
Paul Murray 122
P. A. Nisbet 124
Bruce Peil 126
Tom Perkinson 128
Andrew Peters 130
Julie Gilbert Pollard 132
John Pototschnik 134
Maggie Price 136
Stephen Quiller 138
Don Rantz 140
David Rothermel 142
John Salminen 144
Ed Sandoval 146
Tim Saternow 148
Aaron Schuerr 150
Frank Serrano 152
Valerie Shesko 154
Fred Somers 156
George Strickland 158
Lauren Tilden 160
James Toogood 162
Clive R. Tyler 164
Karen Vance 166
Curt Walters 168
Eric Wiegardt 170
Teruko T. Wilde 172
Don Williams 174
Douglas Wiltraut 176
Michael Workman 178
Dinah K. Worman 180
Keiko Yasuoka & Duncan Simmons 182

Artist Listings 184
Gallery Listings 187
Index 191

Bonus Materials

Enjoy more beautiful landscape paintings by several of these artists at ArtistsNetwork.com/Art-Journey-America

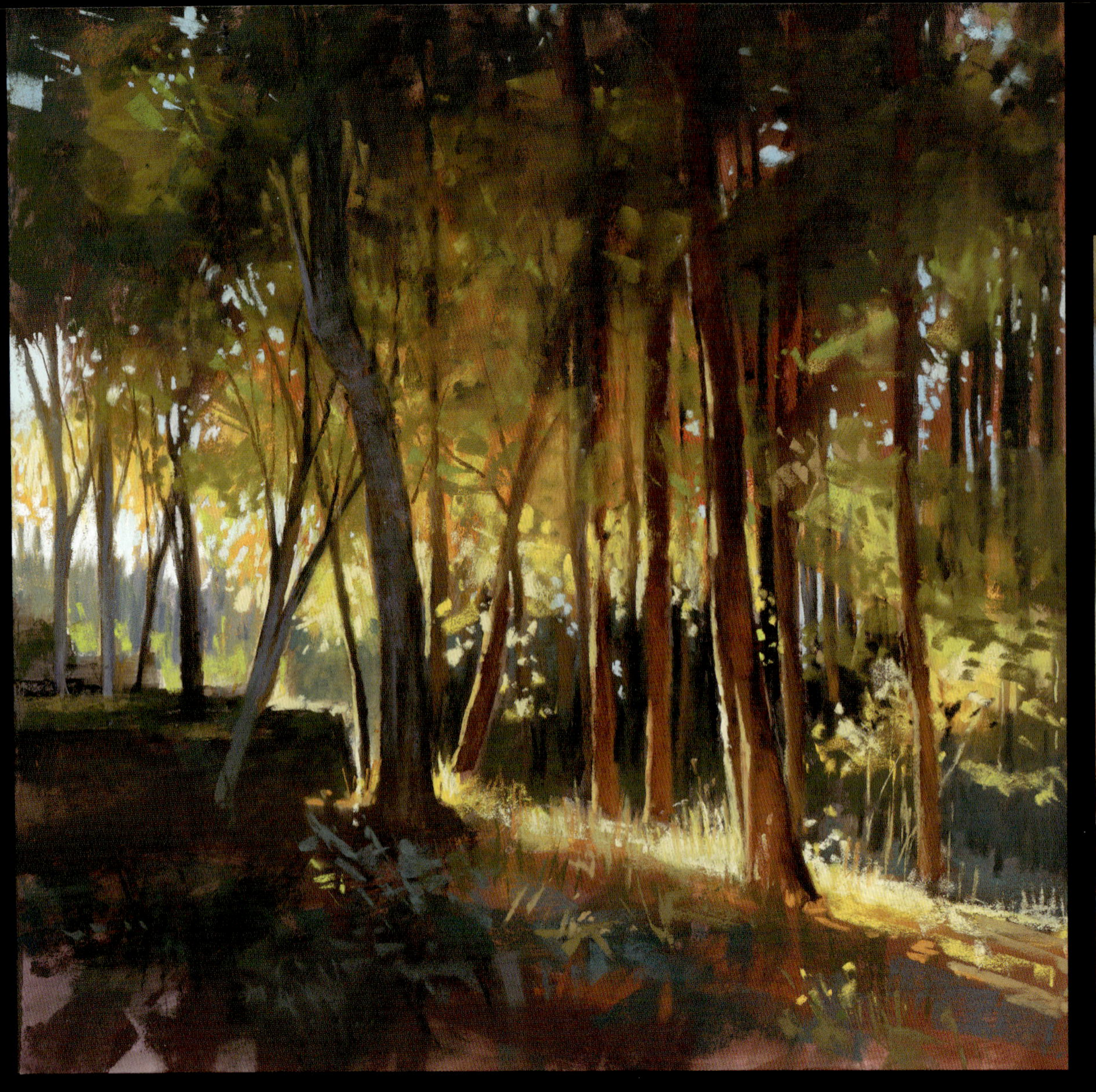

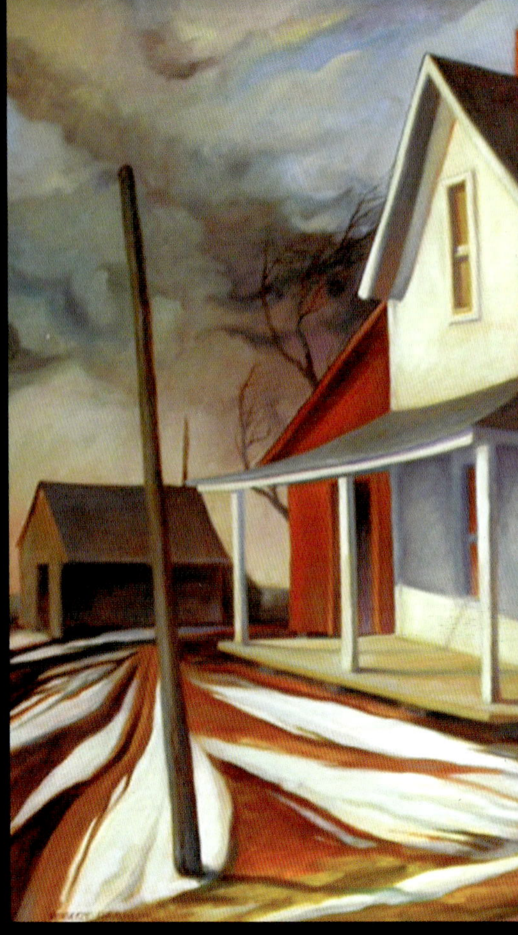

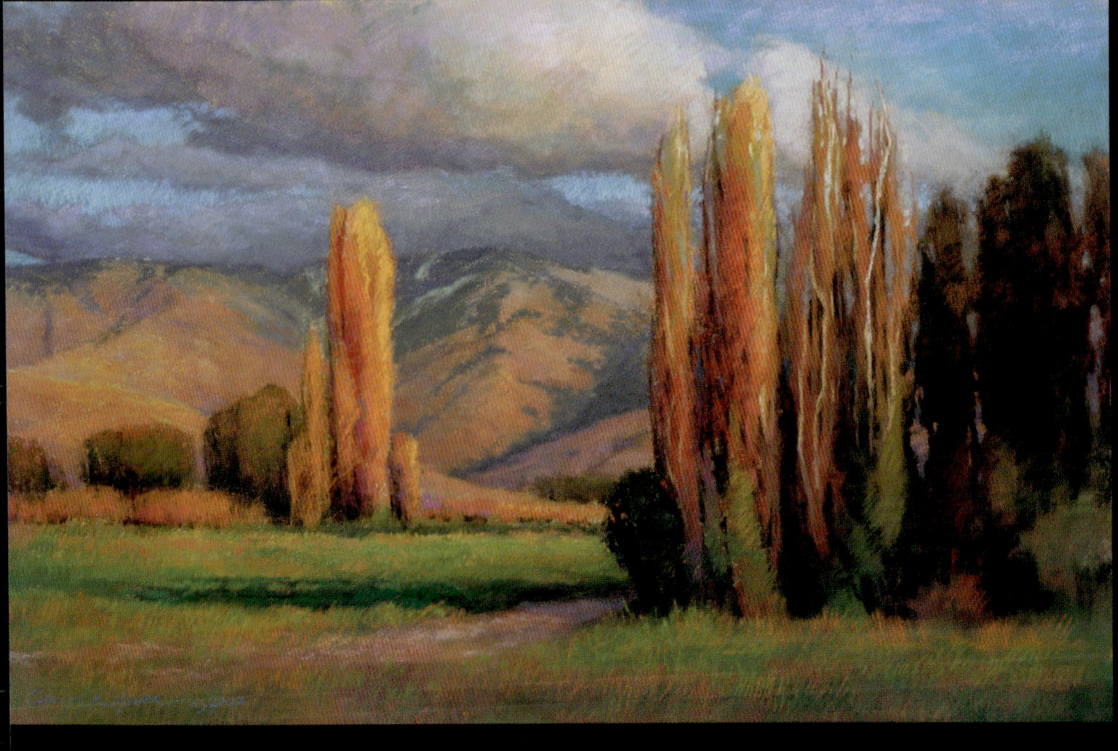

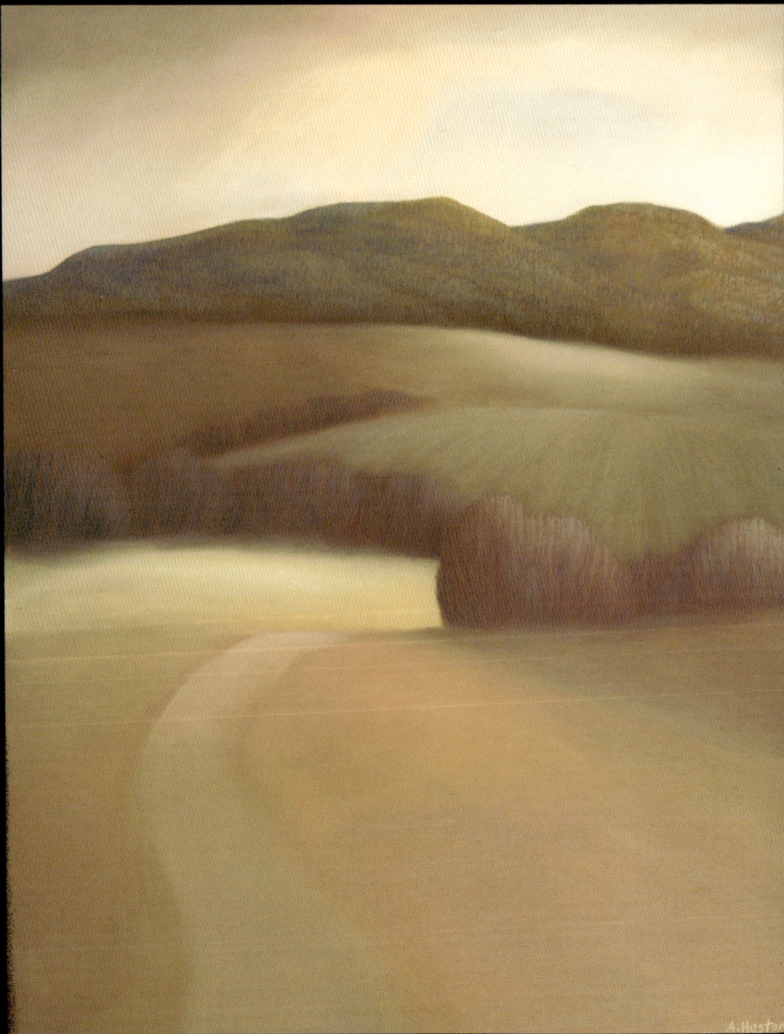

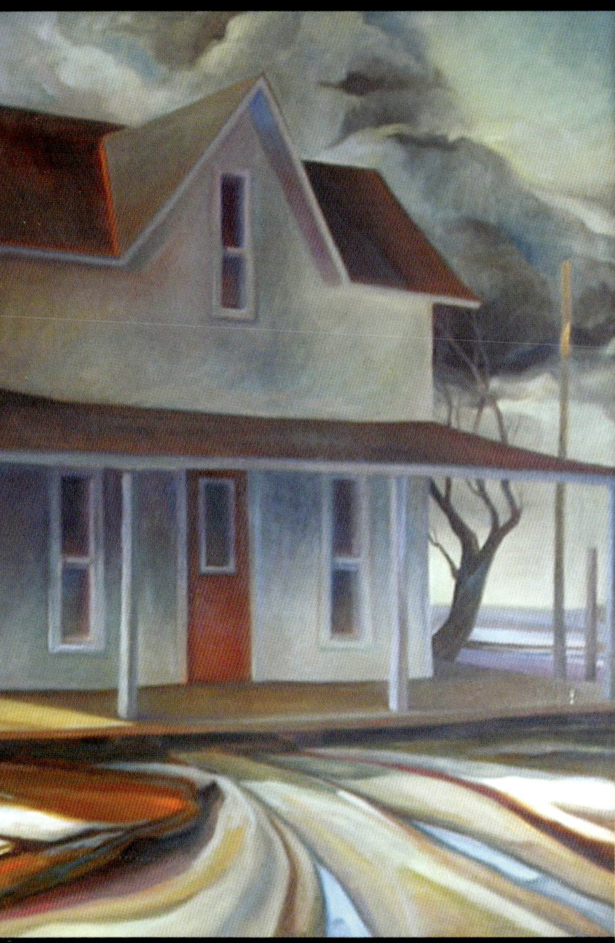

Scenes from the American landscape, clockwise from top left:

THE BRIGHT OF DAY Liz Haywood-Sullivan, soft pastels on sanded paper, page 81

SNOWMIST Robert L. Barnum, oil on canvas, page 13

FIELDS AND WILLOWS Ann Huston, soft pastels on sanded paper, page 99

FALL POPLARS Colleen Howe, pastel, page 93

FOREWORD

THE AMERICAN LANDSCAPE

BY MAUREEN BLOOMFIELD, EDITOR, *THE ARTIST'S MAGAZINE*

A still life is an exercise in design, as the artist arranges the elements; a portrait registers an encounter, but it is planned. What underlies a landscape, less subject to control, is a discovery; coming upon a vista, the painter registers a moment—a quirk of light, a condition of weather, wherein he or she experiences an epiphany. Rendering the shifting conditions as they correspond with the artist's own changing perceptions is the task. Accordingly, landscape painters look both outside and within. From the Hudson River School and the Luminists to Henry Farney and Thomas Hart Benton; from Maurice Prendergast and Childe Hassam to John Twachtman and April Gornick, American landscape painters focus on a luminosity that intimates the spirit of a once new and ever-evolving land. In a trajectory that would have been familiar to Emerson, the mind that knows itself encounters nature and, in an intuitive leap, moves beyond the self to the cosmos. Such is transcendence. We see what's visible and perceive what's not. The artists whose work comprises *Art Journey America: Landscapes* assert the viability and vitality of this rich tradition.

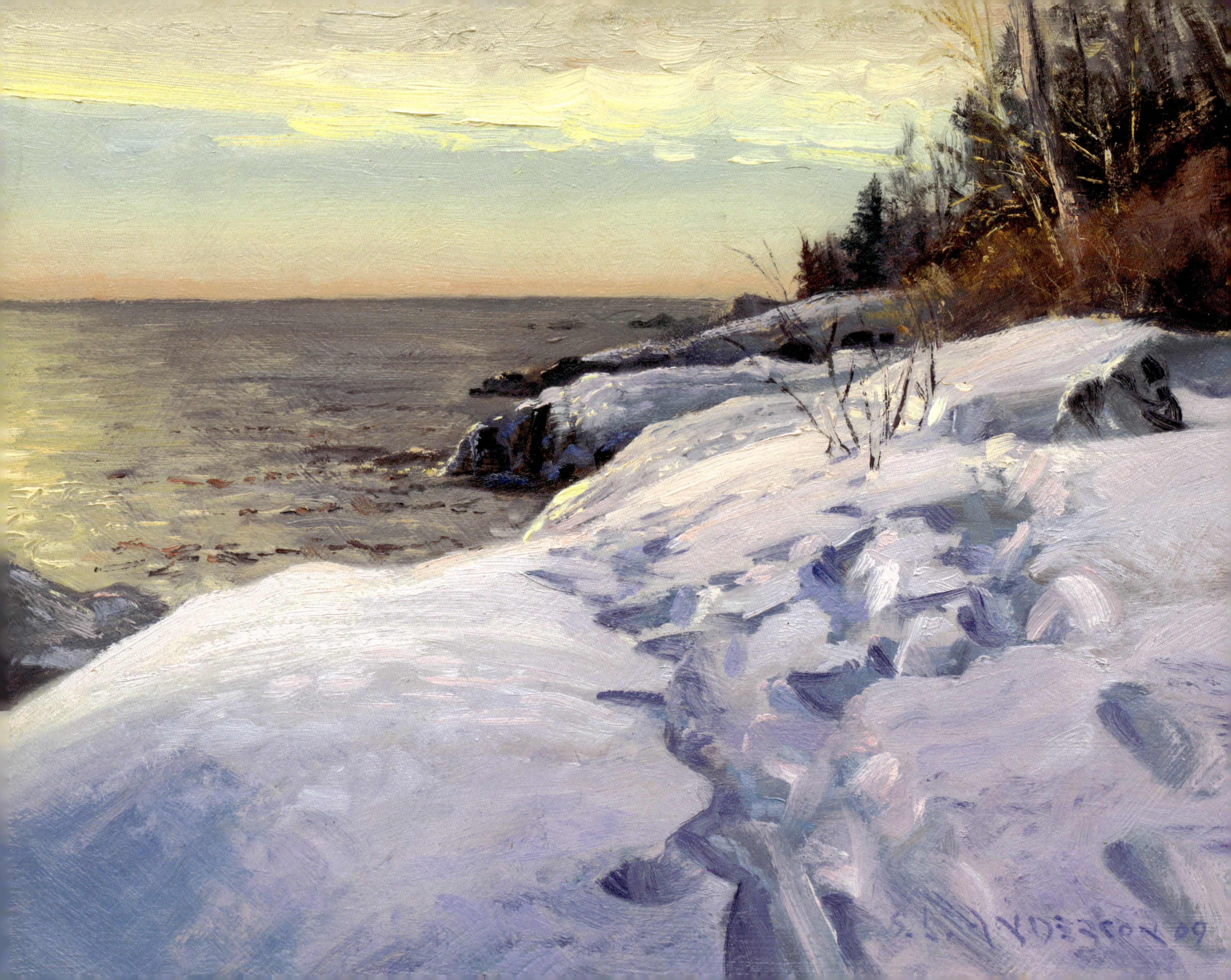

SCOTT LLOYD ANDERSON

When he's not painting, Scott Lloyd Anderson is busy driving his two teenage daughters around and trying to get his golf swing in shape. He also enjoys camping and canoeing in Minnesota's North Woods. Anderson is nationally recognized in the field of plein air landscapes. In 2008, he received local attention for his series of paintings created on the site of the new I-35W bridge construction. In spring 2010 he won best of show in the prestigious Salon International exhibition in San Antonio, Texas. Anderson has also earned top prizes at plein air events in Telluride, Colorado, San Luis Obispo, California, and Grand Marais, Minnesota, and his work has been displayed at the Minnesota governor's residence. Anderson says, "For anyone looking to try plein air painting, I advise them to have the right equipment and dress appropriately. Be prepared. And be patient. It takes about a hundred starts of paintings to get a feel for what you're doing."

What inspired this painting?

I love the drama of Lake Superior's North Shore in the winter. While scouting for a view, my daughter was playing with a friend amidst the mounds of snow and icy boulders. Having settled on a great vantage point looking over the pure, untouched snow, I watched as she tromped right through the foreground. At first I felt she wrecked it, but quickly changed my mind. The steps make the picture.

Do you prefer particular seasons or times of day?

I like painting in the winter because when the sun is out, the colors are so amazing . . . the violet-blue shadows in the snow and pinky-orange in the light.

How do you plan your compositions?

I look for something to catch my eye and turn my head—angles, disparities of scale, contrasts of shapes. I try to arrange pictures in a way that arouses curiosity. When someone walks into a room I want them to notice my picture and spend time with it, and in today's media-saturated world, that's a big challenge.

What mediums do you use and what are your main painting techniques?

My medium is simply oil with turpentine and linseed oil. I paint very thinly at first. When I understand what's going on and want the light to scream, then I pile it on.

What's your best advice to students on painting landscapes?

Understand perspective; recognize that a light effect is about value, not color; start with small canvases; and be patient!

DOUGLAS ATWILL

Since he has lived for many years in the Southwest, particularly Santa Fe, acrylic artist Douglas Atwill finds that the colors of the West interest him more than the green landscapes of the East Coast. "I particularly like the clear air, where a mountain forty miles away is almost as clear as a rock or tree in the foreground, with little sfumato," Atwill states. "Ten miles in any direction from Santa Fe brings up a paintable motif—rivers, high mountains, dry cliffs, fields full of sagebrush, gentle hills covered with piñon pines and red escarpments. Artists are very lucky here."

Q&A

What inspired this painting?

The Elektra Falls is a waterfall off the main highway between Creede and Lake City, Colorado. You drive along through a ponderosa forest and come down into a flat valley with no hint of a waterfall or even a river. The valley floor is covered with low green bushes and grasses. A sign points you to a state park. There, suddenly you see this grand waterfall. In reality, the falls have a different name. I took photos and later, when I started this painting in the studio, I was listening to a Metropolitan Opera broadcast of Richard Strauss's *Elektra*. Somehow, the music seemed to suit the scene, the sharp rocks and coursing water.

Do you paint en plein air?

I do paint smaller canvases outdoors. It's a good exercise for me, particularly to see the exact colors and forms of the midground and foreground. Then, when I extrapolate what I've done out in the open to a canvas in the studio, I try to remember the colors, and I have a small example to refer to.

What mediums do you use and what are your main painting techniques?

I use acrylics almost exclusively, in several different brands but always from a tube for the thick consistency of paint I like. I use brushes of many sizes, and generally try to cover the canvas with paint on the first sitting. Then I can refine and change lines or forms on the second covering. On the third sweep I will refine shapes even more, add shadow colors, insert lines of color and do all the things that make the painting work.

What is your favorite time of day to paint?

Although several friends would say I paint everything at high noon, I actually prefer earlier or later in the day. Shadows from slanting light can bring parts of the landscape into sharp delineation. Late afternoon can offer very dramatic long shadows.

THE ELEKTRA FALLS Douglas Atwill Acrylic 54" × 44" (137cm × 112cm) The Meyer East Gallery, Santa Fe

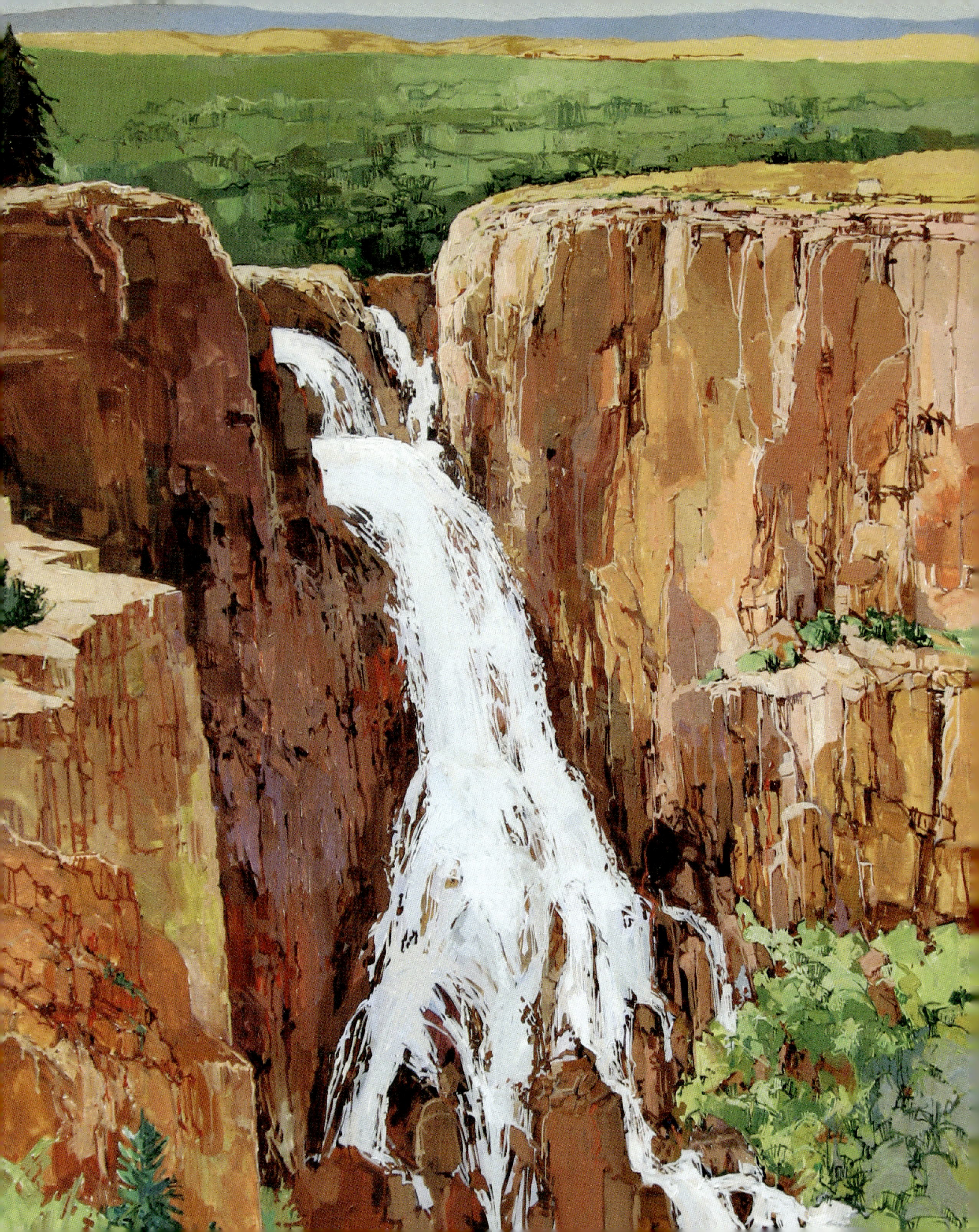

ROBERT L. BARNUM

In the last dozen or so years, Robert Barnum has created and installed seven large public murals and six sculptures in unique and challenging sites throughout the country. His mural *Of Thought and Reason* is a 10-foot high by 130-foot long visual parable that questions how knowledge evolves. *Struggle and Security* is a 2000-square foot, ten-panel painting environment on the human capacity to overcome challenge. A longtime college professor and now teaching at Ferris State University in Michigan, Barnum is consumed with teaching and creating art. But he still makes time for pursuits such as diving and tinkering with a couple of old muscle cars, and considers his four children and first grandchild the most important things he has ever created. A signature member of the American Watercolor Society, the National Watercolor Society and the Watercolor USA Honor Society, he has received more than thirty awards in national and international juried competitions.

Q&A

What inspired this painting?

There is a compelling bond between the land and the people who live on that land. I have lived on the West Coast, in Hawaii and now in the Midwest and it's interesting to note that it is the land that seems to have inspired or defined our character, our look and our beliefs. America's small towns and farms still stand as the best physical example of the remarkable character of Americans to face and overcome challenge.

How would you describe your painting style?

Stylized, figure-intensive, representational but not realistic, and inspired by a visual kinetic that moves beyond the static nature of the medium.

What mediums do you use and what are your main painting techniques?

Snowmist is an oil painting on stretched canvas. By technical tradition my oils are created on canvas treated with multiple layers of acrylic gesso. I first freehand a charcoal drawing of the desired image on the gessoed canvas. Next I do an underpainting into the charcoal with Burnt Umber or sepia brown. *Snowmist* has a Burnt Umber base. I use a thinned-down medium and usually paint four to five layers of oil color over a two- to three-week period of time on a smaller scale painting like this one.

Is your painting inspired by spirituality?

I think all art is spiritual. My paintings are my attempt to visually define, or at least hint at, a unique time and place, and to create a visual dialogue about America and its people. Every once in a while, a painting I create just might have that unique magic that would allow a conversation with a viewer at the highest level. Then there is a good chance that my work has changed someone's life at the emotional and spiritual level.

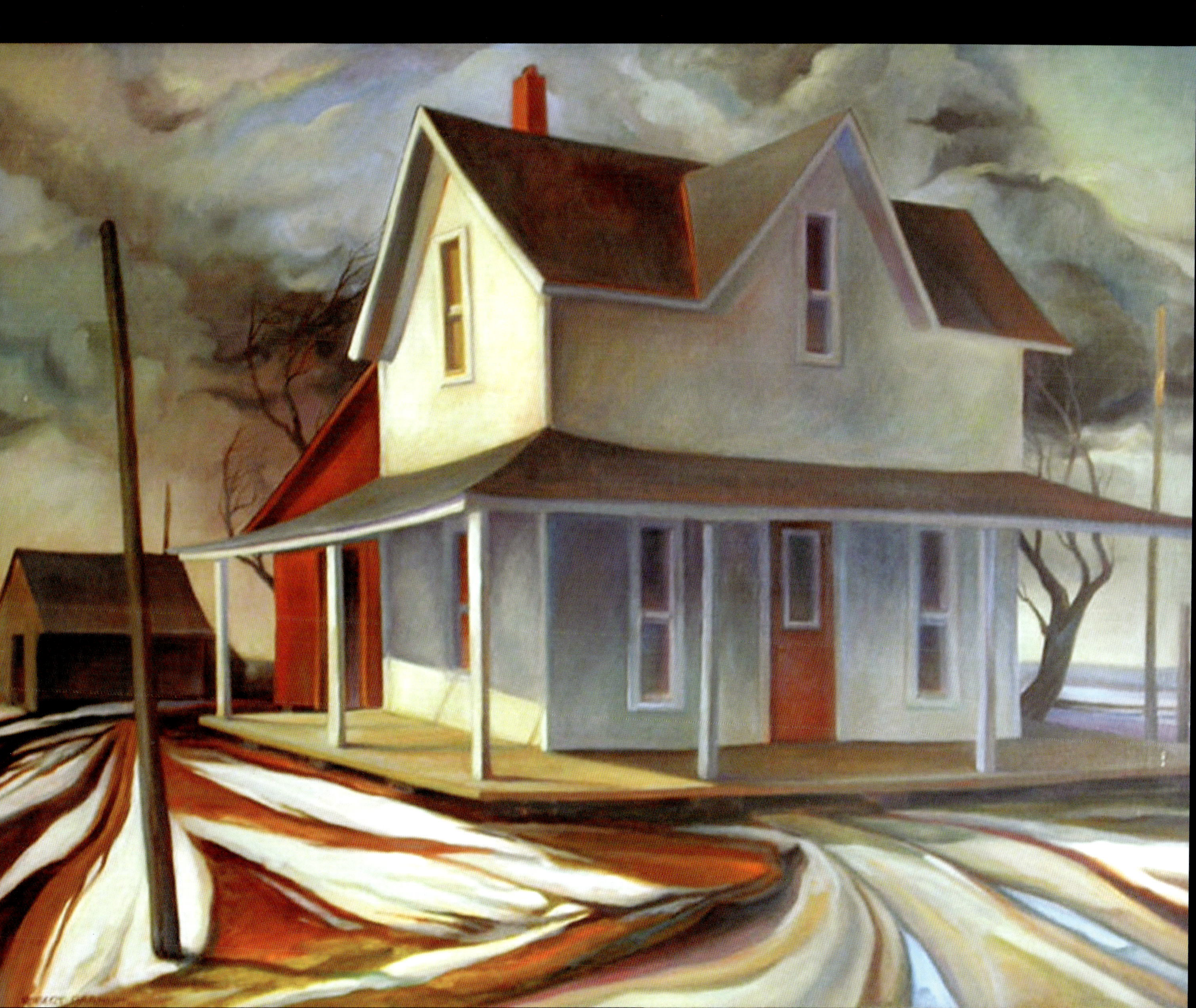

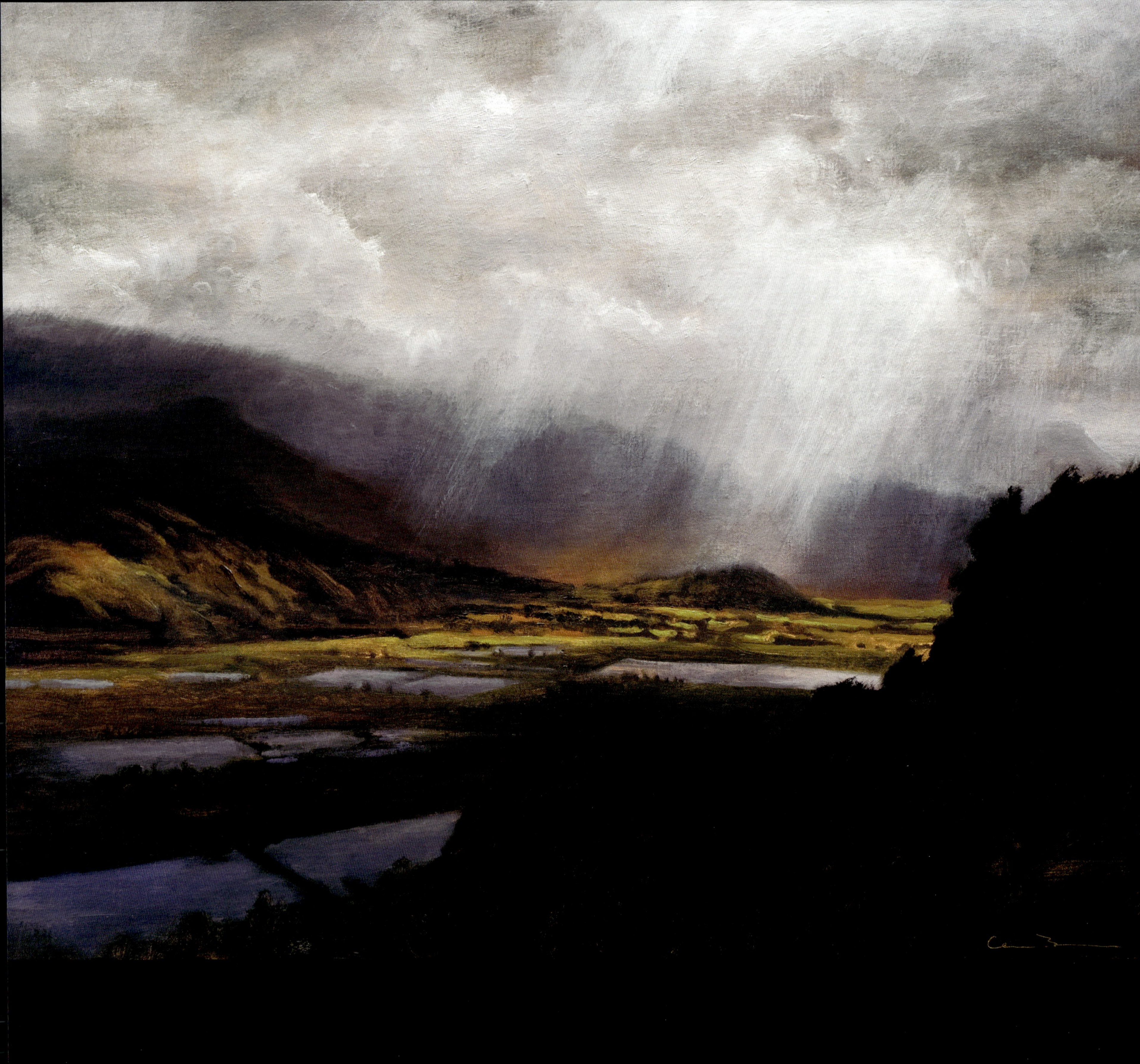

 TARO FIELDS, KAUAI William Berra Oil on linen 24" × 30" (61cm × 76cm)

WILLIAM BERRA

"I live and work in Sante Fe, New Mexico, which initially beguiled me with its magnificent landscape and the painting opportunities it offered," says William Berra. "It's also very inspiring to live in a town that has such a robust art community. I love to travel and paint what I see. Travel leads to reading about history, art and architecture. I paint anywhere I can get a firm foothold. It's nice to be away from the public eye with no one gawking over my shoulder, although that sometimes happens. I prefer to paint someplace where I'm not going to be shot at (that has also happened) and where I am not going to be disturbed. I am happiest when I'm not enveloped in a cloud of mosquitoes, when a storm is not breaking over my head and I have no fear of being struck by lightning. Oh, and I have to enjoy the subject matter and think that I can contrive a good composition from it."

What inspired this painting?

This is painted from the Hanalei Valley Lookout between Princeville and the town of Hanalei on the north side of the island of Kauai, Hawaii. The view is quintessentially Hawaiian in that you look down into a lush, intimate valley of historic taro fields surrounded by mountains swirling with clouds and an ever-changing atmosphere. You see human cultivation and wilderness side by side, and it grabs you emotionally when you see it.

Do you prefer particular seasons or times of day?

I like to study a subject at all times of day to understand it fully and to see how it is affected by changing light. I prefer dawn and dusk for the raking light, the contrasts, and the color. Midday is a whole different story: sometimes its bright, washed-out effects lend themselves to a particular subject. Certain objects cast different shadows midday. Painting is always good after a storm because the clouds are breaking up and the light and atmosphere are clearer. Painting is also good before a storm because it's invigorating to see atmospheric changes as the storm approaches.

What does landscape painting teach us about life and art?

If you drive down the road and see a cottonwood tree, you may not really notice it. But when you see a *painting* of the cottonwood tree, your attention is concentrated upon it. The artist frames a narrow view, studies and records it so that the viewer can give it full and utter attention. Your eye is drawn by the art to what you missed. Landscape painting also teaches us that a subject is infinite. Every moment is different in a landscape: light and shadow change constantly, as do length of days, seasons, weather. Any object is subject to infinite interpretation; it is impossible to look too closely at nature.

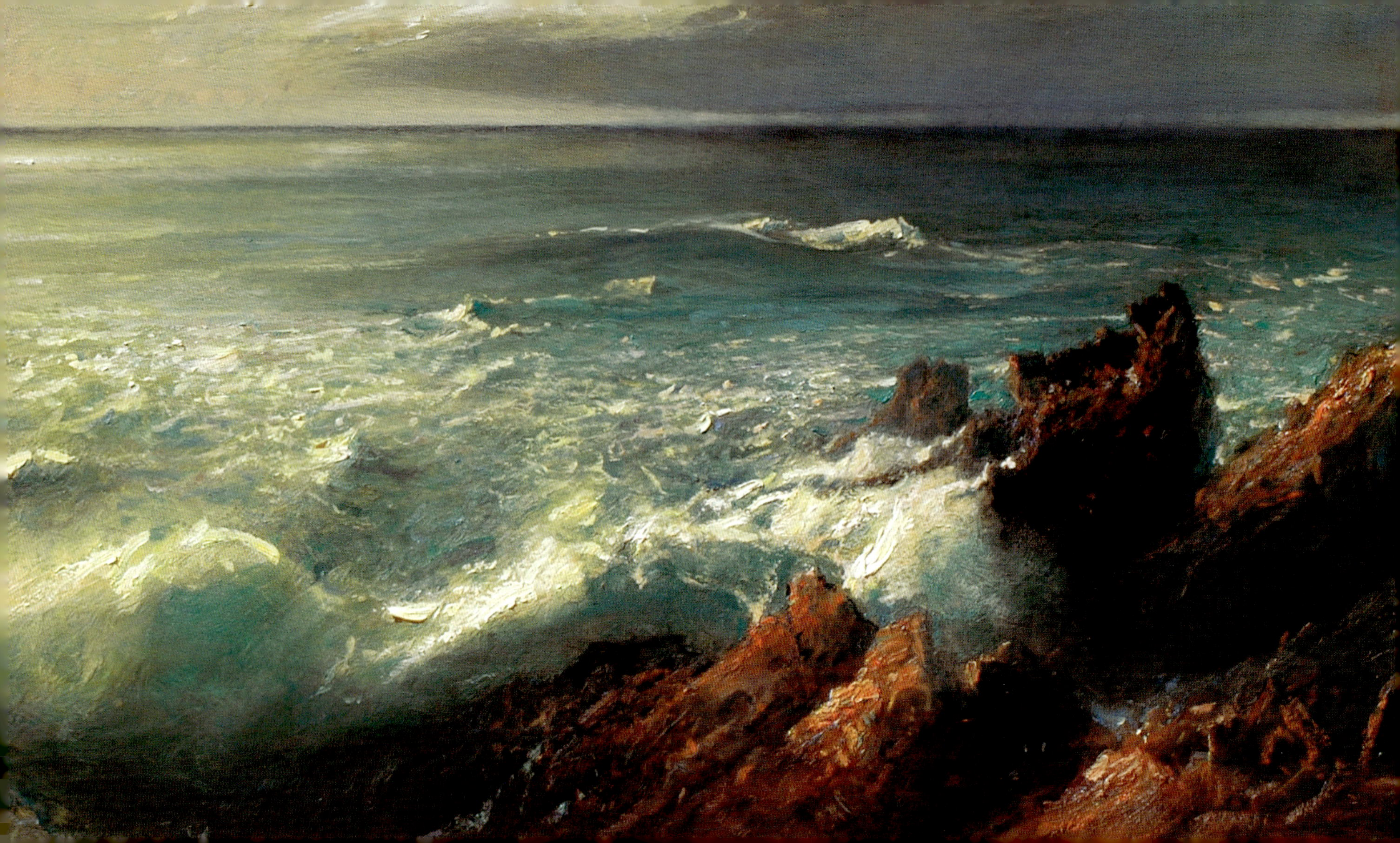

GORDON BROWN

When pressed for information about his painting style, Gordon Brown politely and respectfully responds, "I appreciate when people enjoy my paintings and let the paintings speak for themselves." So begins and ends an interview with the artist. Though short on titles and descriptions, his paintings speak volumes about the American landscapes he relishes. The soothing elements of Brown's paintings are a mere reflection of his life as a soft-spoken family man of great faith. The abstract compositional elements, combined with old-world glazing techniques, illustrate the dedication and passion he has toward his lifelong profession. His work has become the pride of prominent art collections including that of the Denver Art Museum. Of the many awards presented to him, winning the Arts for the Parks competition was the most rewarding. In celebration of the Grand Canyon National Park's 75th anniversary, some 360 paintings were submitted for review including Brown's grand prize winner, *Breaking of Light*. Brown is a native of western Colorado. Every few years he seems to move to the Pacific Coast. After a few years he returns home to the Rocky Mountains.

What inspired this painting?

That place, Point Lobos, I have painted many times. I have painted it in the morning and evening, through the changing seasons. Not all subjects are the same. I don't know what it is about this spot, I just like the way the light is coming in from the left. I like the shape of the wave and how it comes up between and over the rocks and catches the light. In the years I was in California I would watch for storms approaching. I could see the waves from the window in my studio, and when the light was right, I would run down to the water, take photos, hike, experience the storm, the light. It wasn't just painting, it was all of that. That painting was "how it was." It was from life.

What's your best advice to students on painting landscapes?

Spend a lot of time outside. It opens your senses, teaches you how to see and what to look for, and allows the landscape to present itself to you.

NANCY BUSH

Nancy Bush is a native Texan, born in Austin and currently residing in Fredericksburg, Texas. Her pursuit of art has taken her to many beautiful places in the world to study and paint a wide variety of subject matter. "Landscape is my love and is always a challenge, spiritually and emotionally," she says. "The variety and vastness of it can sometimes be overwhelming. Simplification is the answer. The last light of the day or daybreak interests me more than other times of the day." A master signature member of the American Impressionist Society, Bush's greatest influence in her art has come from the nineteenth and twentieth century painters George Inness, Isaac Levitan, Bruce Crane and Russell Chatham. She's a frequent contributor to publications such as *Southwest Art*, *Art of the West* and *American Artist*, and in 2009 was named an "Artist to Watch" by *Fine Art Connoisseur* magazine.

What inspired this painting?

I am very drawn to the twilight hour as it fades into the evening. It seems to be the time of day for reflection and contemplation.

In what locations do you paint?

I paint in many different locations all over America. It's not necessarily an identifiable landmark. Rather, I am always responding to light and atmosphere. I'm drawn to early morning and late evening light, and often the play of light on water at that time.

How do you plan your compositions?

I always consider the structural aspect of the composition in the initial abstract development. Then the energy and mood of the landscape dictates the process from that point on.

Do you paint en plein air?

I love painting plein air and feel it is very important in one's evolution as an artist. Learn to see the truth in nature and it will truly enhance your studio work. My plein air work is different, however, as it is almost always done wet-into-wet, alla prima, as opposed to studio work which is usually wet-into-dry.

What mediums do you use and what are your main painting techniques?

I use turps in the initial stages and will use Liquin or my own mixed medium when and if I do glazes. There are many layers in my paintings in much of my studio work. Layering in my plein air work is more difficult because of the drying process needed. Most of my work in the field is done alla prima.

What's your best advice to students on painting landscapes?

Simplify. No details until the painting is 95 percent complete. Less is more; leave something for the eye and brain to fill in as it wishes.

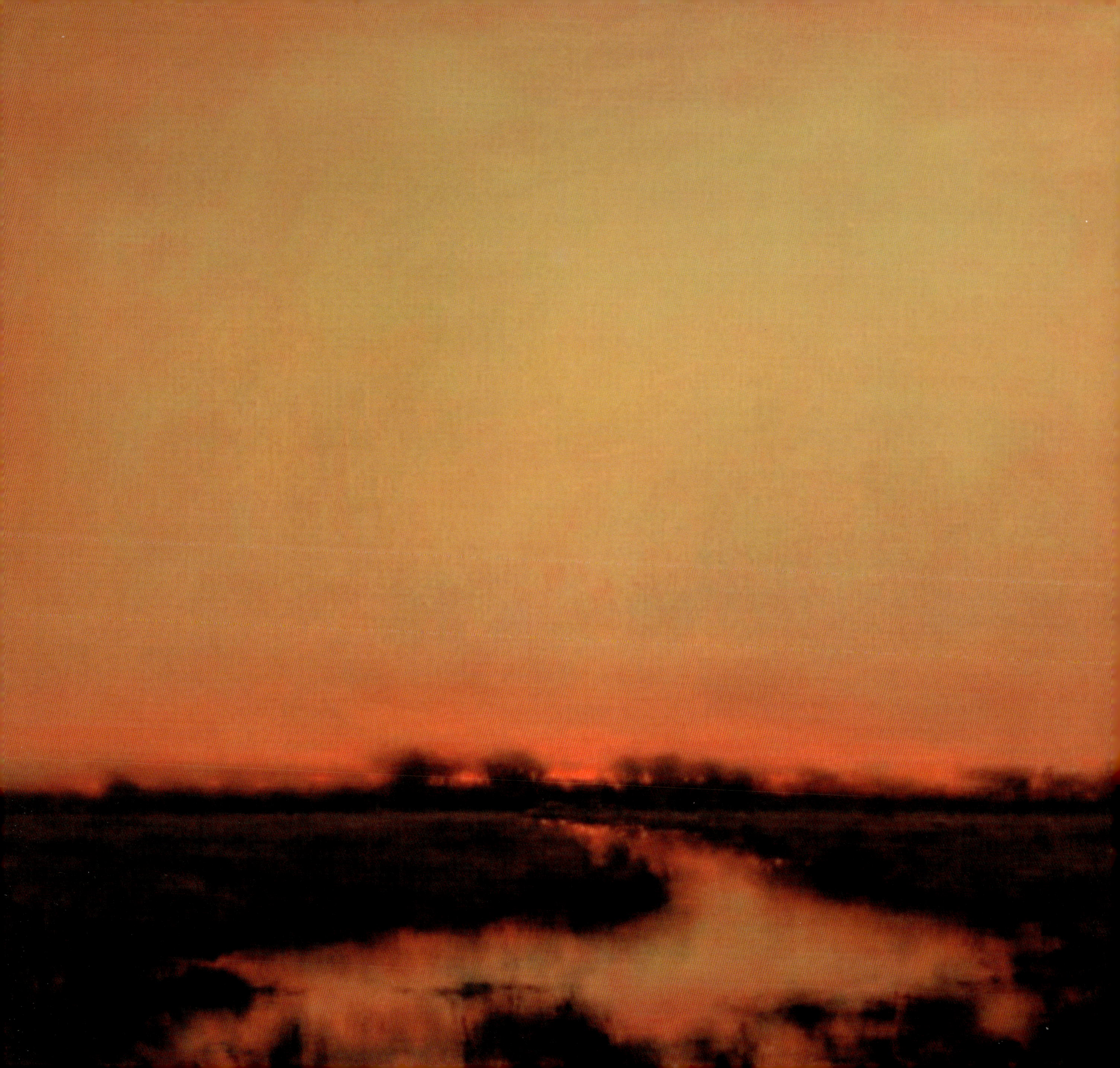

COLE CAROTHERS

Cole Carothers lives and works in historic Milford, Ohio, a bucolic setting east of Cincinnati that was once a mill town. He has taught painting at the Art Academy of Cincinnati and was adjunct associate professor of design at the University of Cincinnati's College of Design, Art, Architecture and Planning. To any student of landscape painting, Carothers says, "Look to the immense history of landscape painting for guidance as a kind of mentorship. Try different approaches with your painting process, such as a variety of mediums like ink, watercolor, oil, encaustics, or acrylic paint. Experiment with different supports like paper, canvas, wood or metal. Do plein air studies, copy artists whom you admire, and be open to using technology if you're comfortable with it. Most of all, be patient." Carothers paints on location and in his studio. *July Grit* reveals the reality of Cincinnati's industrial core, smog and all. The painting is now on loan to the governor of Ohio's executive offices in Columbus.

Q&A

What inspired this painting?

I painted this same location in 2007. Back then, it was a sunny winter morning. Crystalline air illuminated the valley, hillsides and infrastructure. But in July 2010, the air was humid and murky. The Mill Creek that coursed through this valley was usurped by the dense impact of 150 years of industrial growth. Now, the valley divides the city into two distinct sides and the viaduct artery is the only connection. The infrastructure and landscape hadn't changed much in three years, but the power of light and atmosphere made it seem different. In the first painting, the light's clarity was heroic, positive, focused and calm. In *July Grit,* the 2010 version, oppressive heat and humidity coupled with the acidic light is more foreboding. The infrastructure appears to simmer and build up energy as the trailers, trains and storage tanks look like tidal debris swept into the valley.

Why is American landscape painting important today, in the 21st century?

Is painting relevant in the 21st century? Two hundred years ago, photography challenged painting. A photograph could quickly and easily chronicle the landscape. With darkroom skills it could be made to appear painterly. Yet in painting, the scale, preliminary drawing, tactile elements of paint applied thickly or in translucent layers, brushstrokes, scraping, and a matte or gloss sheen alter our perceptions as we view it. These qualities distinguish it from a recorded image. Seen elements (actual) are edited and merged with perceptual ones to create a new experience.

How do you plan your compositions?

I think composition is really about eye movement. With any landscape, I ponder the scene through a viewing window made of two L-shaped pieces of stiff cardboard that can change the size and ratio of the opening. I'll try different formats, crop or increase the landscape, try out different eye levels (horizons) and consider an appropriate size for the painting. Finally, I will make a panel or canvas that is proportional to my viewing window. Working directly on site, the viewing window's four sides help me determine the position and relationship of structures, their edges, sizes and angles.

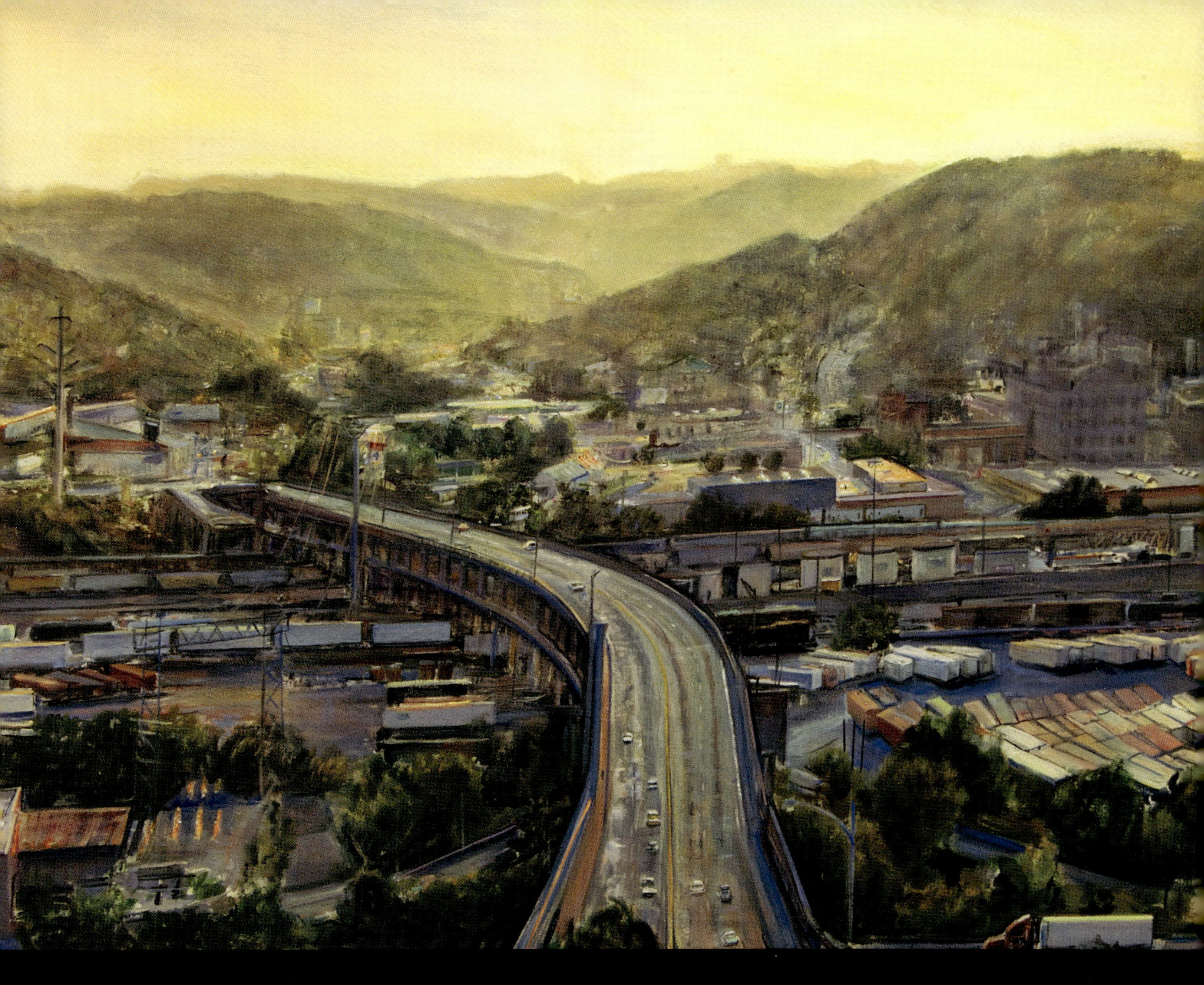

JULY GRIT Cole Carothers Oil on canvas 48" × 65" (122cm × 165cm)

ARTHUR CHARTOW

Arthur Chartow grew up surrounded by art and culture in New York City. He spent many hours at the Museum of Modern Art, which explains the surrealist tinge to his work, and many hours at the American Museum of Natural History, whose animal displays influenced his approach to landscape painting. Chartow attended the High School of Music & Art in upper Manhattan and earned degrees in fine art from Carnegie Mellon University and the Cranbrook Academy of Art. His travels have taken him all over the continental United States, Europe, Canada and Russia, but he now finds his subjects close to his home in suburban Detroit: the lakes and wetlands that dot the local landscape, the Great Lakes within a few hours' drive, as well as the urban industrial environment.

What inspired this painting?

I've been drawn to Detroit's considerable and world-renowned industrial areas since I moved here in 1972. This painting is based on some photography I did back in the early 1990s. There is something about the monumental scale of these buildings that dwarfs me and fills me with a certain awe, but at the same time there is a fragility about them because they are human structures and therefore transitory. The building with the two rows of smokestacks, for example, was a power station that suffered an explosion and fire in 1999. It's mostly gone now, replaced by a new power plant.

How would you describe your painting style?

My work has sometimes been described as surrealistic or even having the flavor of science fiction, although that's not something I consciously strive for. I do look for images that have some unresolved contradictions: the foreboding of an approaching storm on a sunny day. Beauty combined with doom. Attractive ugliness. Decay and rebirth.

What mediums do you use, and what are your main painting techniques?

I use oil paints on canvas or panel. I begin with a rough underpainting and generally build up layers, especially in the sky areas. For scenes depicting architectural elements it's much like a construction project, deciding what elements belong on what planes and painting them in order from back to front. I use glazes sparingly.

What does landscape painting teach us about life and art?

I think we are drawn to the landscape because it gives us a sense of where we fit in in the broader world; it gives us a sense of place, perhaps a sense of belonging, and by extension knowledge of who we are. It can also raise questions such as, "What have we done to our environment?" "What have we built and what does that say about us?" "What does the landscape tell us about the passage of time?" Landscapes can tell a complex human story without the presence of a single human being.

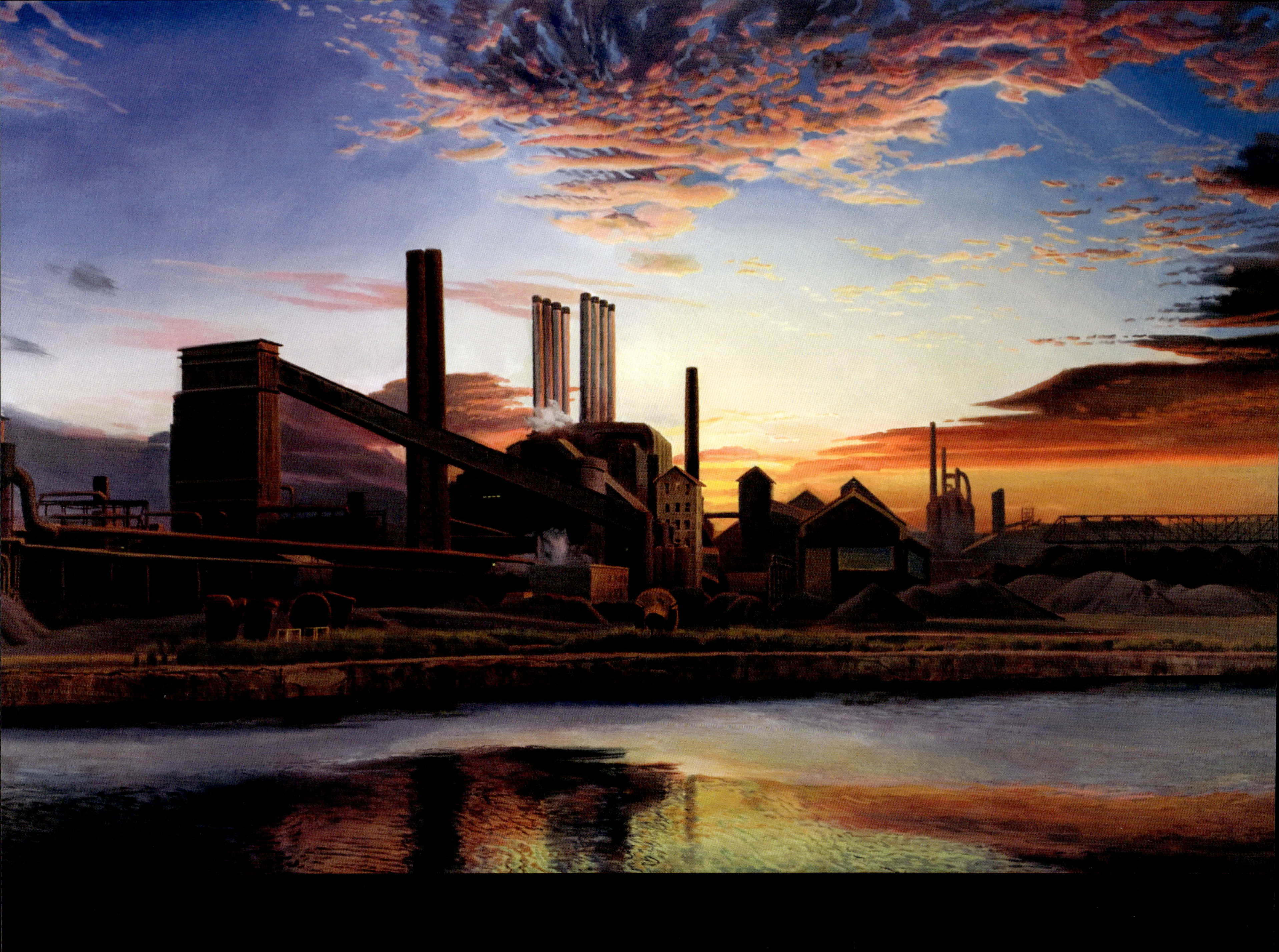

AMERICAN LANDSCAPE Arthur Chartow Oil on canvas 32" × 50" (81cm × 127cm)

ARTURO CHÁVEZ

Born near Taos, New Mexico, Arturo Chávez is a 13th-generation native New Mexican. Raised amid the spectacular vistas of northern New Mexico, Chávez is dedicated to preserving the Western landscape—by painting it. His work has been exhibited in the U.S. embassies in Moscow, Croatia and Guyana. His landscape paintings are in the permanent collections at public and private institutions, including New Mexico State University, the Santa Fe Capitol Collection and the Eiteljorg Museum. "The rough, rocky and colorful Arizona desert is one of my favorite places to paint," Chávez states. "Sedona is built on a bed of Redwall limestone that was deposited about 330 million years ago in a shallow tropical sea. Sandstone is porous, and when water carrying dissolved iron drains through the sandstone, iron is left behind in the form of iron oxide. This red pigment gives the rocks their famous red color and is why we call this area of Arizona 'red rock country'."

What inspired this painting?

In *Mount Wilson Winter*, I tried to convey a sense of the quiet stillness of the fresh snowfall on the red rocks just north of the city of Sedona. As the winter storm passed and the warm Arizona sun emerged, I was moved by the beauty of the lifting clouds that revealed the underlying red rocks of Mount Wilson that had been shrouded in mystery by the winter storm.

Do you paint on location?

My paintings begin on location with small oil color sketches and a series of photographs to document the terrain and to capture the surrounding details. When I return to the studio, I use the color sketches to match my colors and I use the photographs for composition and details. Then I begin work on the intermediate oil painting. If I feel that I need to expand and further develop the painting, I frequently enlarge the intermediate painting to a large-scale work, such as *Mount Wilson Winter*.

What are your main painting techniques?

In a nutshell my painting process encompasses a four-step process: 1) painting on location to ascertain color and color relationships; 2) composition and value drawings in the studio; 3) the intermediate painting in oil; and 4) the final large-scale work. My large-scale format sizes range from 60" × 80" (152cm × 203cm) up to 80" × 160" (203cm × 406cm) and are all derived from the smaller studies.

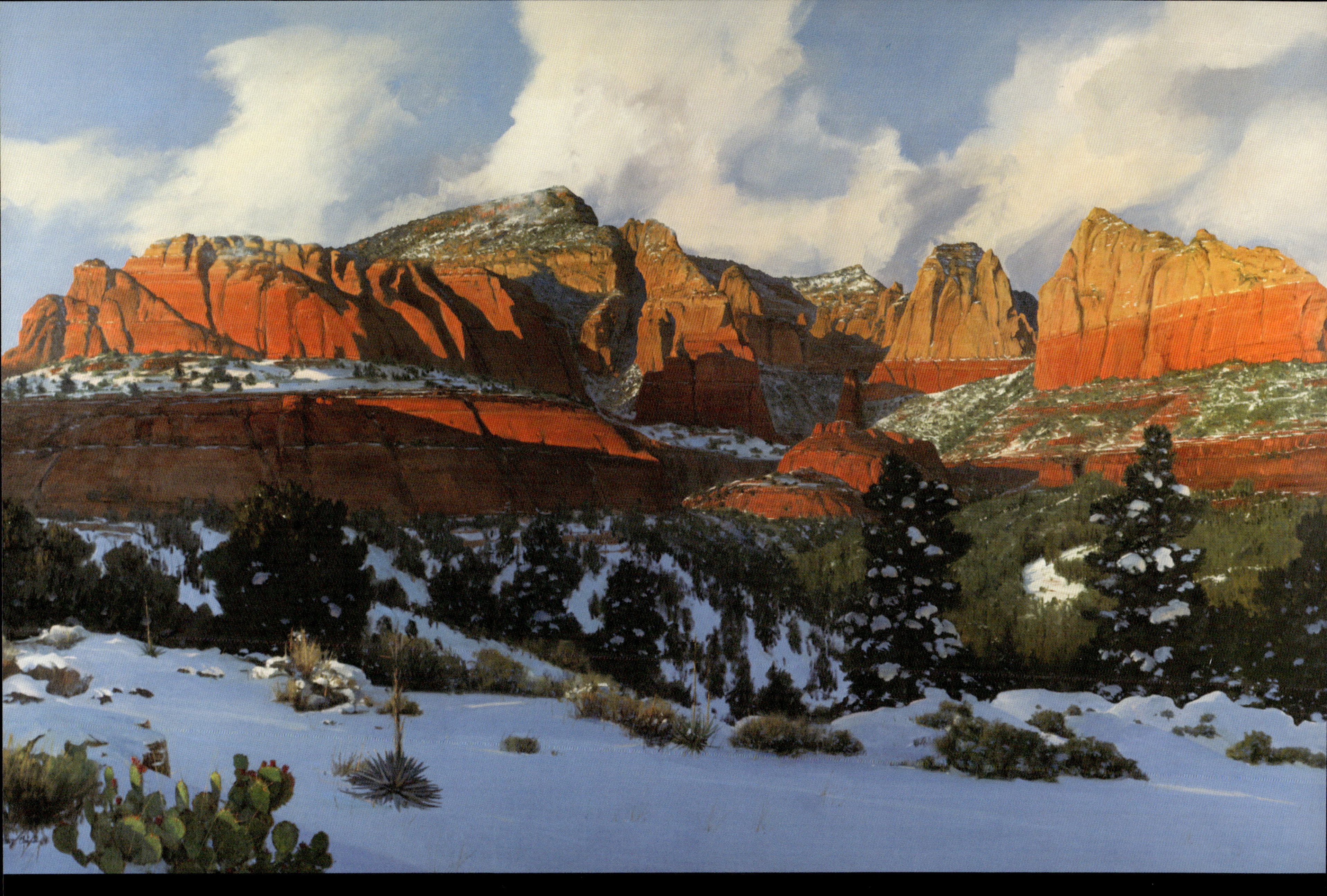

MOUNT WILSON WINTER Arturo Chávez Oil on linen 56.5" × 90" (144cm × 229cm) Courtesy of the Eiteljorg Museum of American Indians and Western Art, Indianapolis

LORENZO CHAVEZ

"I am inspired by scenes of erosion and places where the bare earth exposes the layers of time," says Lorenzo Chavez, "where wind and rain have carved out canyons, arroyos and mesas and left the land rough and barren." Besides painting, Chavez enjoys hiking, collecting books, visiting historic sites, and mindful meditation. "We live south of Denver. It's an ideal place with easy access to a variety of landscape subjects, close to culture and family." His suggestive renderings and fluent technique have earned him numerous awards and many devoted collectors, and he is considered by many to be one of the West's premier pastel painters. A member of the Pastel Society of America and Pastel Society of Spain, among others, Chavez has exhibited nationally with such respected groups as the Plein Air Painters of America, the Pasadena Art Museum (now the Norton Simon Museum), and the C.M. Russell Museum. "The artists I was first exposed to were the Taos Society of Artists and they continue to be a major source of inspiration."

What inspired this painting?

This is a historic adobe church northeast of Santa Fe, New Mexico. Painting there reminds me of my childhood in New Mexico where the church was a place where life is celebrated. Growing up in a Catholic household, we attended weddings, social gatherings, funerals and baptisms at various churches similar to this one. For generations, churches were the center of our community. The cemetery, too, is part of those important rituals and a reminder that life is fleeting; our existence tenuous.

How do you plan your compositions?

My compositions are always about movement. I intend to create a sense of movement through the use of diagonal lines, shape and texture. I would like the viewer to move into and through the landscape and to feel life pulsating within the scene.

What mediums do you use and what are your main painting techniques?

I work primarily in oil and pastel. My main technique is based on an Impressionistic, broken-color style. With pastel, I have a large selection of colors and values available to quickly apply color notes. With oil, I use a limited palette of six colors plus white. Using big brushes, I mix large pools of thick impasto to create broken color and texture.

Do you paint en plein air? What practical advice do you have for those who would like to try it?

I love to paint en plein air. It's exciting to have life surrounding me during the process. It is very stimulating to be outside using all of my senses while painting. My advice is to get outside, paint from life, prepare yourself for the elements, streamline your equipment, work in short, highly focused allotments of time (approximately two hours), and use all of your senses to help create the painting.

CHURCH AT CAÑONCITO Lorenzo Chavez Pastel 18" × 14" (46cm × 36cm) Private collection

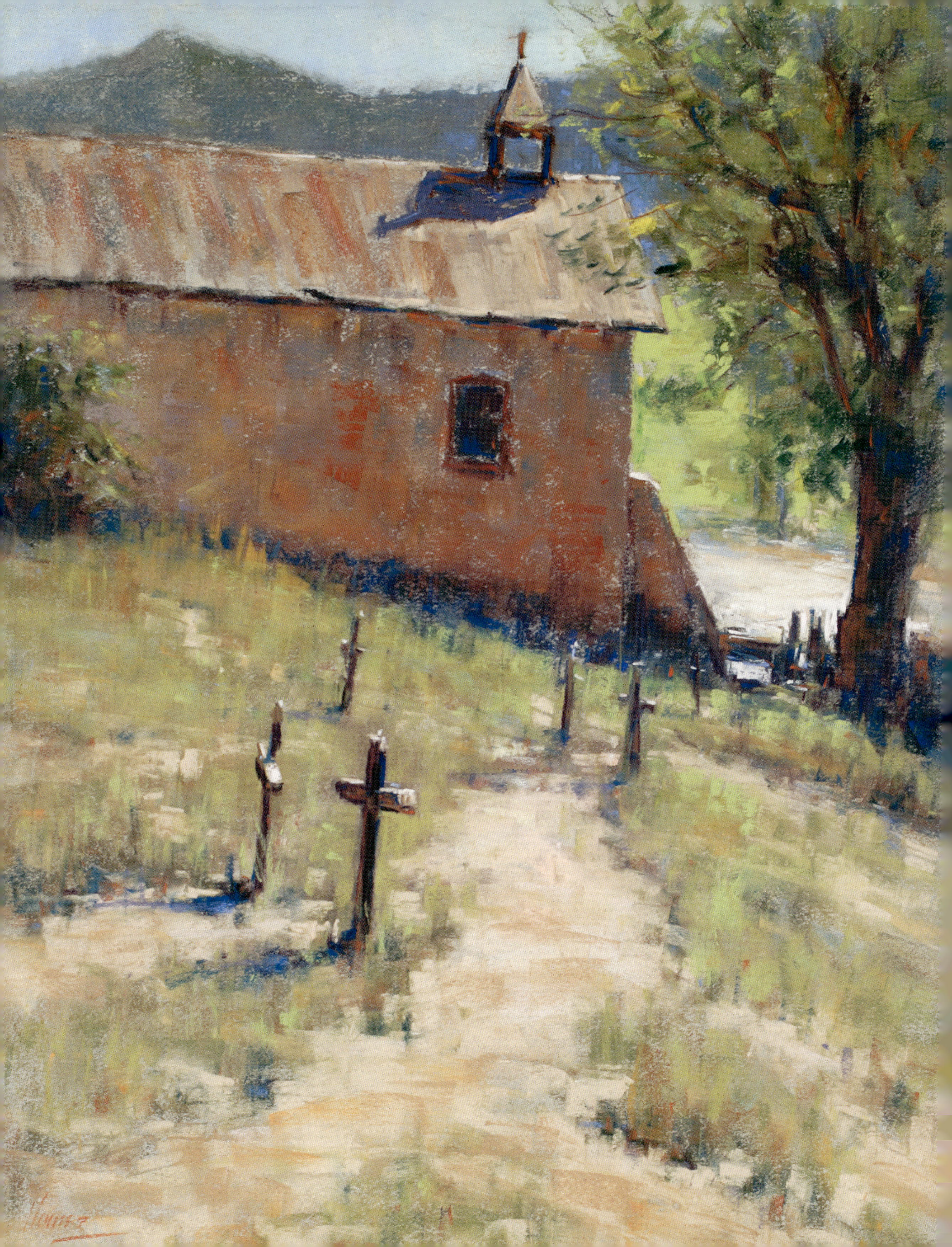

LEN CHMIEL

From an eight-year-old copying Vargas and Petty pin-up matchbook covers, Len Chmiel graduated to painting and pin-striping cars, sign painting and technical illustration in southern California. Weekend and night classes in design, drawing and illustration at the Chouinard Art Institute and the Art Center College of Design in Los Angeles led to an assistant art director job, then to aerospace art departments and freelance advertising design and illustration. Deciding on a life as a painter, gardener, fisherman and hunter, Chmiel moved to rural Colorado where he added viticulture and winemaking to the list.

Q&A

What inspired this painting?

In mid-winter I had seen several bighorn sheep on the iced-over river here. Vitreous glints of reflected sun on winter-darkened water—indications of spring.

Do you prefer painting in a particular season or time of day?

Morning and late afternoon are preferred for the modeling of forms in summer. However, midday and I are not strangers; it just presents a different challenge. I like challenging subjects. Any season, any time with enough light to see will do.

Is your painting inspired by spirituality? How is that seen in your art?

Eyes and mind open, head in the clouds, fingers in the soil or holding a brush—celebrating my human connection with the planet informs my work.

How do you plan your compositions?

Composition reflects one's basic instincts, one's personality. I witness nature as organized chaos. That would be me. I avoid placing the subject in the middle of the canvas unless I really mean it.

Do you paint en plein air?

En plein air? The painters who did that were French and are all dead. I pick a spot, dive in and paint an American "on-the-spot"-er. My advice for an artist contemplating painting outdoors is to wear a wide-brimmed hat, minimize your gear, be fearless! Then get the first hundred paintings over with, as it's a learning process. Save all one hundred.

What's your best advice to students on painting landscapes?

Assuming an intellect, use it; copying verbatim what is seen, is not. No one sees through your eyes; therefore, criticism from another is colored by that person's belief of what is correct.

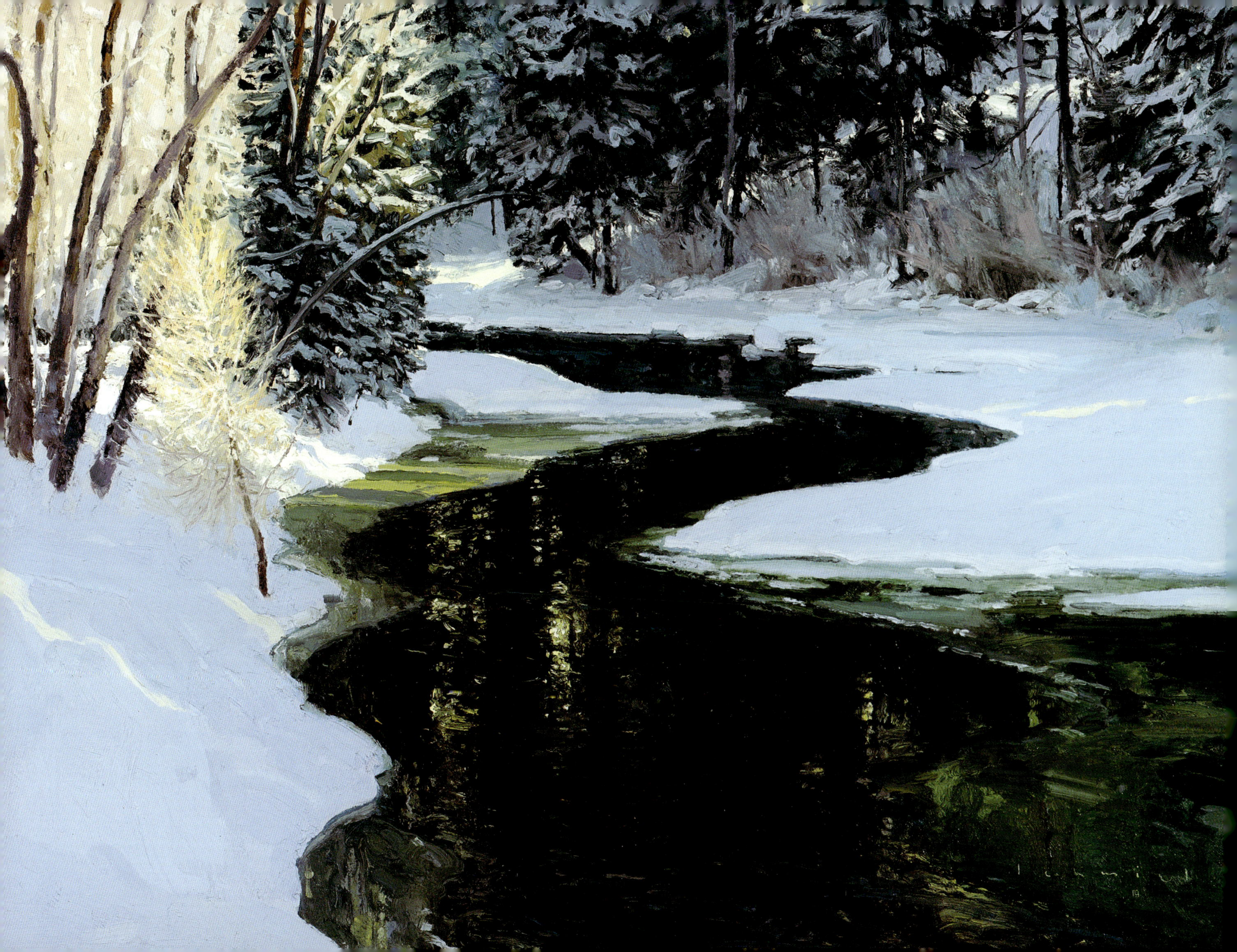

BRIAN COBBLE

Since he has lived in or spent time in several parts of the country, Brian Cobble feels he's a bit schizophrenic in the landscapes that inspire him. Recent work has been drawn from the Southwest (New Mexico, Colorado, Texas, Utah), the Midwest (Nebraska and Kansas), New York (NYC and Long Island) and the Northwest (Oregon and Washington). Often he is attracted to places where the old interfaces with the new, or the man-made with the natural world, with an eye out for that which feels mystical, or surreal, or perhaps just slightly quirky. Cobble attended New Mexico State University (BFA), Southern Methodist University (MFA), and the Skowhegan School of Painting and Sculpture. He was a MacDowell Colony fellow twice, and is a signature member of the Pastel Society of America, and a Master Pastelist. He lives in Albuquerque with his wife, Julie, a biologist, and a passel of dogs, all of whom are forced to pose occasionally. When he's not painting, Cobble is hiking, camping, biking and exploring the canyons and mountains of the Southwest.

Do any historical movements, periods or artists inspire your painting?

Probably most people have a chauvinistic feeling, a special tie to their native land. With me it is the same with art. I have always loved the American landscape and those who have depicted it, especially some of the late 19th and early 20th century painters such as George Inness, Charles Burchfield, John Twachtman, Edward Hopper and Maynard Dixon, to name a few. When I lived in New York, I used to prowl the basement of the American wing of the Metropolitan Museum of Art, where they had hundreds of American paintings by artists both famous and obscure, displayed salon-style—a crash course in landscape painting.

How do you plan your compositions?

Pastel is often thought of as a medium of spontaneity and speed. Unfortunately, my methods are the opposite. My paintings are built very slowly. When I find a possible subject, I usually take a number of photos, capturing different angles, lighting, weather conditions and times of day. It's not unusual for me to mull over a subject for months, if not years, working the composition in my mind, rearranging, adding and subtracting, borrowing elements from somewhere else, or just making them up.

Do you prefer particular seasons or times of day?

Many of my paintings, especially the Southwestern images, are set in the early morning or late evening. The western sun tends to flatten objects and bleach out color during the height of the day. But as the afternoon turns to evening, the colors grow rich and the shadows darken and lengthen, adding mystery and softening the harshness of the desert. I have often used a winter setting to enhance the starkness of a painting—the muted color and bare trees can enhance the emptiness of a scene.

What does landscape painting teach us about life and art?

I've always thought of landscape painting as a way to relate to the world we live in. Often it is not unaltered nature that attracts me as an artist as much as the raggedy places where the "natural" overlaps the man-made, the darkness on the edge of town. Even in these most mundane places, light and shadow can elevate the ordinary into something almost profound.

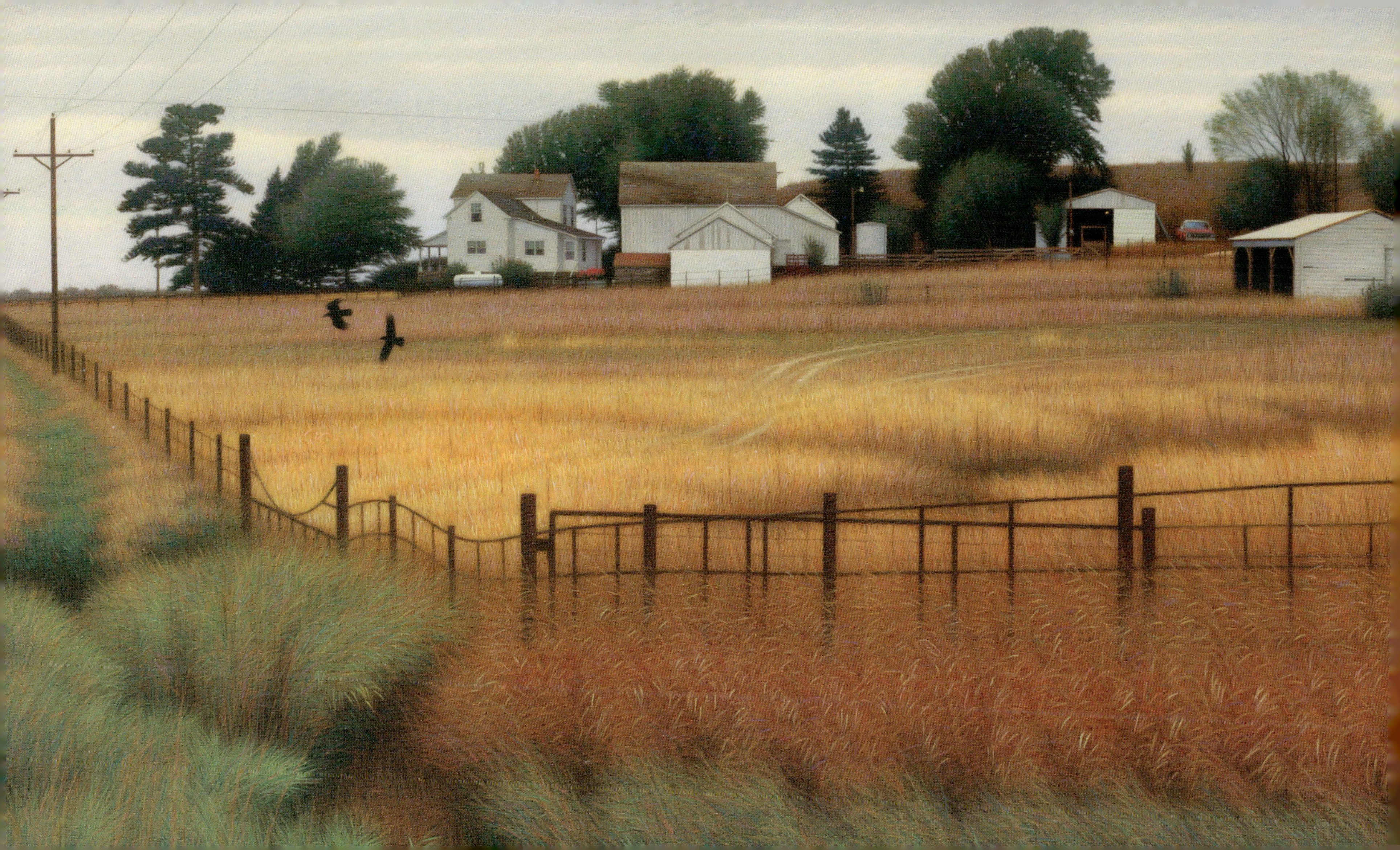

GIL DELLINGER

After graduating with an MFA from San Francisco State in 1971, Gil Dellinger went to work at the University of the Pacific in 1972, teaching drawing, figure drawing, painting, printmaking and design. He eventally became a full-time tenured professor and in 1992 won the Distinguished Faculty Award for his teaching and professional contributions. During the time he was teaching, he had a studio on campus and worked four hours per day, six days a week. He retired in 2001 to paint full-time. Now he paints from twelve to fourteen hours a day. Dellinger concentrates on painting Americana and in 2011 had a one- man show on the glories of California's Central Valley. Constantly working to improve quality, Dellinger says, "At 68, I think I am finally hitting my stride!"

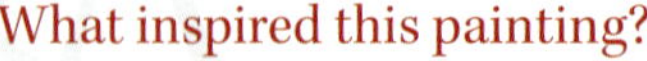

What inspired this painting?

Our area of California's Great Central Valley is rife with vineyards, orchards and magnificent fields of grain. The whole process of growing and harvesting is thrilling to me.

In what locations do you paint?

I paint in many locations across the country, but the more I travel the more I come to realize that the most startling images can come from right around me.

Do any historical movements, periods or artists inspire your painting?

Seeing the light in a Vermeer painting changed my life. Although I seldom paint the figure, his treatment and obvious transcendence have had a great effect on me. The light of Frederic Church and space and grandeur of Albert Bierstadt have also moved me deeply. Our local museum, the Haggin Museum in Stockton, California, owns twelve Bierstadts, several Inness works, and paintings by Thomas Hill and Jan Monchablon. I have studied them quite closely and often.

Is your painting inspired by spirituality?

I try to make my love for God primary and tangible in my work. I am a firm believer that beauty is a tangible way that God makes His presence clear. Beauty is an example of hope, that something exists beyond us.

What's your best advice to students on painting landscapes?

Learn how to draw! Draw, draw, draw. Learn how to use values with great skill, for it's my contention that the secret to great color is the understanding of values and neutrals.

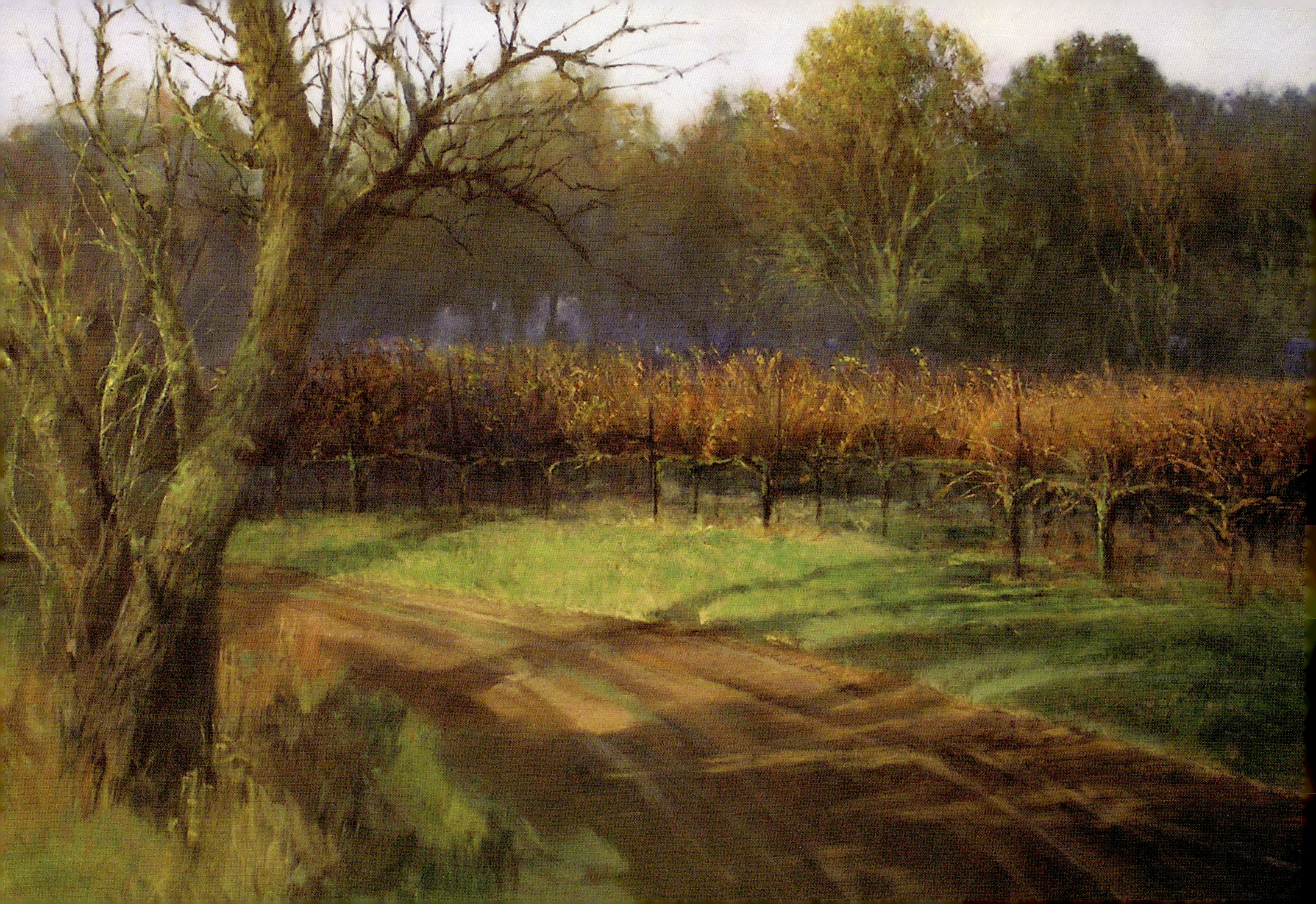

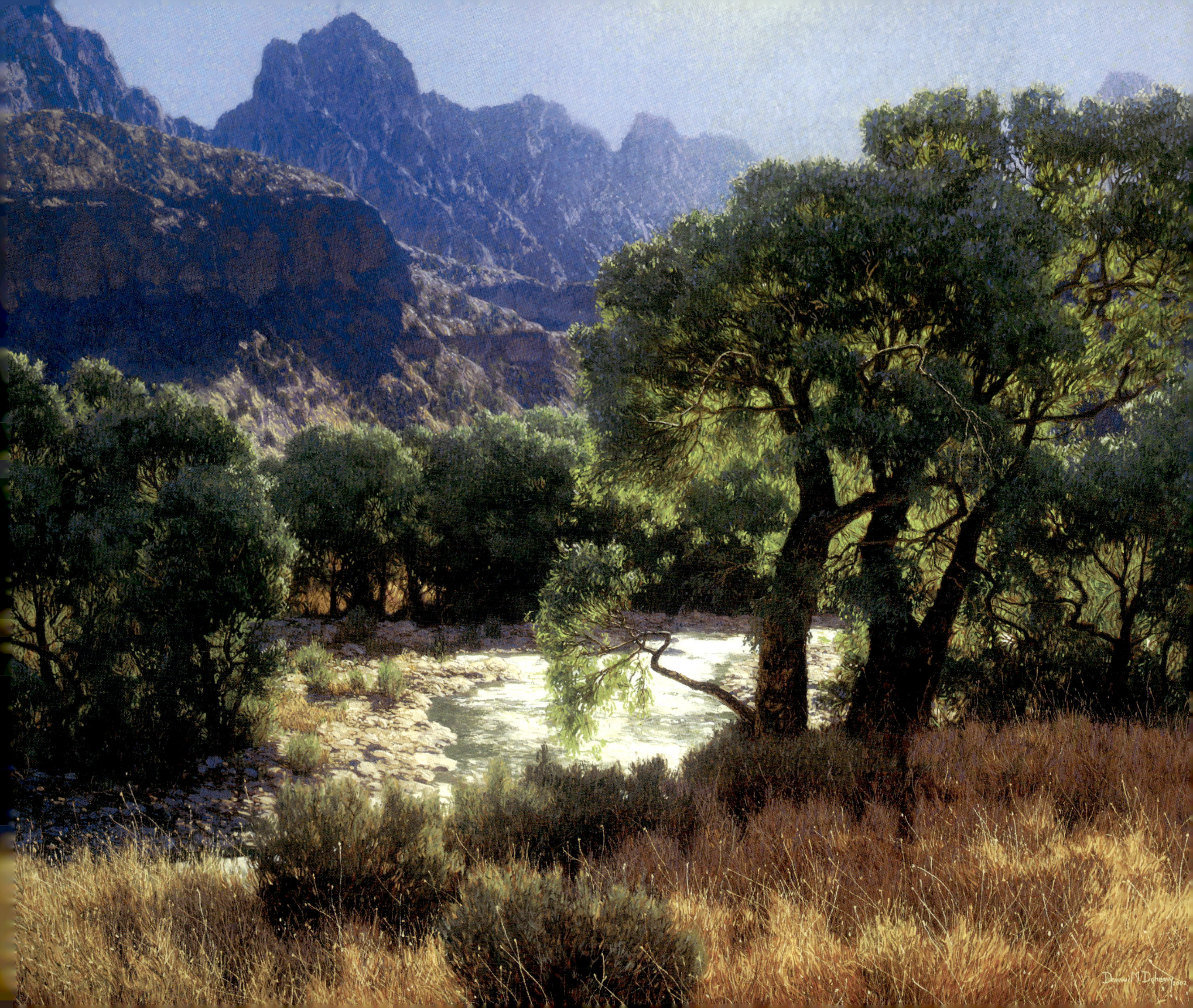

DENNIS DOHENY

A third-generation Californian, Dennis Doheny was born and raised in the Los Angeles area and currently resides in Santa Barbara. Growing up with an innate love of art, he spent much of his childhood drawing and painting. Although he studied some art in school, Doheny is largely self-taught. For ten years, he supported his family with a steady career in commercial art until his passion for painting prevailed. A signature member of the California Art Club, Doheny won their Edgar Payne Award for best landscape at the 2009 Gold Medal Juried Exhibition. He has also been honored to receive the Frederic Remington Award given in recognition of exceptional artistic merit in the Prix de West Invitational Art Exhibition in 2006 and again in 2008. Doheny was also recognized by the Autry National Center and awarded the Masters of the American West Award in 2003. His painting was acquired by this exceptional museum for its permanent collection.

What inspired this painting?

We were in Zion National Park in the fall and although the surrounding area was extremely dry, the contrasting water of the Virgin River really drew my attention.

In what locations do you paint?

I paint throughout the West from mountains, deserts and coastal areas. It's where I've grown up and it's what I love!

Do you prefer particular seasons or times of day?

I'm drawn to all four seasons. I feel each one has its own unique charm.

How would you describe your painting style?

I would describe my style as realism, but if one were to examine the paintings closely, there is very much an element of Impressionism.

How do you plan your compositions?

I plan my composition based on whatever strikes me at the time as far as patterns and colors.

Do you paint en plein air? What practical advice do you have for those who would like to try it?

Although I am probably better known as a studio painter, I very much enjoy painting outdoors. My advice for those who want to try it is to experiment with different subject matter and colors and to step back and view the painting often.

DAVID DRUMMOND

Widely recognized for his realistic watercolors of Lake Powell and western landscapes, David Drummond concentrates on detail and mood in his paintings. After retiring from the Air Force as a career physicist, he began painting full-time, returning again and again to Lake Powell where he created a unique process for capturing the subtle variations of light and shadow on water, which he teaches today. Drummond was born in Virginia and raised in Philadelphia, but even as a boy he always looked at *Arizona Highways* magazine and wanted to paint those scenes. He couldn't believe it when he moved to Colorado and later to New Mexico: those places actually existed, and the air was so clear, the sunsets and sunrises so bright! Then he found New Mexico green chili and Lake Powell, the Grand Canyon, Capitol Reef, and his current home, Albuquerque, and has never thought about living anyplace else. Now, besides painting, Drummond still does some physics research, and likes to hike and ski. He earned his American Watercolor Society membership in 1986. Sixteen of his paintings have been included in the national Arts for the Parks Top 100 show, and in 2007 he was commissioned to paint the White House Christmas card.

Q&A

What inspired this painting?

I've always been fascinated by the moving abstract patterns in waves. This particular painting has a very strong design (partly from a photo, but mostly fiction) leading the viewer's eye into the scene.

In what locations do you paint?

I paint mostly at Lake Powell and other desert areas, but occasionally in the mountains and around Albuquerque in the river and metro area. I paint Lake Powell because it is one of the most dramatic areas that I have ever been to in the Southwest; and it has water, which I love to paint, and it is more accessible than the Colorado River in the Grand Canyon. Lake Powell has dramatic sandstone walls, constantly changing light and shadows, and miles and miles of clear water for reflections. I paint the mountains of New Mexico and around Albuquerque because I see them every day and love the shifting light and shadows. It is a different feel than the desert. The Rio Grande Bosque runs through Albuquerque and provides a great backdrop for painting the mountains in their evening and afternoon colors.

Do you prefer particular seasons or times of day?

I like to paint sunrise, sunset and winter, but these obviously make plein air painting difficult. I often try to memorize a scene and make a small watercolor sketch later. I like the light during these times and the feeling of the day and evening. I also like the feeling of light on snow, and try to capture the contrast of sunlight, snow and a cold, crisp winter's day whenever I can.

What mediums do you use and what are your main painting techniques?

I use watercolor, and try to use the textural contrast between very wet washes and more precise dry techniques to convey a feeling of realism.

Do you paint en plein air?

I paint plein air as often as I can find the time. However, most of this work is small, rough sketches used as reference material for later paintings. Painting plein air and from memory is the best way to hone your observational skills.

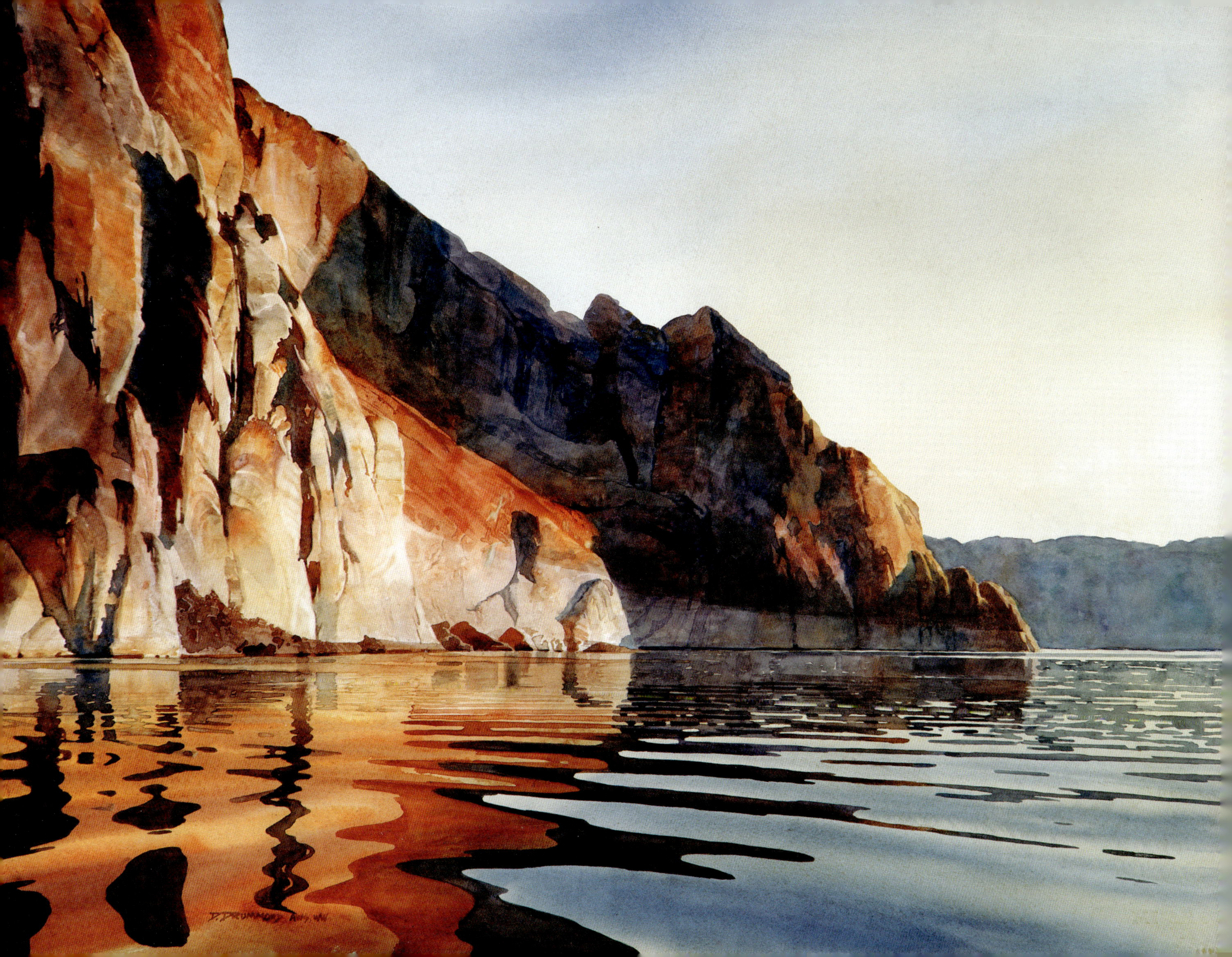

JOELLYN DUESBERRY

"I am a self-taught painter except for a very influential month spent with painter Richard Diebenkorn in 1986," says Joellyn Duesberry. "Before that year of moving west, I was an atmospheric landscape painter, obsessed with light and the East Coast veil of moisture where natural forms share edges. When I moved to Colorado, the absolute light and dark and sculptural clarity of waters, plains and mountains completely changed my focus to formal construction of landscape compositions." In 2000, the Denver PBS television station filmed Duesberry and her oil painting/oil-based ink processes. The resulting 32-minute film is used by teachers all over the country. Besides painting, she loves to bicycle, ski and accompany her husband on fishing trips to the western rivers. Their old farmhouse home of big trees and gardens affords her a huge studio from a one hundred-year-old restored barn with skylights.

Why is landscape painting important today, in the 21st century?

Landscape painting is often the last testament to a beautiful place on the planet before it disappears to development or neglect, beneath a road, or to trophy homes of the rich. I have watched lupine fields, wild waters, abandoned quarries, the crests of striped hills, wetlands and forests begin to disappear even as I finished recording them. The ultimate vanishing act was the view north and east from my studio on the 91st floor of the North Tower of the World Trade Center on 9/11, imploding with friends, some of my work, and the perch in the high air that had enthralled me for six months of painting the maze of cubes that was New York far below, never to be captured again from such a height.

In what locations do you paint?

The Northeast has afforded me the stern coastal rocks and trees of Maine, rock quarries with their man-made cuts and angles, and the striped hills of farmland from my rural upstate New York studio in Millbrook, all veiled in the soft, humid light of the coast. By contrast, in the West, the mountains and waters, the hogback red ridges near Denver, and the adobe forms and pink desert dotted with piñon pines in New Mexico have provided rock and land forms revealed in absolute light and dark in the arid clear air.

How do you plan your compositions?

I crave painting big canvases, often splicing them and re-assembling them on site, en plein air. A wide and tall canvas (actually, primed Belgian linen) involves my peripheral vision and I become embraced by my subject. I start with a charcoal draft, brush those lines with medium and a shadowy rose tone, make wide swaths of neutral washes for the lights and darks, then build up layers of paint.

What's your best advice to students on painting landscapes?

Try to avoid "scene" painting. Rather, stalk a subject that galvanizes your attention and you don't know why. Intuition and the unconscious are the best guides. Save old 37ml tubes to squeeze to the minimum for a paint box, so that your plein air experience does not lack for subtle color. Use a hand truck or caddy with stretching straps so you can go anywhere.

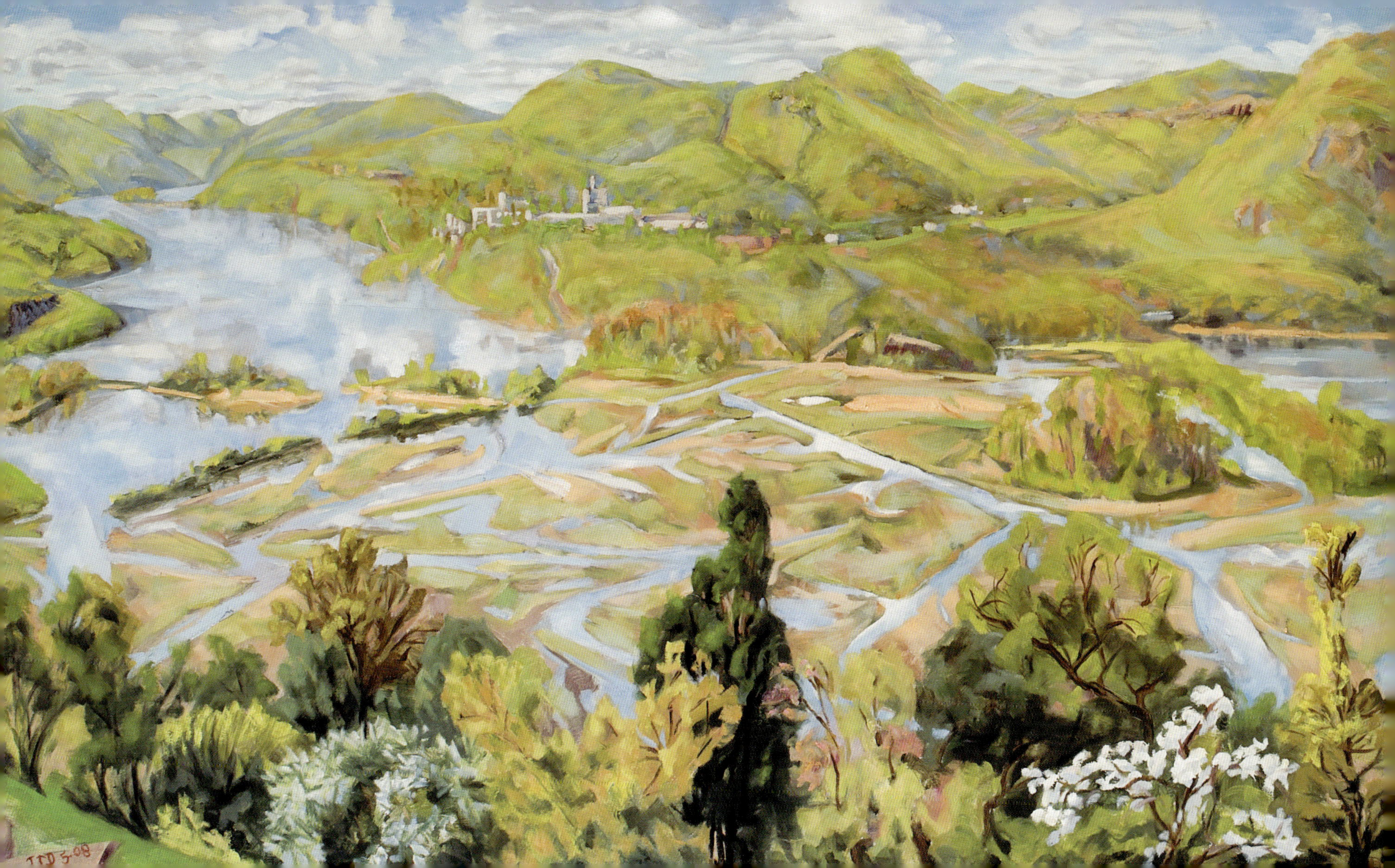
TCD 5-08

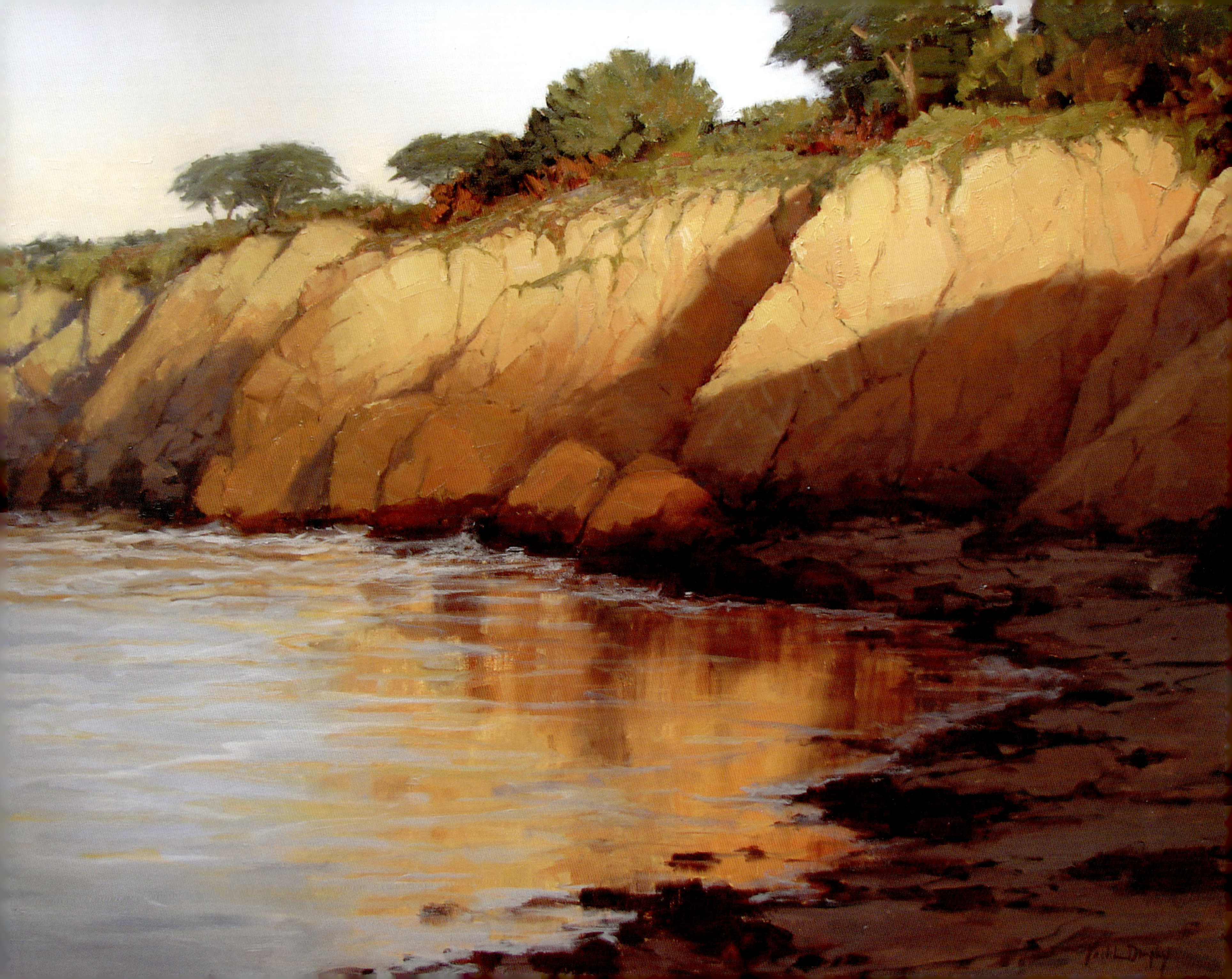

KATHLEEN DUNPHY

Maryland native Kathleen Dunphy has been drawn to the coast of California ever since she first saw the sun set over the ocean. She now lives in the foothills of the Sierras and travels several times each year to paint in Carmel, Pacific Grove, Cambria and Laguna. "There's something elemental and powerful about the juncture of land and water that inspires me any time of year and in any weather conditions," she says. "Nothing is ever boring or predictable at the coast." Dunphy's rapid success in the competitive art world was predicted when *American Artist* magazine recognized her as one of the Top Ten Emerging Artists in 1998, just two years after devoting herself full-time to painting. Her honors include Best of Show from the American Impressionist Society; an Award of Excellence from the Oil Painters of America; seven California Art Club Gold Medal Shows; the Federal Duck Stamp Competition; Birds in Art; Art for the Parks and many others. Her highest honor to date came when she was selected by the Plein Air Painters of America as a guest artist for their exhibit in 2011.

What inspired this painting?

I painted *Evening Sun* in my studio from a study I did on location in Pacific Grove. My trips to the coast usually turn into a marathon of painting, with so much inspiring subject matter at hand. On my last day at the beach, I was packing up my gear to head home after a full day of painting when I saw the rays of the setting sun gilding the rocks. I set up my easel one more time and painted a quick 20-minute study to capture the light and color that I knew no photo would ever accurately depict. Although the study was rough and far from complete, it provided invaluable information for me back home in my studio, where I had the luxury of time to work up a large rendition of the scene.

Do you paint en plein air?

I paint outside at least once or twice a week, and every studio piece that I paint has its genesis in a plein air study. I started out as a studio painter, and heading outside was at first intimidating and frustrating. It took many tries before I painted anything even remotely presentable en plein air, but I truly believe it was the single greatest thing I did for the improvement of my work.

Do you prefer particular seasons or times of day?

The main theme that runs through my work is dramatic light. Those fleeting times at the cusp of day or close of evening make for such exciting painting: the clock is ticking and it's a race to the finish to capture the feel of the moment.

What's your best advice to students on painting landscapes?

Get outside! Too many artists rely on photos for painting landscapes, and their work inevitably looks flat and lacks emotion. The human eye can capture subtle nuances that the camera can't. To paint a scene believably, you have to have been in it with your senses fully engaged—seeing it, smelling it, hearing it, feeling it. Turn off your iPod and listen to nature when you're painting. Find things that are exciting to you and paint with your heart and your emotions. Excitement in a painting can't be faked and viewers can sense when you're just going through the motions.

STERLING EDWARDS

Sterling Edwards is a contemporary watercolor artist born in Kansas City, Missouri, in 1951. At the age of twelve he was introduced into the world of art through private art lessons and began experimenting with every medium at his disposal. In 1985 he began studying transparent watercolors and was captivated by the freshness and luminosity of the medium. Influenced by watercolor master and friend, Zoltan Szabo, Edwards spent several years developing his own unique style of painting that focuses on bold designs with slightly abstract undertones. Edwards lives and works in the town of Hendersonville, in the mountains of western North Carolina. When he's not in the studio painting, he likes to fly fish and take black and white photographs. In 2010, he was awarded a signature membership in the esteemed Transparent Watercolor Society of America, and his book, *Creating Luminous Watercolor Landscapes: A Four-Step Process* was published by North Light Books.

What inspired this painting?

I have been visiting Naples, Florida, for many years and have always been attracted to the colors of the water and the architecture of the buildings. *Neapolitan Life* is a visual statement that focuses on the beautiful aqua colors of the water and the white stucco buildings that are so prevalent there. I wanted to create a painting with rich colors and extreme shifts in value to exemplify the tropical nature of the area. The addition of palm trees and red tile roofs add to the feel of south Florida.

How would you describe your painting style?

I paint in many styles ranging from slight impressionism to total abstraction. My favorite style is what I refer to as "representational abstract." That's actually an oxymoron because a painting is typically one or the other. I've tried to marry the two styles and produce a painting that has slight abstractions but is still representational with an identifiable subject or theme. I think these paintings are my best pieces because they allow me an opportunity to create rather than replicate. I spent many years as a photorealist. During this time I would work feverishly to replicate every nuance of the subject that I was painting. Since then I have learned to focus most of my attention on the large shapes rather than the details. This has been a major epiphany for me because it freed my creativity.

In what locations do you paint?

I am predominantly an indoor painter. I find that plein air painting is difficult with watercolor unless you are working on a relatively small painting. Since I paint mostly large watercolors, there is the problem of the sun or wind drying my paper too quickly. The beginning stages of my paintings are often painted with wet color on wet paper. If the paper dries too quickly I don't have sufficient time to get all of my initial colors and shapes established before it dries. I have also noticed that insects are attracted to wet watercolor paper. There are few things more aggravating than having a bug land on your freshly painted and still wet sky!

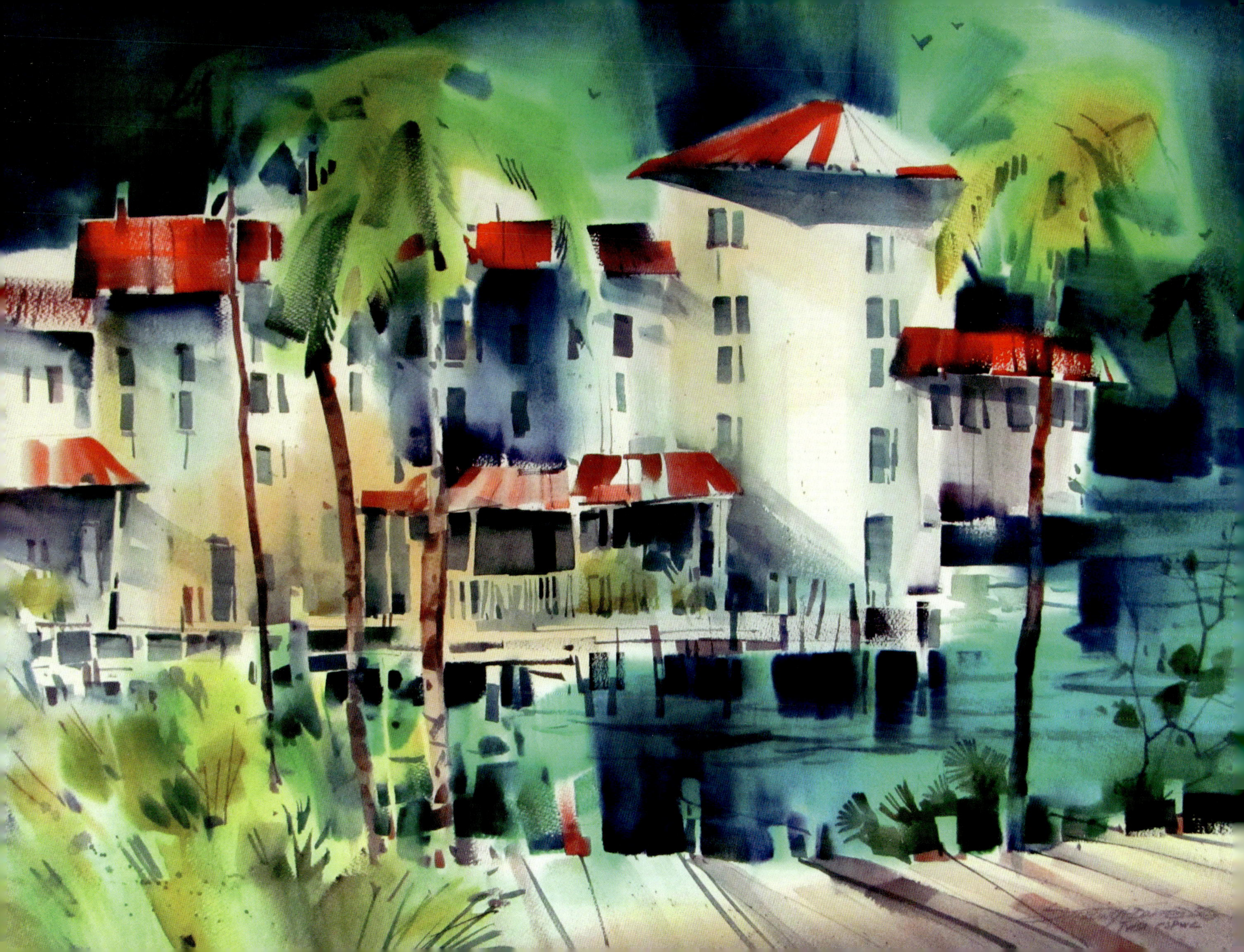

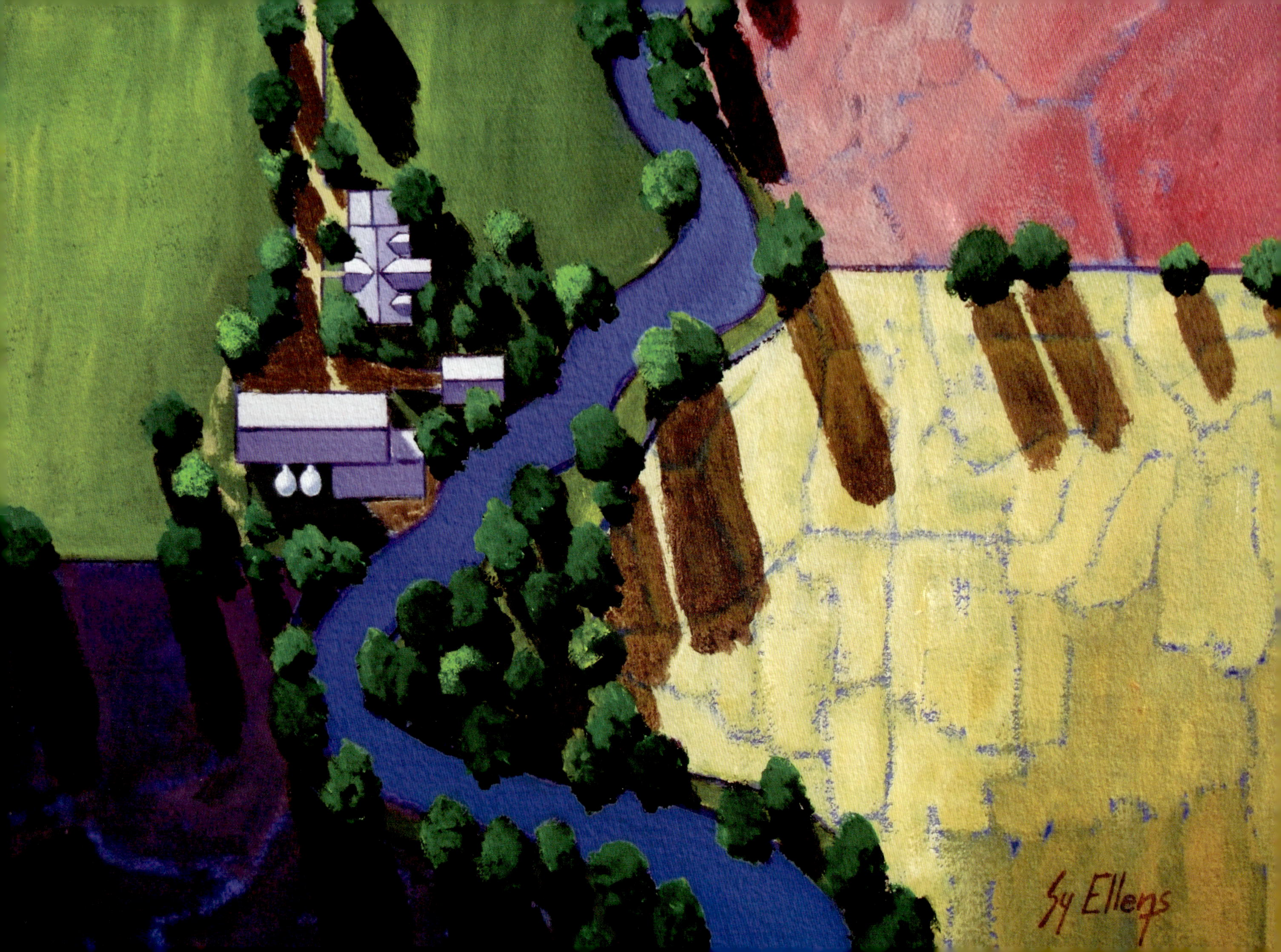
Sy Ellens

SY ELLENS

When asked where he finds inspiration for his paintings, Sy Ellens responds, "Usually I don't paint a particular place. I paint images that I have in my mind as the result of doing a lot of traveling, especially by plane." Hence the bird's-eye view seen in this painting, *By the River.* Ellens continues, "From an aerial perspective, one can see how people divide the land and establish spaces for themselves which they call their own. One can also see how this little space then relates not only to the other many spaces, but also to the unpredictable natural areas of rivers and lakes. As this creates both challenges and opportunities in one's daily life, so it does in the ordering of shapes, colors and textures in my paintings." Ellens has been a commercial artist, a teacher, and since 1980, a freelance artist. He has created a 2,200-square-foot *Fantasy of Flight* mural in the Children's Room and a 62,500-square-foot floor mural in the new Air Zoo in his hometown of Kalamazoo, Michigan. He is a signature member of the National Watercolor Society, and has recently been a contributing artist to the book *Strokes of Genius, The Best of Drawing,* published by North Light Books.

What inspired this painting?

After traveling extensively by plane, I have been able to look at the earth from a distance. This gives me a new perspective of the land that I know so intimately. Everything looks peaceful and harmonious on the land. I wish that people could also live that way.

Why is American landscape painting important today, in the 21st century?

Landscape artists capture the changes in the landscape that are affected by natural forces and also those caused by the intrusions and inventions of humans. The artwork of the past is a great help in discovering what past civilizations were like, and what we create today will help future generations understand our present society.

Is your painting inspired by spirituality? How is that seen in your art?

Having grown up on a farm, I have developed a special relationship with the land. When I was a child, I picked stones, cultivated crops, pulled weeds, milked cows, and did many other chores. I helped with seed planting, pest control and harvesting. I learned what it is to go through a frustratingly dry season and patiently wait for rain or wait for the rain to stop. I know what it is like to have an abundant harvest and almost no harvest at all. This made life on the farm both interesting and difficult, challenging and unpredictable. And it is this special relationship which God has given me that I am trying to explore and creatively express in my paintings. I also want to enrich the experiences of the viewers. I want to express a positive mood in my paintings through color: warm, fiery reds, yellows and oranges to brighten or inspire, and hues of blue, green and purple to calm or soothe.

What mediums do you use and what is your main painting technique?

Usually I paint with acrylic. I paint the canvas or watercolor paper with an undercolor first, often red or blue. Then I start to lay in the shapes by taking a pointed brush using Dioxazine Purple. I start to fill in the shapes with various colors, leaving the undercolor showing through. In some areas I add more layers of color, always leaving some of the previous layers showing through. At this point my painting is still abstract. When I paint in trees, buildings and other items, suddenly my painting appears realistic. I fill in the shadows and then it takes on a three-dimensional appearance.

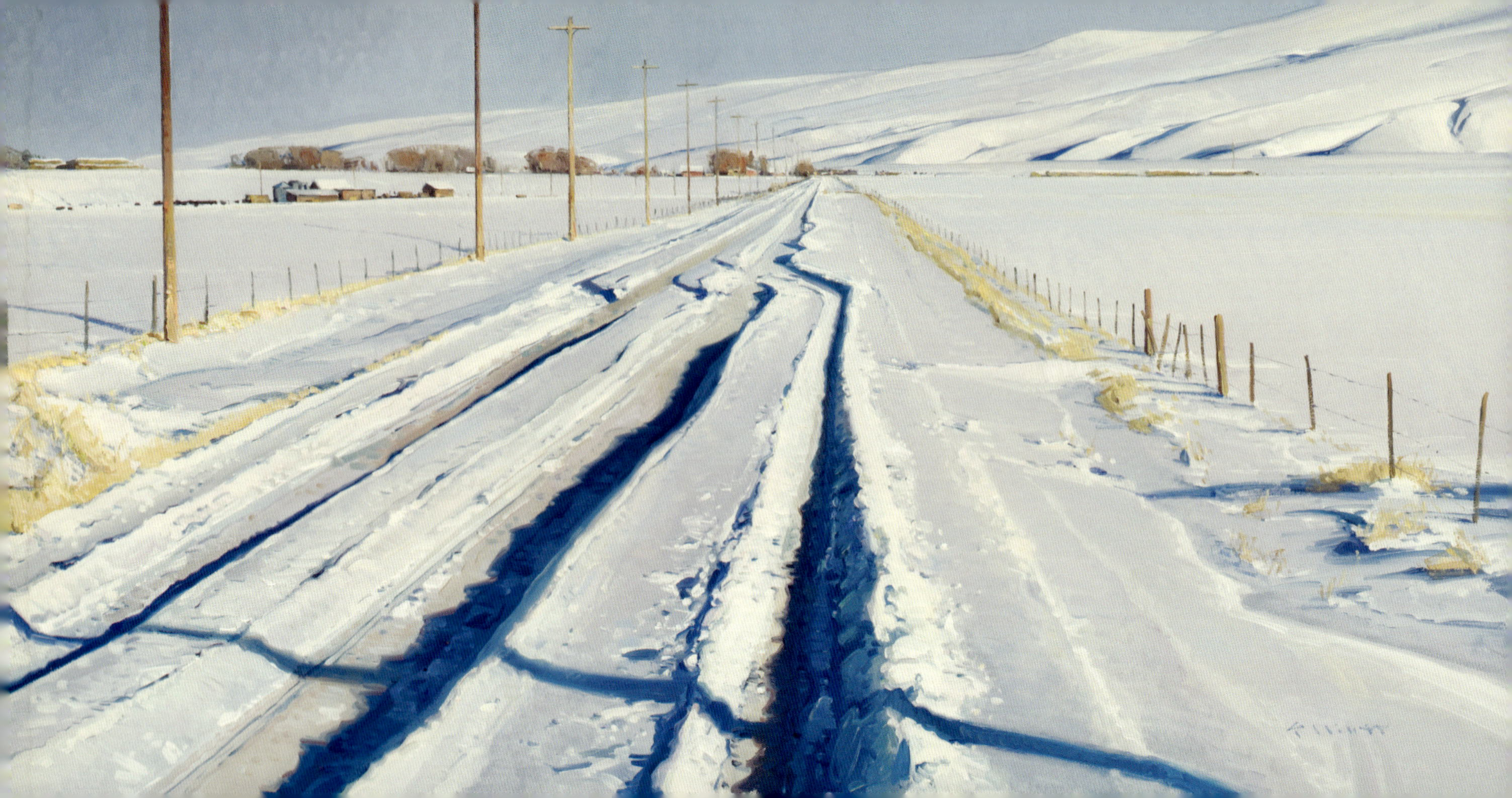

JOSH ELLIOTT

For Josh Elliott, a native of Great Falls, Montana, art-making is a family affair. His grandfather studied with Grant Wood and dabbled in all sorts of artistic pursuits. His father, wildlife artist Steve Elliott, gave up a successful career as an ER doctor to become a full-time artist. Josh learned the importance of painting from life and discovered his passion for painting outdoors. He lived out of state for some time but always felt a deep connection with Montana's landscape and people. He and his wife and two daughters now live in Helena, Montana. Josh is a member of the Salmagundi Club in New York City and the Northwest Rendezvous Group of Artists.

What inspired this painting?

I liked the bold and simple nature of the one idea of tracks in snow leading you into the painting. Also appealing was the tonal nature of the scene: variations and harmonies in blue. Finally, I liked how it told a story of rural life in the American West.

Do any historical movements, periods or artists inspire your painting?

I am inspired by the Canadian Group of Seven and Tom Thomson, the Taos Society of Artists, and the California Impressionists. They all painted from life and interpreted the landscape in their own unique voice. To me, a good painting is nature's truth filtered through the artist.

How do you plan your compositions?

I try to design my paintings so the viewer's eye can travel through the painting more than once on different paths, ultimately resting on the center of interest. I like to explore different motivations for design as well. For example, I may focus on an overall color scheme or harmony, creating a sort of tapestry. Sometimes I might opt for a dynamic painting with a more quirky composition, such as a high horizon with lots of thrust in the foreground. Or I may combine these elements as I did in *February's Blanket*.

Do you paint en plein air?

I painted outdoors almost exclusively when I first started—I think it heightened my level of observation. Although I still paint on location often, I paint in the studio more, where I have more time to contemplate what I would like to paint and how. I'll spend more time designing and drawing. However, without frequent sessions outside, I would lose the ability to paint light convincingly. For those wanting to try it, I would advise that they paint in all types of lighting conditions, and paint what inspires them, not what they see other people paint.

MAX FERGUSON

Max Ferguson learned the discipline for his meticulously rendered oil paintings while doing animated films as a teenager, graduating from the NYU film school in 1980. But it was while spending a year at an art school in Amsterdam that his interest switched to painting. He was, and continues to be, greatly influenced by Dutch 17th-century painting. Upon Ferguson's return to New York, H.W. Janson, author of the classic text *History of Art*, acquired one of his paintings for his personal collection. He has worked on a number of series over the years, including ones on subways, Coney Island, nocturnal imagery, and Jewish scenes. "My work is essentially autobiographical," says Ferguson, with his two most frequent models being his father and himself. His works are in many prominent public and private collections, including the Metropolitan Museum of Art, the British Museum, the Crystal Bridges Museum of American Art, and the Albertina in Vienna. Ferguson divides his time between New York and Jerusalem. He is also very passionate about music and languages, especially etymology.

What inspired this painting?

I try to see the positive and the beautiful in all things. This image struck me as exceptionally beautiful and romantic. I have done many nocturnal scenes and paintings of Central Park in New York, and this fits well within these parameters.

Do you prefer particular seasons or times of day?

I very often find that the most commonplace of scenes, in the right circumstances, can take on a magical quality. That's why I often paint scenes at night, or in the snow or rain; I feel this adds another element that makes the ordinary extraordinary.

Do any historical movements, periods or artists inspire your painting?

My two greatest influences are Dutch 17th-century, and early 20th-century American realists (the Ashcan School, the WPA-era artists, etc.). Specifically, my ideal artistic marriage would be Vermeer and Hopper. I recently told an art dealer that I was somewhat stuck in 17th-century Holland, and he replied, "That's not the worst of places to be stuck."

What mediums do you use, and what are your main painting techniques?

I work in a variety of media, but my strong suit is oil paint. While I approach every painting a little differently, generally I begin with a monochromatic underpainting and then work up in layers (usually two or three or more) of color, until I feel the painting has achieved a degree of finish with which I am reasonably content. I am yet to do a painting with which I am 100-percent satisfied. I suppose if I were to, I would find the *experience* unsatisfactory.

CENTRAL PARK NOCTURNAL SNOW II, 2005 Max Ferguson Oil on canvas 44" × 30" (112cm × 76cm) Private collection / The Bridgeman Art Library

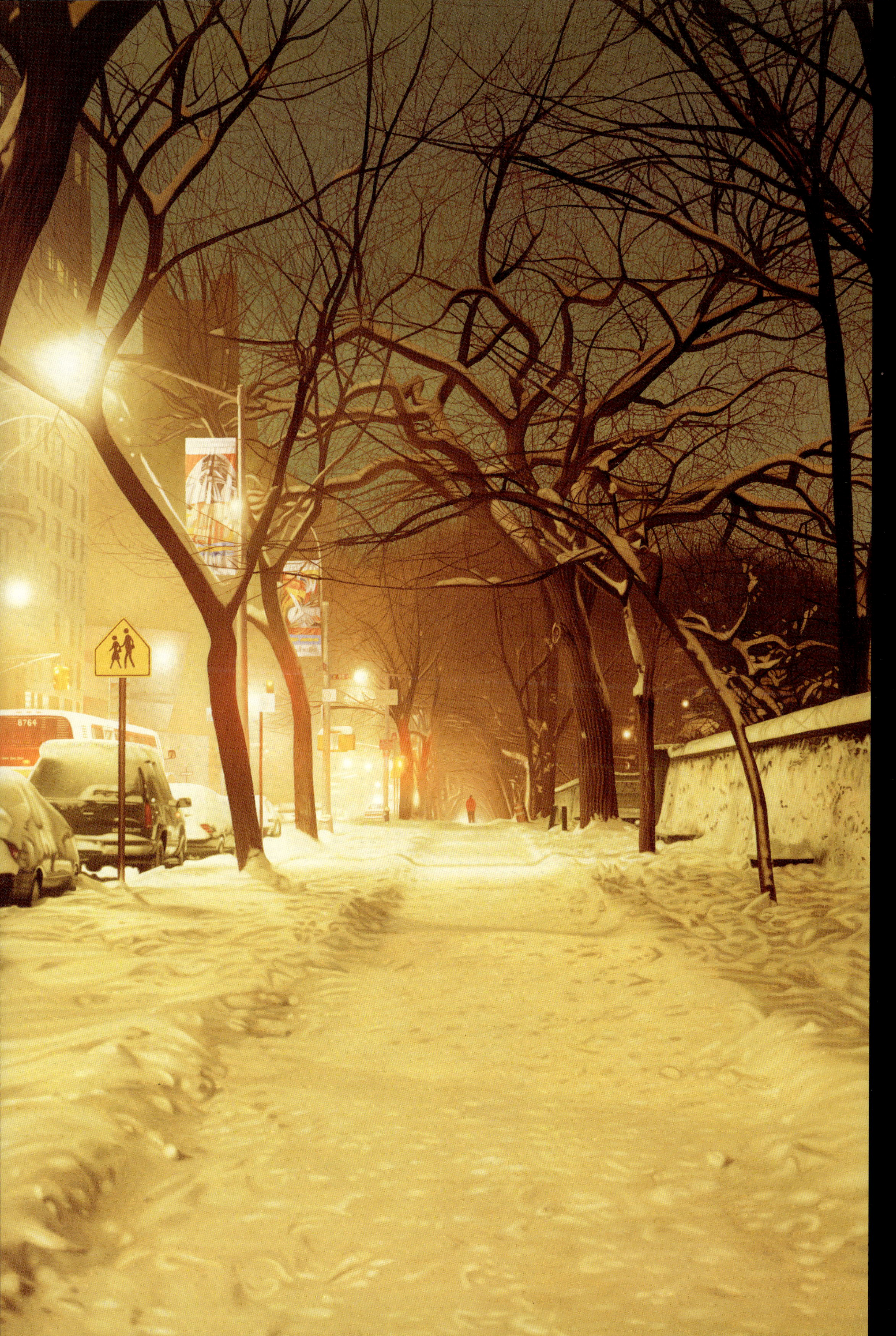
6764

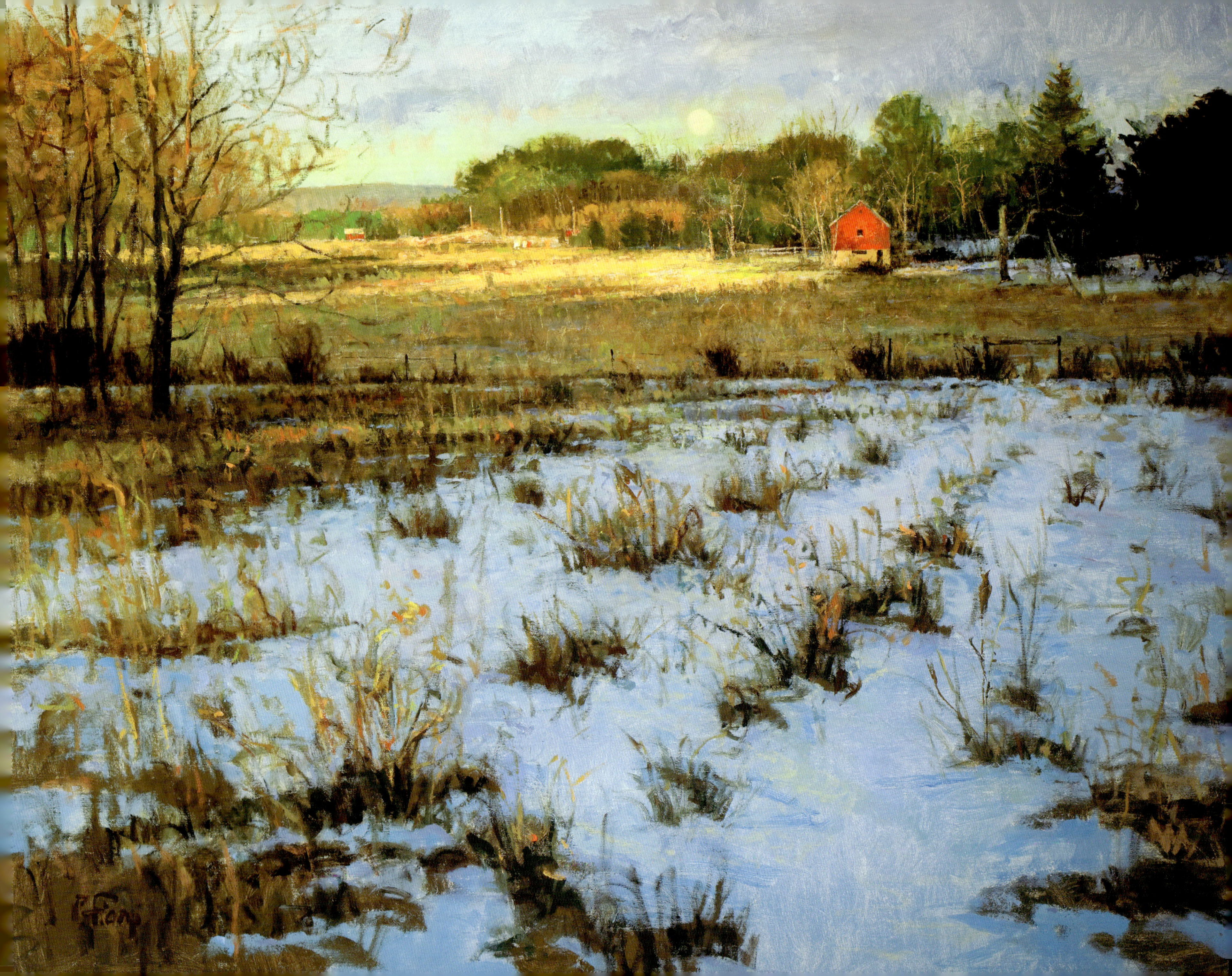

PETER FIORE

"My first love was photography and I continue to read and learn about it every day," says Pennsylvania artist Peter Fiore. Previously, he worked as a professional illustrator where he collaborated on thousands of projects and won numerous awards. Today his landscape paintings are widely collected. He's best known for painting light and for his striking use of color. "I live and work in northeastern Pennsylvania but I endeavor to create eternal statements," Fiore says. "All of my paintings are created in the studio. All of my subject matter comes from my immediate world. I take the raw materials of my environment and re-orchestrate to create the world that I want my viewers to see and feel. I used to think that I had to travel far to find interesting landscapes, but I have found that my own backyard can be inspirational. I just walk out my door and it's all there."

Q&A

What inspired this painting?

This particular landscape has been the subject of many paintings for me. The field, the trees, the spot of red of the barn, the distant hills, the light and the weather have all been major contributing factors to the variations and moods of these paintings. In this particular painting, there is a certain kind of quietness that I responded to that sets it apart. The inclusion of the moon makes it, for me, a timeless statement.

Do you prefer particular seasons or time of day?

Winter has always been a magical time for me. The light in winter is most varied; there are days when it's clear and bright, carving the earth into light and shadow like a razor. Yet, at times, the light can be soft and quiet as a whisper, with color of the most intense chromatic variations. In particular the light at the last moments of the day fills me with a sense of tranquil resonance.

What mediums do you use and what are your main painting techniques?

My paintings are structured in a traditional sense. I work mostly direct, including areas of impasto, scumbling, abrading the surface and whatever else I deem necessary, and later maybe a judicious harmonizing glaze when called for. I work in oil on oil-primed linen and most recently on oil-primed panels.

What's your best advice to students on painting landscapes?

Spend a lot of time waiting for a subject to evolve. You get more by waiting than you do by moving. You wait for the light to come and it will change the world in front of you. The true subject of any painting is light. If you have good light, anything can be made beautiful.

ALAN FLATTMANN

Although accomplished in oil and watercolor, Alan Flattmann has become best known for his work in pastel. His classic book, *The Art of Pastel Painting*, is still considered by many as the definitive guide to pastels. "Cities tend to be my favorite subject matter," says Flattmann. "I grew up in New Orleans and have been painting the French Quarter since I attended art school there in the mid-sixties. I love painting 'old things.' I've also done a lot of paintings of Europe, mostly Greece, Italy and France. The countryside is particularly appealing in these locations because the old architecture and the landscape tend to dwell together as one." Flattmann is a member of an elite group of artists elected to the Pastel Society of America's Hall of Fame and the Masters Circle of the International Association of Pastel Societies. He is also the founder and current president of the Degas Pastel Society.

What inspired this painting?

This is a fantastic panoramic view of the French Quarter in New Orleans from atop a high-rise building. I love how it shows the rugged character of the old port city. I used the approaching storm to create dramatic mood and lighting.

How do you plan your compositions?

The most important factors in planning a composition are choosing a center of interest, placement of the objects, and locating the borders. I use a viewfinder on location. In the studio, I experiment with cropping photos different ways to achieve the most interesting arrangements.

Do you paint en plein air?

I greatly enjoy painting en plein air. There is nothing more satisfying than coming back from a trip with a batch of sketches and small paintings done on location. I recommend working relatively small so that you can complete (or nearly complete) paintings in about three hours or less. The lighting and conditions change too much after three hours to continue on the same piece without getting confused. Most of my plein air paintings are about 80 to 90 percent completed on location, then I finish them in my studio from memory or sometimes by referring to a photo taken at the location. Pastels and watercolors are the mediums I find the easiest to work with outdoors.

What mediums do you use and what are your main techniques?

I paint with oils, pastels and watercolors. Pastels for me are the easiest and most fun to work with, but I love the challenges of oil painting and watercolor is my favorite sketching medium. My pastels are built up in layers, starting with a strong value underdrawing, followed by a lay-in of overall color, and a gradual development of forms with a thick application of pastels. Each layer is isolated by spraying with fixative to secure the pastel and allow for additional color buildup.

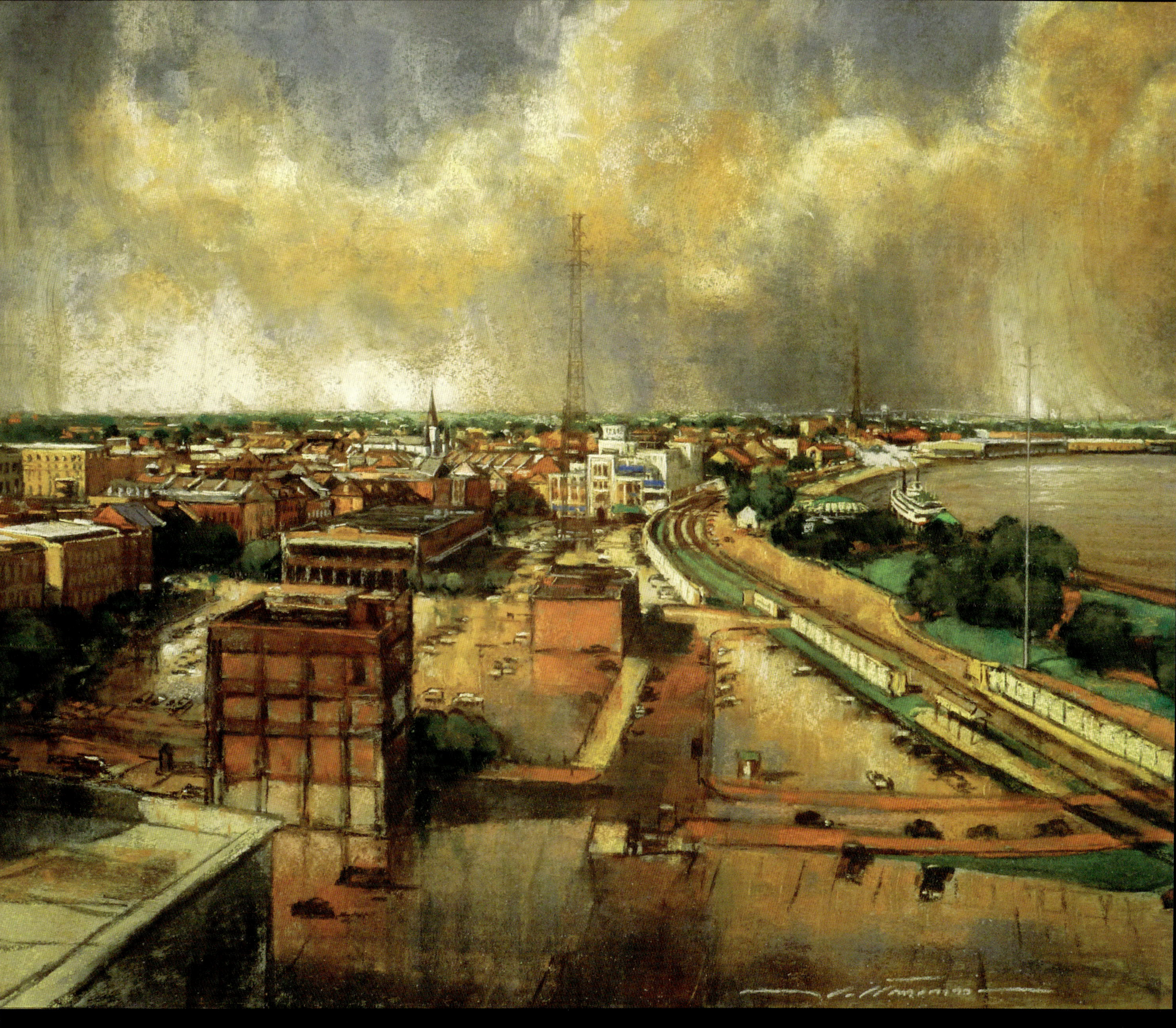

APPROACHING STORM Alan Flattmann Pastel 24" × 30" (61cm × 76cm)

TERRI FORD

San Jose, California, artist Terri Ford discovered pastels in 1987 and has worked with them ever since. She says, "My passion for pastels never subsides. It becomes more intense as I continue my journey with them." Ford is a signature member of the Pastel Society of America and received the title of Masters Circle by the International Association of Pastel Societies in 2007. Of her favorite painting locations, Ford says, "The landscape of California is so diverse. We have the coastline, mountains and high country, desert, lakes, streams, eucalyptus, palms and so much more. The dunes of Carmel Beach are a standout favorite subject of mine. They seem to possess natural design and don't depend on ideal weather to be paintable." She describes herself as a representational painter with an Impressionistic feel. "I want the strokes and colors that I use to be as apparent and effective in the painting as the subject itself."

What inspired this painting?

I have always been attracted to barns and other old buildings as painting subjects. I painted this Sonoma, California, barn en plein air. The morning light and shadows were so lovely. I've visited this barn at various times of day and it really comes alive in the morning light.

How do you plan your compositions?

I'm not a big planner when it comes to painting. I have certain approaches to getting the information that I need on the surface but I usually let each painting experience take its own course. I think that composition comes to me instinctively. I don't have a formula for it.

What mediums do you use and what are your main techniques?

I work exclusively with dry pastels. I have done some oil painting and worked in acrylic years ago but pastel is my medium. I work on sanded paper that is mounted to acid-free museum board so I have a nice rigid surface. I begin with harder stick pastels and make a point of establishing the darks and lights. I then use a stiff bristle brush dipped in denatured alcohol and apply this to the pastel, which creates a wash/underpainting. This dries very quickly. Once dry, it is set and I then layer a variety of pastels using different types of strokes to develop the painting. The underpainting often shows through in the final painting.

What's your best advice to students on painting landscapes?

Get a good sense of what you want to paint. Sometimes it's best to take on a smaller part of the big picture until you feel comfortable with your medium. Students often try to paint everything they see. It's valuable to simplify, simplify, simplify.

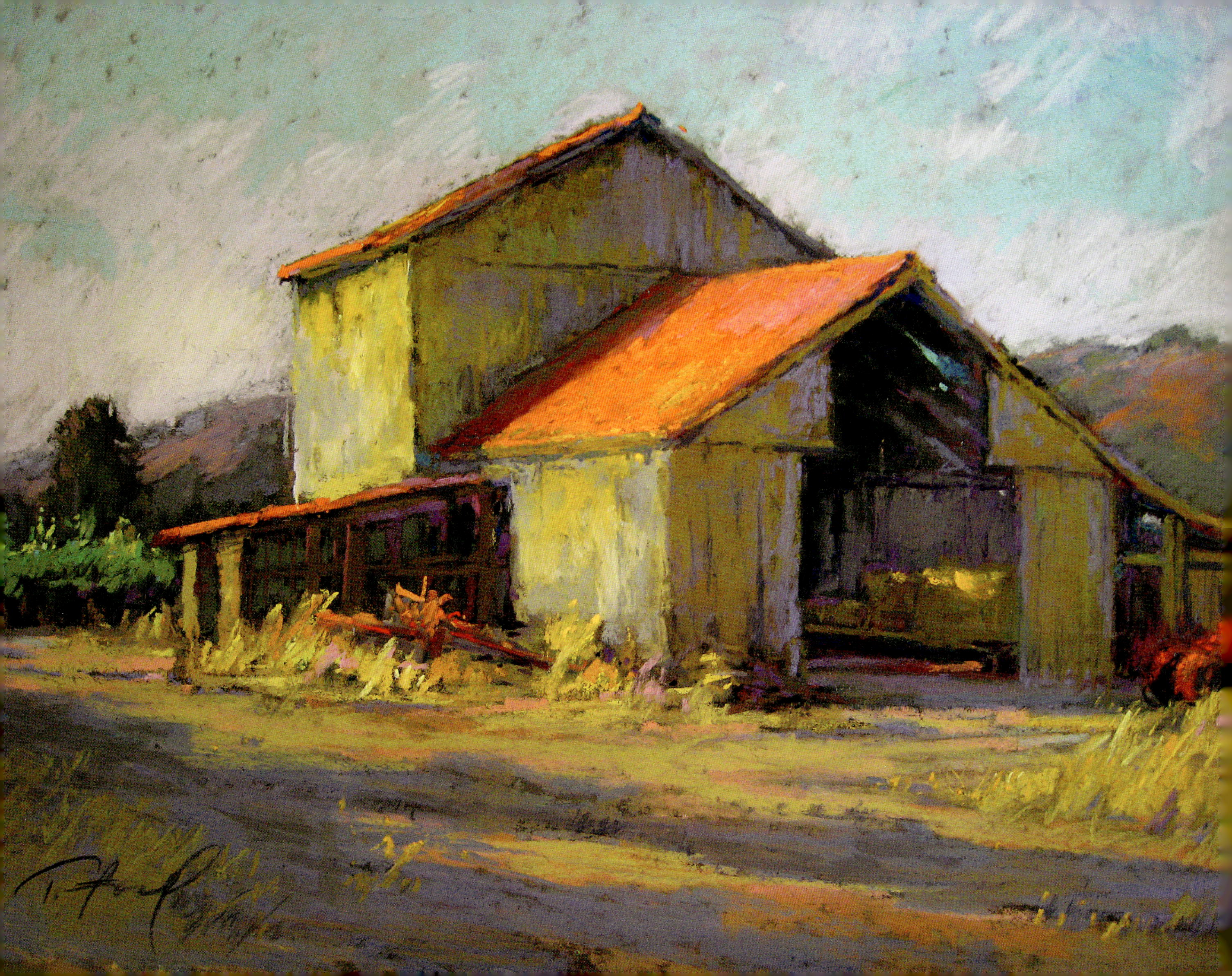

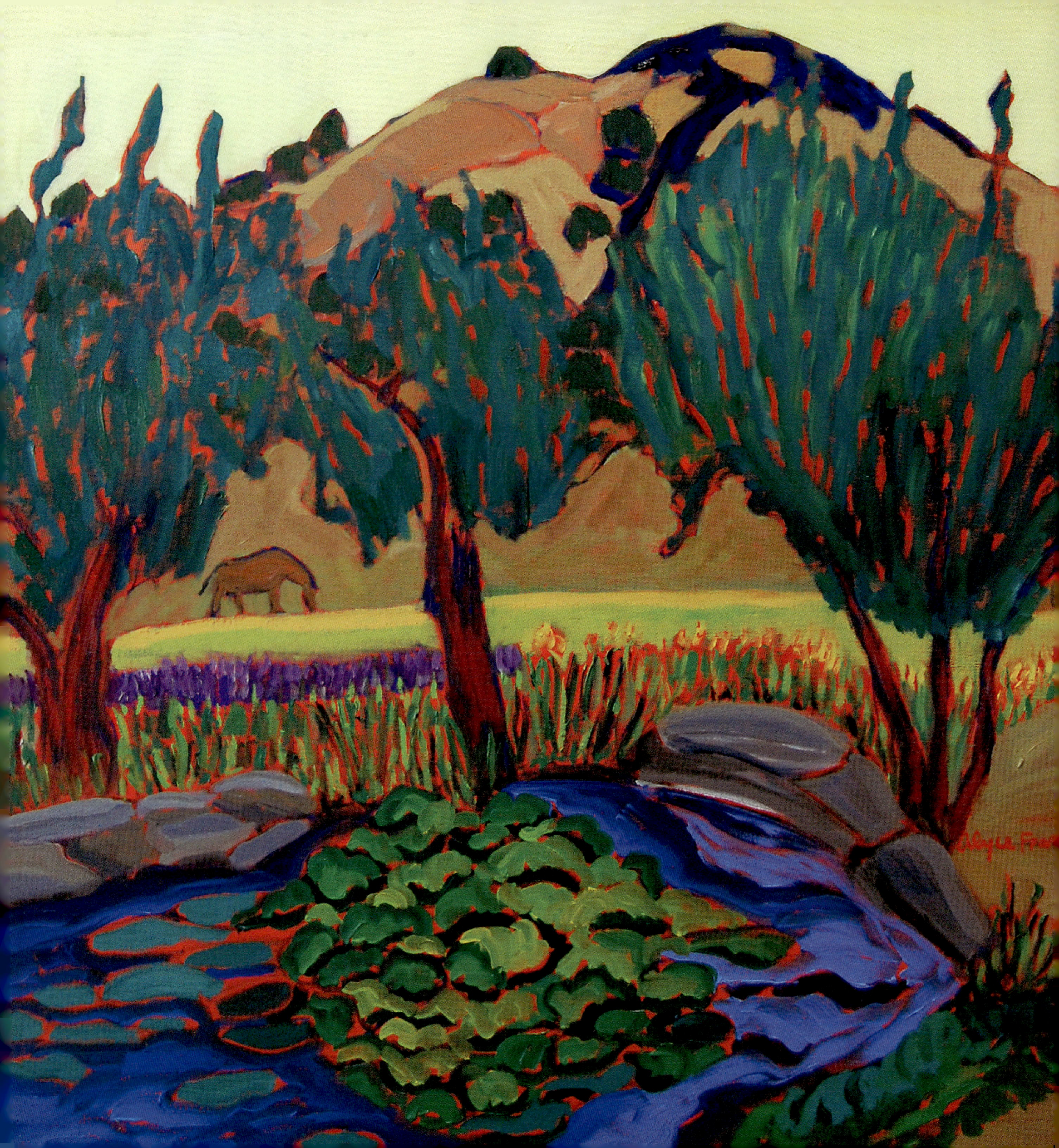

ALYCE FRANK

It is often said of longtime landscape artist Alyce Frank that she "will not paint what she sees." She does not limit herself to depicting only what is observed. Frank's colorful and playful interpretation of the land is uniquely her own. Every piece is begun on site, as she takes in her surroundings then rids herself of limitations, such as the actual colors in the landscape, and lets her imagination guide her to an emotional finish. She often underpaints her canvas in red, a practice that emphasizes her non-realistic approach and heightens drama. Though she was never formally trained in a university setting, Frank has studied with local masters and was selected for a master class with renowned abstract expressionist Richard Diebenkorn at the Santa Fe Art Institute. She continues her art training to this day, still attending workshops despite her many artistic accomplishments.

Why is American landscape painting important today, in the 21st century?

Land is permanent, always interesting, eternal. It's ever the same and ever changing.

In what locations do you paint?

While I mainly paint in northern New Mexico where I live, I have painted in many western states: California, Utah, Nevada. There have been series of paintings from Yellowstone National Park, where I was an artist-in-residence, the Canyonlands, Canyon de Chelly (my all-time favorite) and Alaska.

Do you prefer particular seasons or times of day?

Because I paint plein air, I prefer the spring and fall when the weather is fine and the colors superb. Winter storms have also been successful subjects, however.

How would you describe your painting style?

I consider myself a Taos expressionist, a term I coined. Lately my work has been abstract and based on color and form.

What mediums do you use and what is your main painting technique?

Oil is my primary medium with a layered stroking technique. I am known for a red ground or undercoat which serves to heighten the colors and emphasize emotion in the landscapes.

JONATHAN FRANK

Living in Moab, Utah, in the heart of red rock country, it's no wonder that watercolorist Jonathan Frank feels a deep, spiritual connection to his surroundings. "I become awed, humbled, energized and inspired, all with a deep sense of peace," says Frank. A signature member of the National Watercolor Society, his watercolor process involves painting hundreds of abstract shapes, all with hard edges, within a representational framework. He paints layer over layer, floating pure color into clear washes, letting the colors blend visually on the paper. When the colors reach the desired richness and the painting is otherwise finished, he takes the extra step of outlining every shape he's just painted with India ink and a Rapidograph technical pen. The practice of outlining his paintings began as a spontaneous extracurricular experiment on a high school art class assignment. Frank was so impressed with the results that he adopted the concept into his general artistic thinking from that day on.

Q&A

What inspired this painting?

I'm continually amazed by the combination of red earth and blue sky that is so prevalent in southern Utah. This was the view from our first campsite on the White Rim Trail in Canyonlands National Park. I sat here for an hour or so with my coffee through the warming sunrise of a cold November morning, all the while imagining how I would paint this scene to convey this amazing experience.

Do you prefer particular seasons or times of day?

Like most landscape artists, I love low angled light that you typically get in the early morning or late afternoon hours. However, I'm not above altering a scene to create a mood, or combination of seasons that doesn't actually exist. I'll use whatever it takes to express my vision and make the painting more interesting. This also supports my creativity, and keeps me from being merely a copyist.

Do any historical movements, periods or artists inspire your painting?

I've always been particularly inspired by the art of Maynard Dixon. The bold colors and outlining were inspired by the art of Peter Max.

How do you plan your compositions?

I always start a composition from photos that I've taken on hikes or various trips. I try to do most of my composing through the camera lens, but usually end up adding or eliminating some elements in the final piece. I start by sketching out the image on a sheet of newsprint the same size as the painting. Here I can experiment with ideas, erase, change, and arrange elements to my heart's content. This drawing is usually just the primary shapes with very little detail. When I'm satisfied, I trace it onto the watercolor paper using graphite paper.

What does landscape painting teach us about life and art?

Our planet Earth *is* the landscape and to paint it is the unique opportunity for me to express my feelings of gratitude toward the planet, and my place on it.

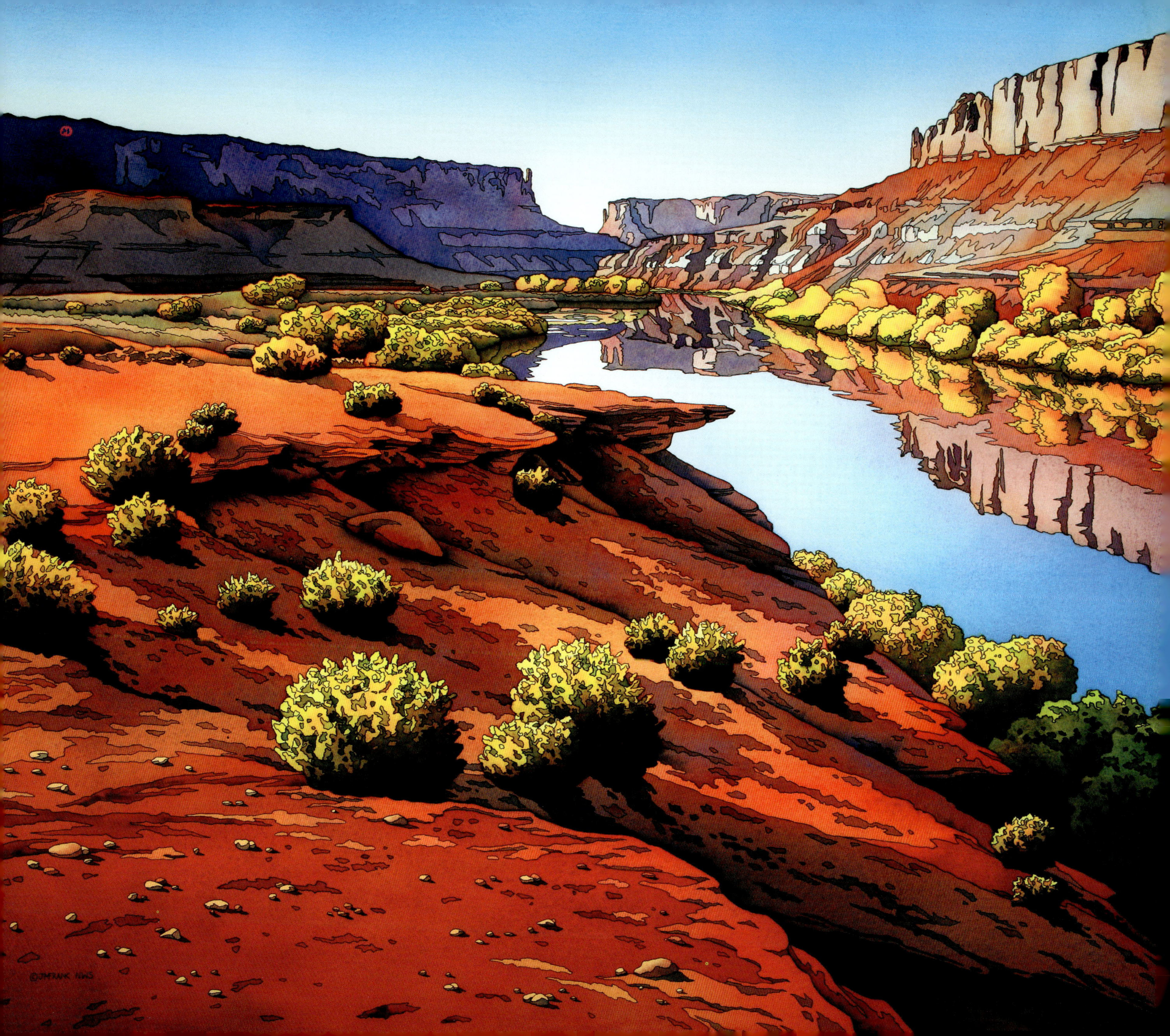

GUIDO FRICK

Born in 1947 in Germany, Guido Frick spends half of the year painting in Europe and the other half painting in the United States. He received his art education as a student of Czechoslovakian impressionist Karel Hodr, but he considers the influence of Russian-born painter and instructor Sergei Bongart as the most important, and of a life-changing impact. Bongart encouraged him to become a full-time painter. Besides his art studies, Frick worked as a newspaper journalist and broadcaster. Success came along, like winning the Prix de Salon in the early 1980s in Fontainebleau, France, but the final push toward life as a painter came from Bongart's encouragement. Today, Frick is represented in several galleries in America and abroad, has been published in art magazines and enjoys teaching workshops in the United States. He never gets tired of traveling through the American West and nurtures a great interest in the history of the Plains Indians.

What inspired this painting?

For days it was raining like crazy and never seemed to stop. I had had all my painting equipment shipped over to my place in the Hawaiian Islands, and there I was, sitting on the porch, staring into the rain, not able to do a single brushstroke. After days of this, suddenly a bright sun broke through the clouds. The breeze blew the clouds, and my frustration, away and it looked like a color explosion. What had been subdued, dull and sad suddenly started to shine brightly and glow with light. I felt a color explosion within myself and tried to put that on the canvas in this painting, titled *Harmonies of Hawaii*.

How would you describe your painting style?

I always have a problem labeling my "style" because it is not abstract—it is realistic, but in a loose, non-photorealistic way. I paint loose, sloppy, careless, generous—but controlled loose, sloppy, careless and generous. My motto: Swing a big brush, symbolically and literally. Don't paint with a brush the size of a toothpick, and avoid getting overwhelmed by details. Think big, paint big. As my former teacher, the great master Sergei Bongart, said: "First paint the dog, then the flea, then the signature."

Do you paint en plein air? What practical advice do you have for those who would like to try it?

I paint exclusively outdoors. I have a nice studio where I can do anything I want, except paint. As soon as I grab a brush, I get claustrophobic. I miss the smell and the sound and the atmosphere of the great outdoors. I will never forget a perfect painting day on the Oglala National Grassland along the border between Nebraska and South Dakota. Endless golden knee-high grass stretches in all directions like an ocean without a horizon. The wind waves it and creates a smooth and gentle sound; a meadowlark now and then can be heard, but no noise. It's a complete quiet that our ears are not used to anymore. And for a hundred miles around, there's no sign of civilization, not even a telephone pole. My advice for those who want to become outdoor painters? Be prepared to not only struggle with your painting subjects, but also with the elements. Be prepared for wind, rain, heat, cold, sandstorms, dust devils, thunderstorms. Learn to read the language of nature, become a part of nature, then you might be rewarded with a good painting.

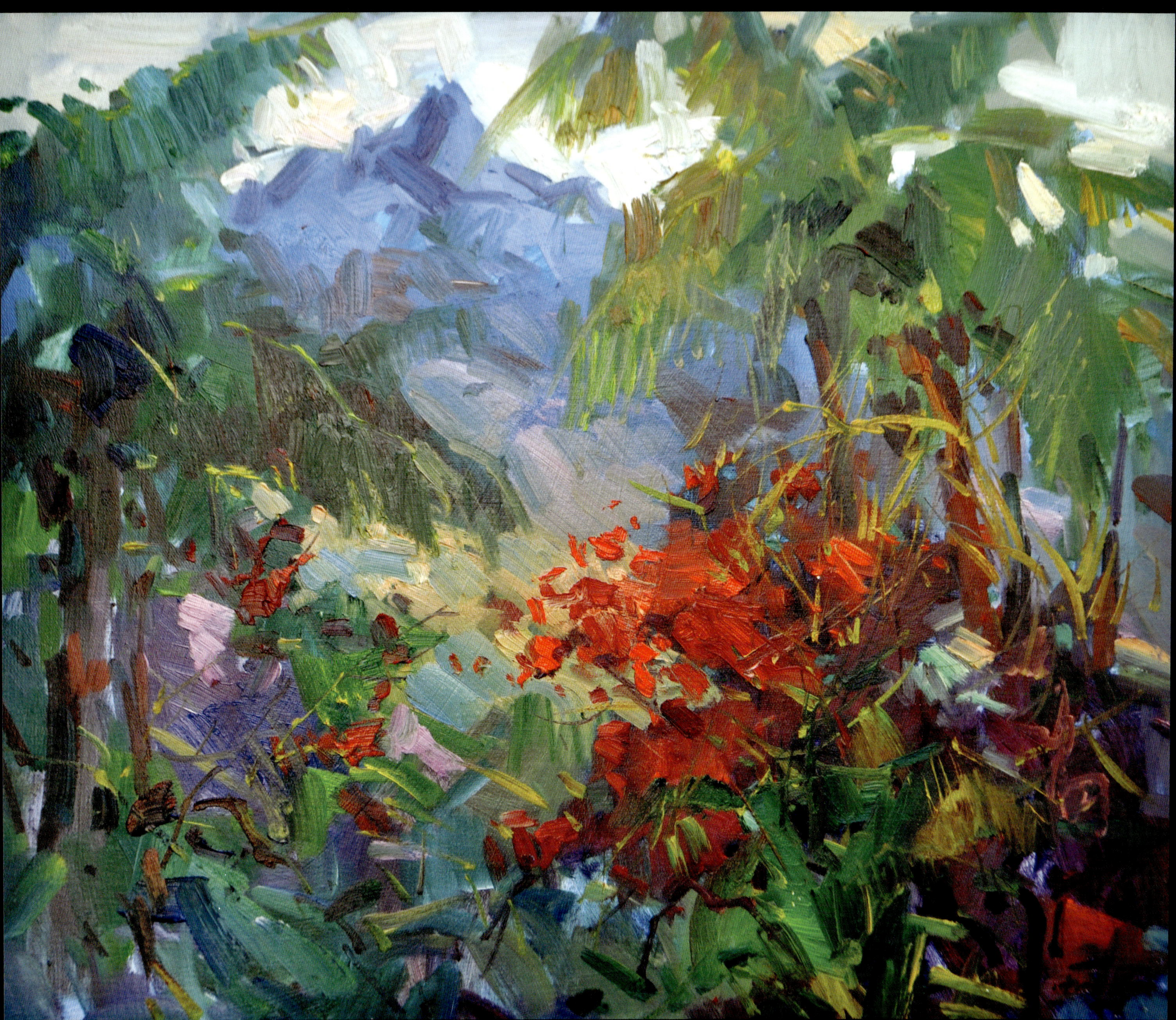

JON R. FRIEDMAN

When asked why he believes American landscape painting is important today, Jon R. Friedman replies, "The beauty of the natural world is a solace and a reminder of our connection to something deeper and more durable than the increasingly frenzied routines of our 21st century civilization." Friedman and his wife divide their time between New York City and Cape Cod, Massachusetts. Therefore, it follows that he paints the locations he's most familiar with. In recent years, these have been the beaches and tidal marshes of coastal New England, and the forests and parks of the Mid-Atlantic states. "They are, for me, an inexhaustible source of wonder and surprise," Friedman says. "Each time that I set out for the beach or the woods, I am full of eager expectation and I am never disappointed. It makes me want to sing. Since I can't sing, I paint."

Q&A

What inspired this painting?

I like the fact that the image is both very real and very abstract; intricately complex in its detail, and very simple—light, dark, light—in its overall structure. This commingling of representational complexity and formal abstraction is a quality that I try to discover and articulate in all of my landscapes.

How would you describe your painting style?

Realistic, but not photorealistic. This is not so easy to tell in reproduction. From a distance, my paintings often appear strikingly detailed and realistic, but as you move in to examine them more closely, that impression dissolves and the material details of the paint surface seem surprisingly unanchored from the descriptive content of the painting—abstract and suggestive rather than local and literal. I am very interested in having the material—paint, surface, the physical stuff of the painting—exist in a lively dialogue with the illusionistic representation. I want the observer of the painting to ping-pong back and forth between the illusion of the painting and the physical facts of the painting.

How do you plan your compositions?

Most of my landscape paintings are fairly large and painted in the studio. I rely on a combination of quick thumbnail sketches made on site and digital photographs. I do a lot of cropping and collaging of my photographs on the computer, exploring different compositional possibilities before beginning a painting. I block in the composition on the canvas, working very quickly, using thin turpentine washes. Once underway, I alter and revise the composition as the painting progresses.

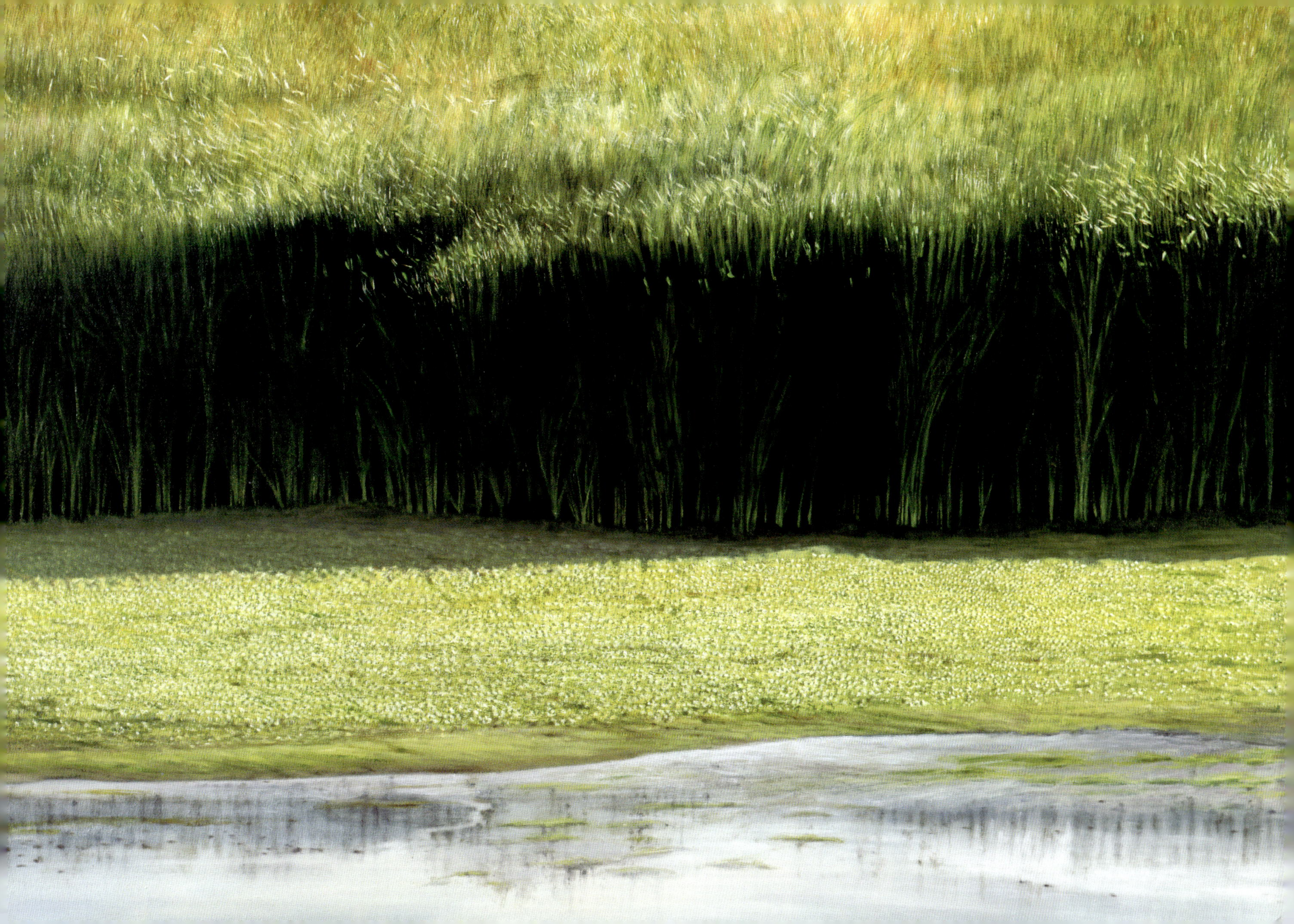

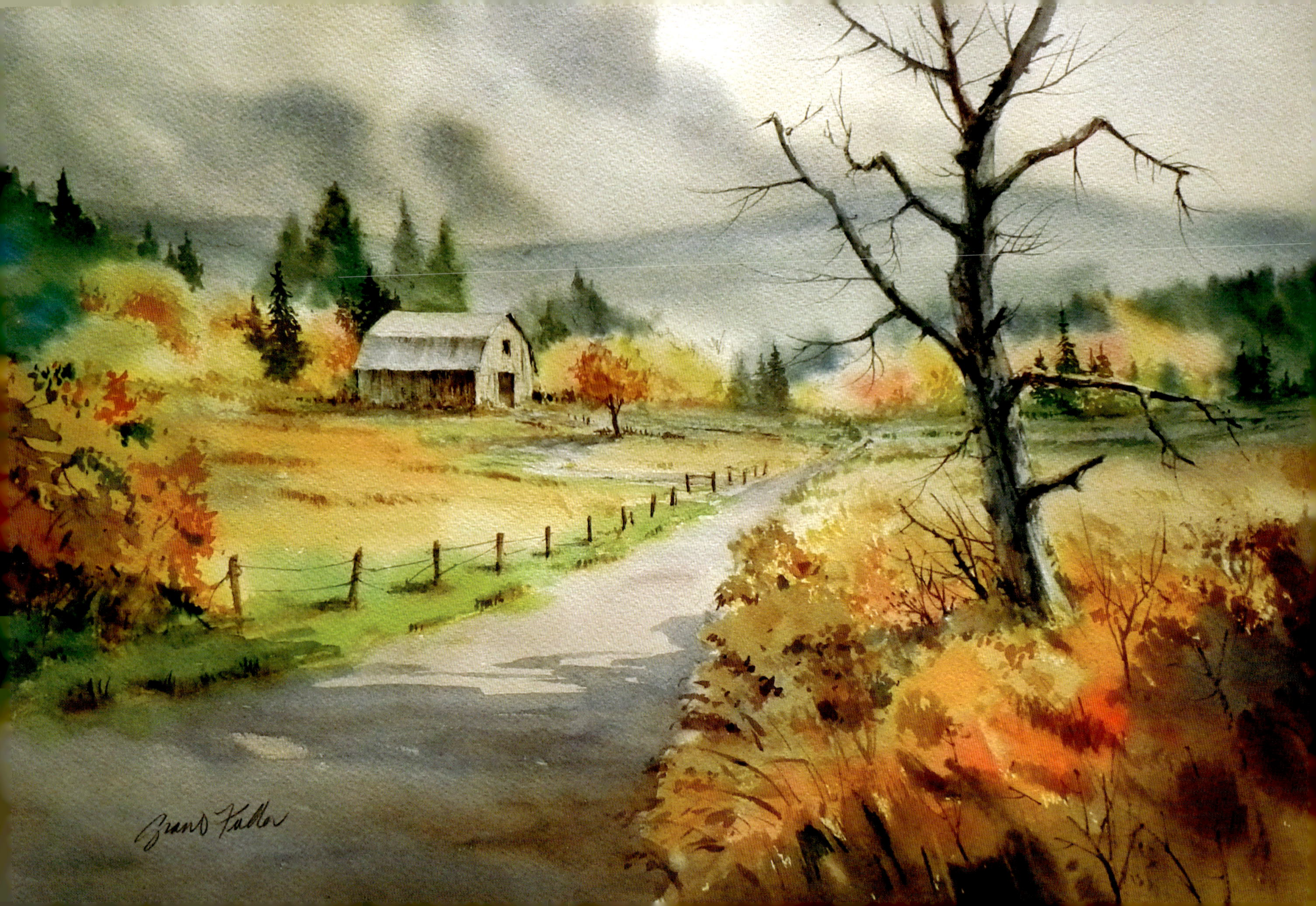

GRANT FULLER

Even though he loves painting seascapes as well as farmland, rivers and lakes, Canadian artist Grant Fuller calls himself a "fair-weather painter." He says, "I do not enjoy fighting with the elements. Wind, cold or rain will send me into the car with the heater on or home to the studio to work from photos. A rainy day in the studio is heaven for me." After four years of college at the Vancouver School of Art, Fuller went to Toronto in 1965 to begin a career in commercial art. He started as a layout artist and soon was promoted to art director and later to advertising manager for Sears, working with top photographers and artists in New York, Montreal and Chicago. Then came the opportunity to manage broadcast production. His experience in art directing took him to location shoots in Florida, Arizona, Puerto Rico and California. These days, Fuller teaches watercolor workshops throughout the U.S. and beyond, from Hawaii and Alaska to the Cotswolds, England, and has written two art instruction books, *Watercolor A to Z* and *Start Sketching and Drawing Now*, both published by North Light.

What inspired this painting?

This is such a well-worn subject but I cannot resist the country road and the old barn in the field. It just cries out to be painted time and time again. I always see something different—the misty hills in the background, the fall colors, the afternoon light, and the road that never fails to lead us into the story.

Why is American landscape painting important today, in the 21st century?

These old buildings and farmlands are being lost as development moves in. A graphic record in photos and paintings is not just important for historical reference, but the art makes a visual retreat from the hectic urban lifestyle of our time.

Is your painting inspired by spirituality? How is that seen in your art?

I can't say my painting is motivated by any religious beliefs but I must admit that many of my works seem to have been helped by a higher power. Some of my paintings fail and I will destroy them but the really successful ones are often mysteriously beyond my usual skill level.

What mediums do you use and what is your main painting technique?

Aside from pencil drawing, I work mainly in watercolor. In the studio I will do a lot of wet paper work. I paint on a drawing board, almost flat but at a slight angle. Outdoors I work on dry paper, vertically on an easel. This is a much looser treatment than studio painting; splashes and runs are common and expected.

What's your best advice to students on painting landscapes?

The first thing to study when starting landscape painting is elimination. It is so tempting to put everything you see into the picture. Use a small piece of cardboard with a window cut out so you can frame a scene as though you were looking at a photograph. Even then you will need to simplify the contents. This is where a sketchbook comes in handy.

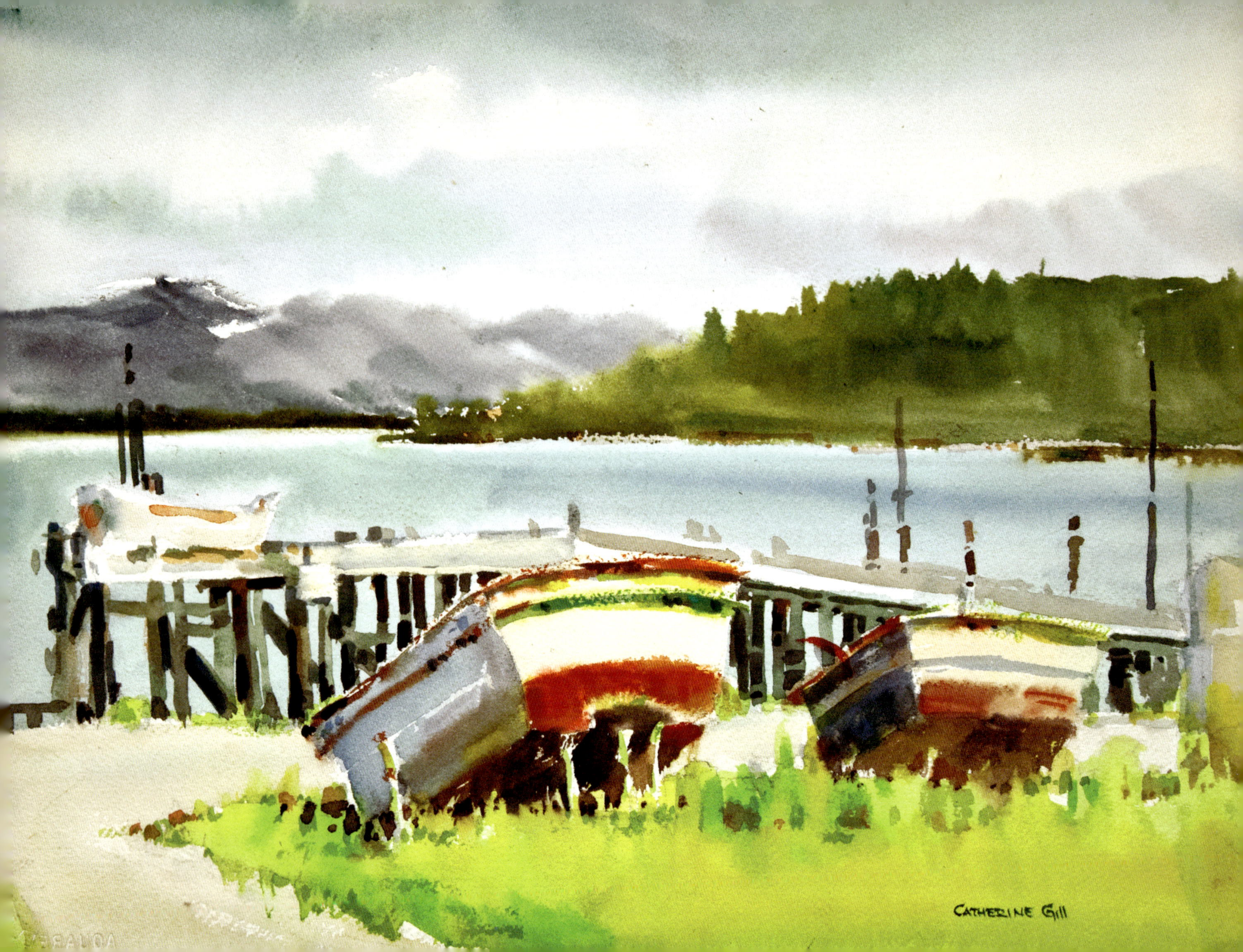
CATHERINE Gill

CATHERINE GILL

Catherine Gill has lived and worked in the Pacific Northwest for thirty years. She paints on location in watercolor, oil and pastel, and is also a printmaker. "I relish painting landscapes in rural areas, often seeking out places that are small, remote, quiet," says Gill. "Some of these landscapes show grand vistas, but many do not. I'm attracted to places that evoke the power and endurance of the land and of the people who have lived there; this endurance is certainly not only an American characteristic, but it is a personal and cultural one for me, and is representative of much of America's immigrant history." Gill teaches painting and printmaking at her studio in Seattle, Washington, and throughout the United States, Europe, China and Australia. She is co-founder of Art Partners International, an organization dedicated to bringing together artists and art of different cultures. She is also a member of the Northwest Watercolor Society and the Plein Air Painters of Washington. Her book, *Powerful Watercolor Landscapes*, with writer Beth Means, was published by North Light in January 2011.

What inspired this painting?

The imagery in this painting is so suggestive of many small communities in southeast Alaska, with its endless small, quiet, hidden bays, old wooden docks, and small boats scattered everywhere. The remote community of Craig is on the west side of Prince of Wales Island, and is truly way "out there," removed from most urban challenges, but steeped in its own. Painting and teaching in this area for many years offered me the opportunity to witness this laid-back and independent way of life; to experience the endurance of folks tied intimately to the land and water, folks who judge you by how well you do your job. It is a place of hard, satisfying and valuable work done mostly with the hands, and of living in a more direct relationship with nature. Here there is a solitude and a hard-won peace that I see and admire in many small communities that exist on the edges of the land. It has made its mark on me, and my painting.

How would you describe your painting style?

My style is impressionistic. The painting starts as a simple design with an abstract pattern, and then gains relevance to the actual landscape more through suggestion of color interplay and pattern of shapes and lines than from rendering exactly the objects before me. I often interpret and exaggerate. I have no issue with moving mountains, altering landforms, reducing dimensional space, and changing color and value. If the painting calls for it, I'll go there.

Do you paint en plein air?

What attracts me to painting on location is the firsthand and totally present connection to the land, feeling the energy of a place that provokes an emotion in me, and powers my painting. When my feet are on the ground, and I know the direction of the light and the sound of the wind, I have so much more information to help me with the challenge of painting landscapes.

What mediums do you use and what are your main techniques?

I use many different media. I was an oil painter first, then took on watercolor. That led to mixed media (pastel in wet watercolor). I added printmaking about ten years ago. I generally start by doing a simple value sketch of the design, keeping the shapes minimal. Then I draw it out on canvas or paper, and with paint start to build the painting in a few more layers, going from large blocked-in shapes to smaller areas of refined shapes. When the painting "feels" like my initial take on it, it is done. Not a stroke more.

MICHAEL GODFREY

Born in Germany in 1958 and raised in North Carolina, Michael Godfrey is a representational landscape artist whose work hangs in many private and corporate collections. After earning his BA in Fine Art, he began his painting career in oils and watercolors. Godfrey spends hours field sketching and photographing, preparing for a well-thought-out painting. Typically, he starts a major work using small oil studies done on location. These field studies provide color accuracy, and the photographs capture special details. In his studio, work progresses in successive layers of paint, and light is orchestrated to create a painting that appeals to his internal sense of order. "Landscape artists must have some knowledge of many disciplines (geology, chemistry, physics, architecture) to understand the world they're trying to create," says Godfrey. "An artist must observe with the idea that what is observed must be interpreted and distilled. It's just as important what you do not include in a work as what is eventually laid down."

What inspired this painting?

I look forward to fresh snowfall. Our snowfalls in the East tend to be wet and sticky. Whenever it snows I go to a nearby wooded pond area to see what treasures are exposed by the blanket of snow. Snowfall reveals the underlying structure, reflects and bounces light, and presents many possibilities for painting compositions. *Winter's Splendor* is a composed studio work that distills the essence of my experience during a recent snow in Maryland. Because of my preference for strong lighting effects, I composed this painting facing into the sun.

In what locations do you paint?

I paint the things and places that speak to me. When I go to a locale, I spend lots of time studying how the scene reflects the quality of the light. What is the sky's color? How does it affect the land or water? Is there moisture in the air? How does that affect the visibility?

What medium do you use and what are your main techniques?

I paint exclusively in oils. I prefer the medium's forgiving nature and the ability to layer and glaze. I imply detail, rather than state it directly. Light and mood are the most important aspects of a good painting.

Is your painting inspired by spirituality? How is that seen in your art?

Any ability I have is God given. I want my paintings to reflect what God has already done. My motivation to create comes from my relationship to Him. I want the viewer of my work to feel the sense of awe that I experience. There is much that is beautiful in this world and I think that art—my art—should lift the spirit of the viewer. Artists have a choice as to what they create. I want the work of my hands to glorify God and cause people to think of the beauty of this wondrous creation.

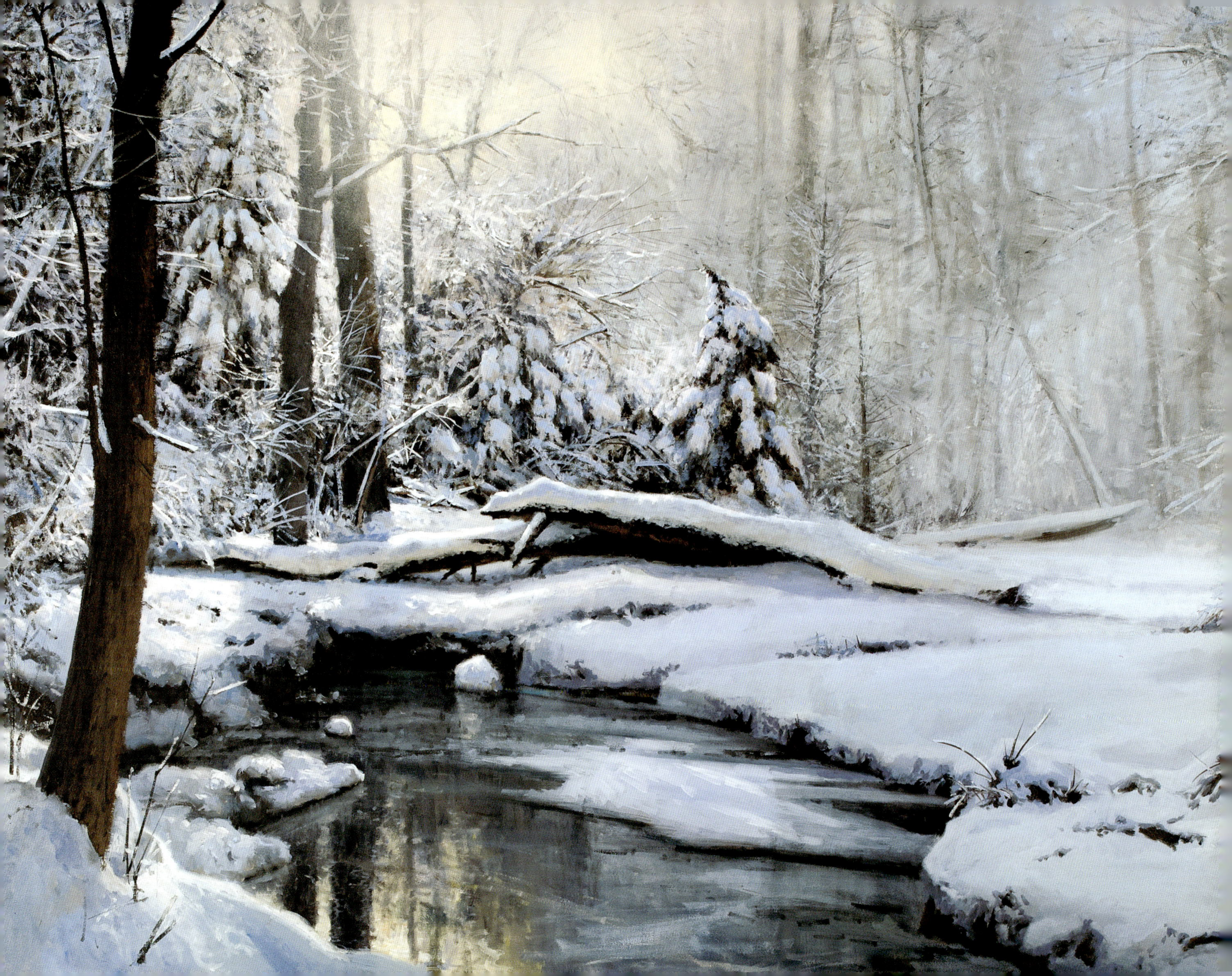

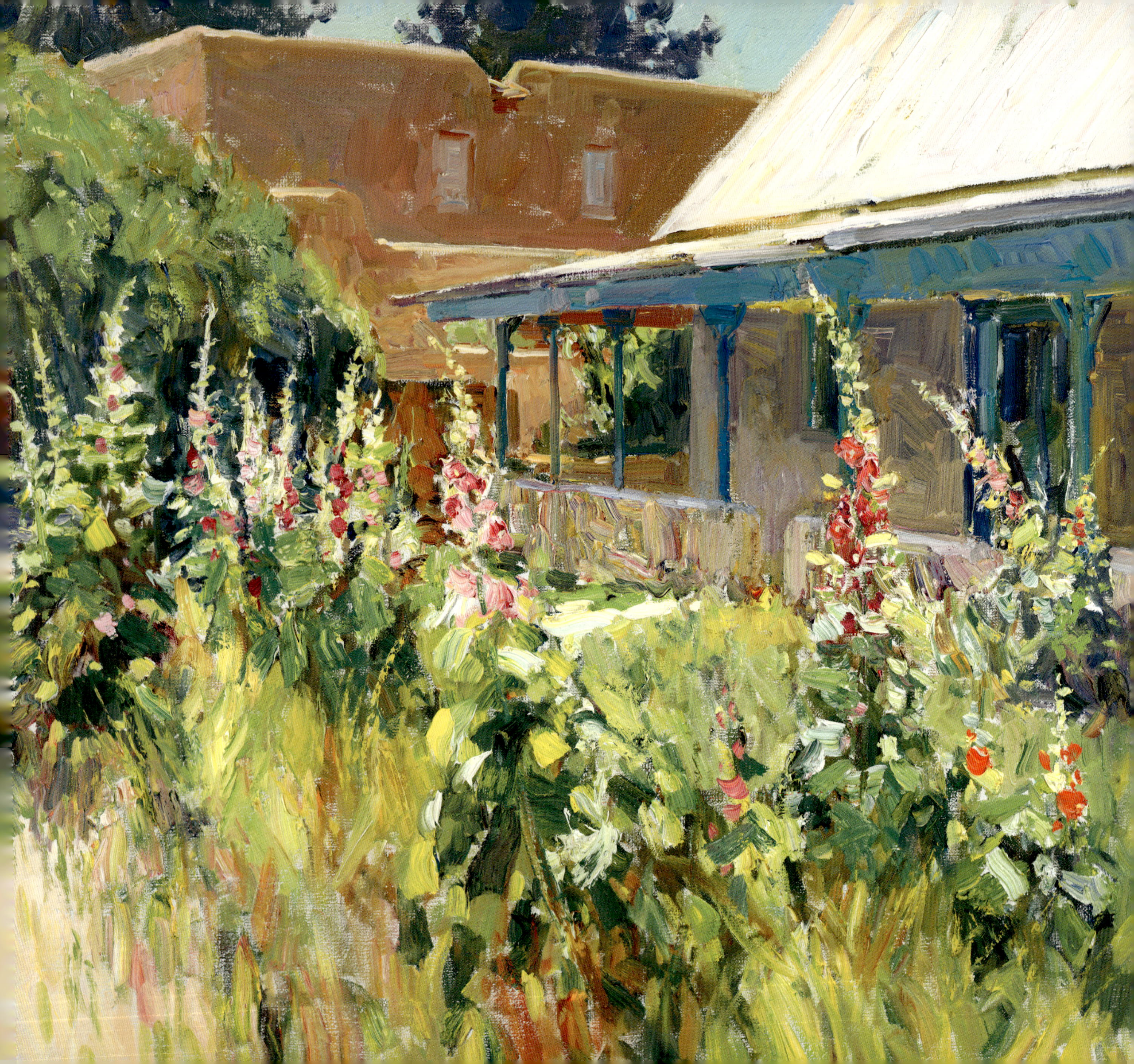

WALT GONSKE

Born and raised in New Jersey, Walt Gonske began his art career working at advertising agencies and doing men's fashion illustration in New York City. But in 1971, he flew out to New Mexico with his parents to visit his sister, and discovered the many art galleries in Taos and Santa Fe. "I was thrilled to see so much representational art on the walls," says Gonske. "In New York it was all modern art." That's when the dream of living and painting in New Mexico began, and in 1972 his dreams came true. "The Southwest has been good for me," he says. "To have my work be my joy is a precious gift." Gonske feels fortunate to have been invited into some prominent museum shows such as the Prix de West at the National Cowboy & Western Heritage Museum in Oklahoma City for the past 34 years, and more recently at the Gilcrease Museum in Tulsa. His work can now be seen in galleries throughout the West, from Santa Fe and Taos to Denver and Vail, Colorado.

Q&A

What inspired this painting?

The Padre Martinez Hacienda is built in what's known as "Territorial Style" and is located in the historic part of Taos. The subject of adobes and hollyhocks has inspired me for the last forty years.

In what locations do you paint?

I enjoy painting all over northern New Mexico and western Colorado. I can think of no greater pleasure than to fire up the Paintmobile (a custom-built mobile studio) and go off on a painting trip. I'll be driving along, looking, really seeing the land and something will draw my attention. I'll get what I call an emotional jolt. I need to trust that response and act upon it right away.

How would you describe your painting style?

I work in a loose, painterly style. I respond more to art that looks like paint on canvas and leaves something to the imagination. Each brushstroke is a record of the moment, an impulse, and I want the viewer to see that, to feel it.

Do you paint en plein air?

I would say that a little better than half of my yearly output of paintings are done outdoors, on the spot. Anyone who's interested in learning how to paint outdoors should consider taking a weeklong workshop with a professional instructor in the area.

What's your best advice to students on painting landscapes?

The single most important piece of advice I can give is to paint from life. There certainly is a place for using photo reference, but a student's work will progress so much faster working directly from nature. And a personal technique will evolve more naturally without any conscious effort.

MARK GOULD

When Mark Gould thinks about painting on location, he feels most comfortable in "less densely populated landscapes." He knows his own limits and strengths and while a city or an urban environment is often beautiful and vibrant, he can always find more of what he needs somewhere outside the city limits. A field, grove, gravel road or path are equally potent places, come with fewer distractions, and provide a good amount of gratifyingly unoccupied space, all of which helps him to think through and define his aesthetic choices. These decisions will then be carried forward into his studio, which is, of course, another less-densely-populated place geared mostly for his own contemplation and creative process. Gould has been regularly featured in such magazines as *Watercolor Artist*, *Southwest Art* and *American Art Collector*, and his paintings are in numerous collections from Arizona to Canada, as well as Germany, Japan, New York, the United Kingdom and Washington, DC.

What inspired this painting?

The topography of this meadow was made mystical by strong progressions of light, atmosphere and organic space, all of which led me visually into and then back out of this particular place. I had walked a short trail towards this grassy area and stopped in some trees right before an edge of full-on sunlight. Good initial access to any subject puts me at ease and I was immediately enticed by this spot. Adding to my comfort level here was a balance of various elements such as "distant" versus "near," color phrasing, and simplified arrangements of light and shadow. Because no one facet demanded too much attention, my initial attempts at experimentation were freed and risking something on canvas was easy.

Do you prefer particular seasons or times of day?

I have a preference for sunrise or sunset, with their somewhat extreme low-angled lighting and often colorful prismatic contortions. Much of my work loosely relies on what Italian schools call *controluce* or "backlighting," and low slanting light provides an abundance of this.

How do you plan your compositions?

First I try to set aside any preconceived ideas I might have developed; those are the kiss of death for my process. If I'm out in the field I'll pan through all views available from one place, searching for some small visual intrigue. In the studio I'll gather any reference materials together that fascinate at that moment and begin to study their relationships. Eventually some subset of visual elements captures my interest. Eventually I'll turn out what might be called an "attempt," designed only to break the ice between that young painting and myself.

Do you paint en plein air?

Painting in the field for me is more about reconnecting with outdoor sensual experiences than with creating an accurate rendering . . . breeze in my hair, sun on my face, a wave of quiet in place of a flood of human noise. I never worry about producing a completed painting in the field. My advice to anyone wanting to venture out? Determine what you need to enjoy painting outdoors and what you need to return with. Be realistic: painting outdoors is not the same as a Hollywood movie set—good does not always triumph over evil. Enjoy it all and learn from it.

COPPICE 874 Mark Gould Acrylic 24" × 18" (61cm × 46cm)

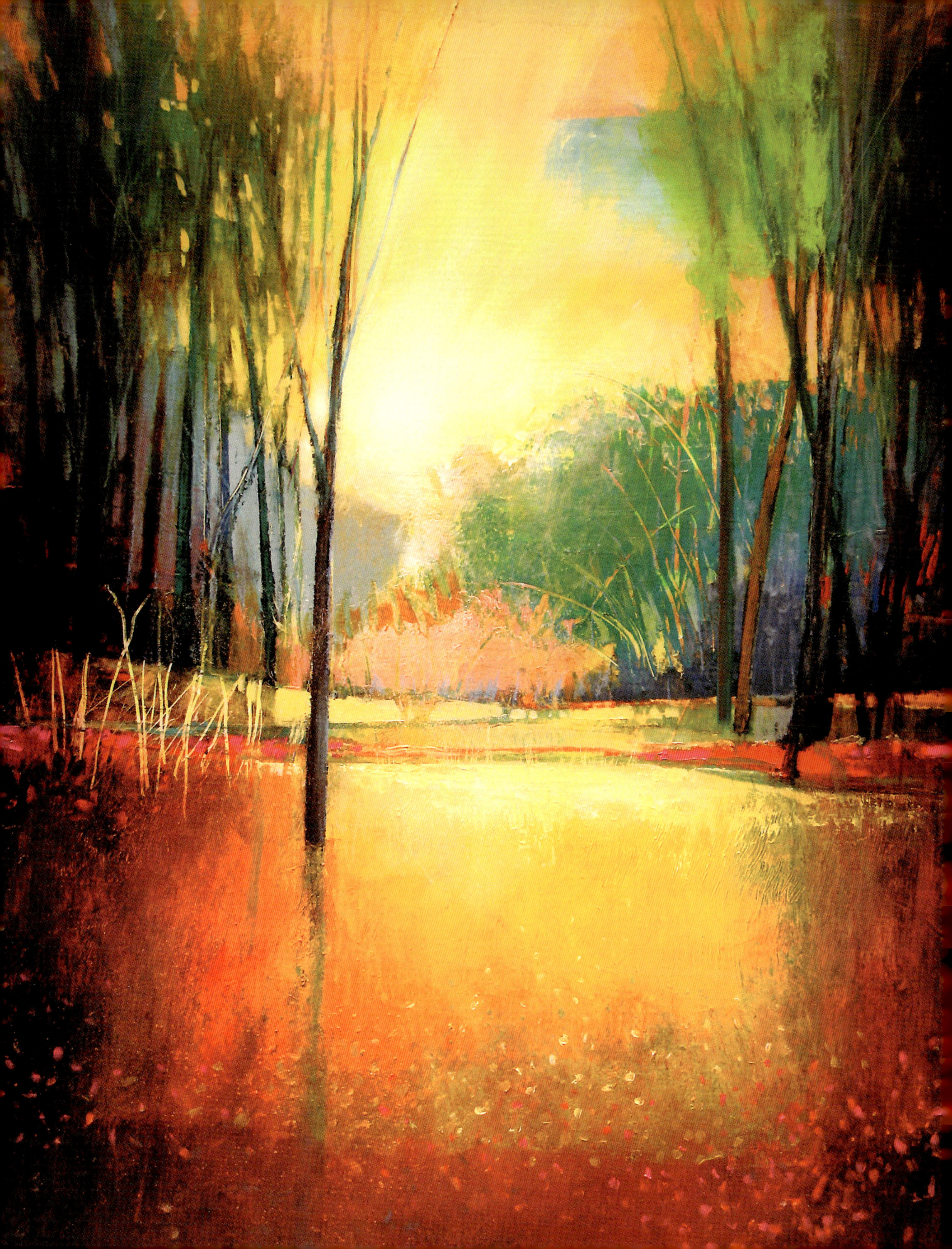

HUGH GREER

Hugh Greer grew up in Kansas City, Missouri, and has been painting since the first grade. In the beginning, it was a way for him to keep busy and out of trouble with his teachers. It proved to be a win-win for everybody. Greer's love of dramatic weather and textural vistas was influential in his decision to become a full-time landscape artist. Acrylics provide him the versatility to fully express the variety he sees in nature. He uses acrylic paint as both an opaque and transparent medium, and loves the permanence, ease of manipulation and dependable results acrylics provide. A four-time top awards winner in the Arts for the Parks exhibitions among others, Greer has published two books on painting as well as three instructional videos. Besides art, he loves bass fishing and baseball. He also likes to get a big bag of M&M's and drive around in the country. And he has been lost more than once.

Q&A

What inspired this painting?

Quiet, peaceful scenes appeal to me. *Back Porch* is not only quiet and peaceful, but also nostalgic and patriotic. I discovered a similar scene while driving around in the Kansas Flint Hills. The house had been abandoned but its character was still intact. At one time it had obviously been a well-cared-for home. In this painting I tried to re-create the feeling of how life used to be and that "all is well with the world" outlook. The trees and flowers are backlit, adding a palette of luminescent, vibrant color.

How would you decribe your painting style?

My style has developed over many years of architectural rendering and working with the fast-drying properties of acrylics. My style is not exactly realistic, but it is tighter than impressionistic.

What mediums do you use and what are your main painting techniques?

Acrylic lends itself very well to layering. I use thin washes to achieve depth of color, particularly when I want luminescent color.

Do you paint en plein air? What practical advice do you have for those who would like to try it?

I'm not sure acrylic paints are best for plein air, but it is my medium of choice. It dries fast indoors and it dries even faster outdoors. Soft edges are hard to achieve with acrylics, and almost all plein air paintings have to be touched up indoors. Still, I highly recommend painting outdoors—it seems to pry things out of you that you didn't know were there, particularly colors. My advice to anyone painting in Kansas? Carry an anvil to hold your easel down. The wind blows here a lot! Bug spray isn't a bad idea, either.

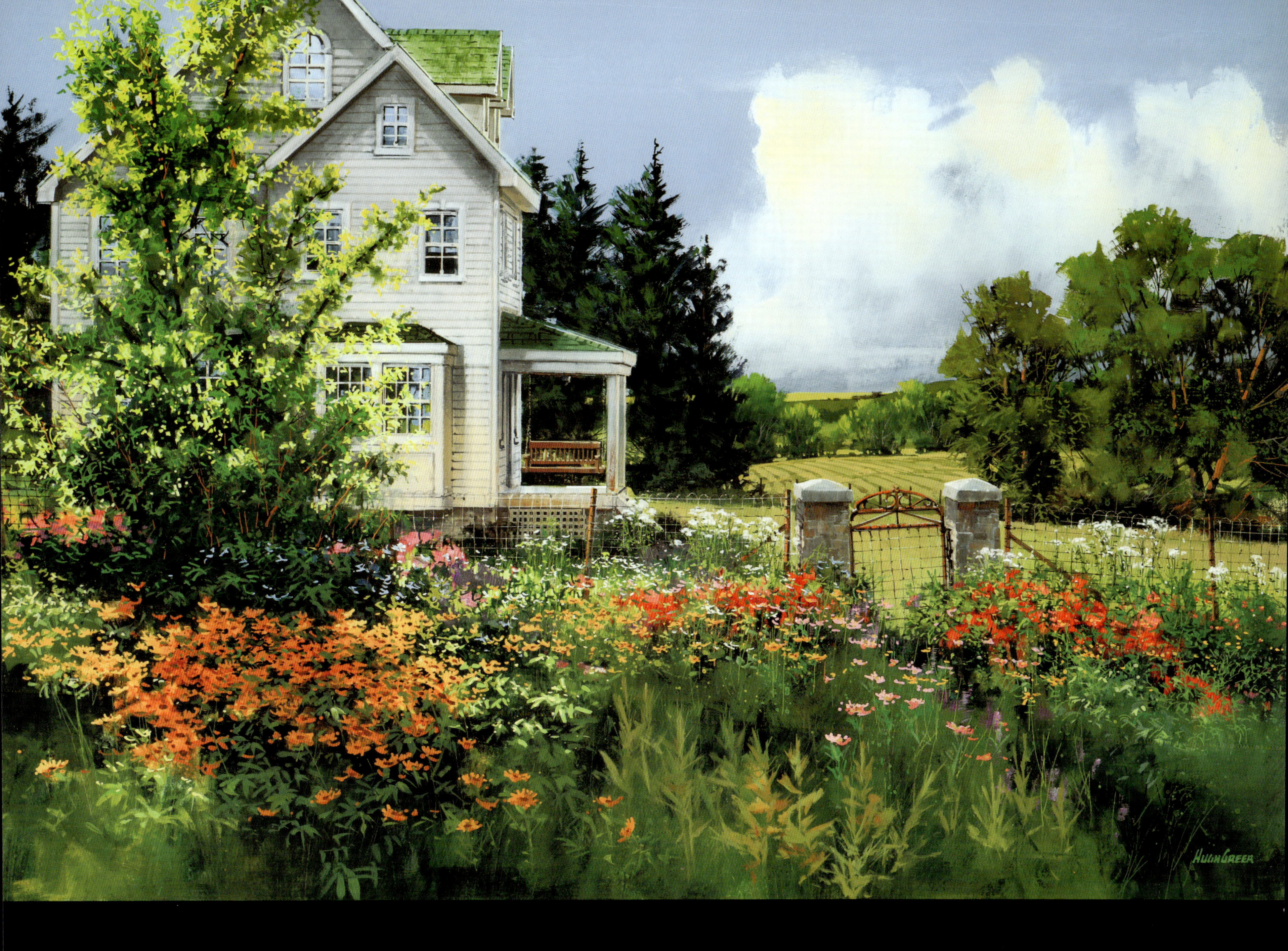
HUGH GREER

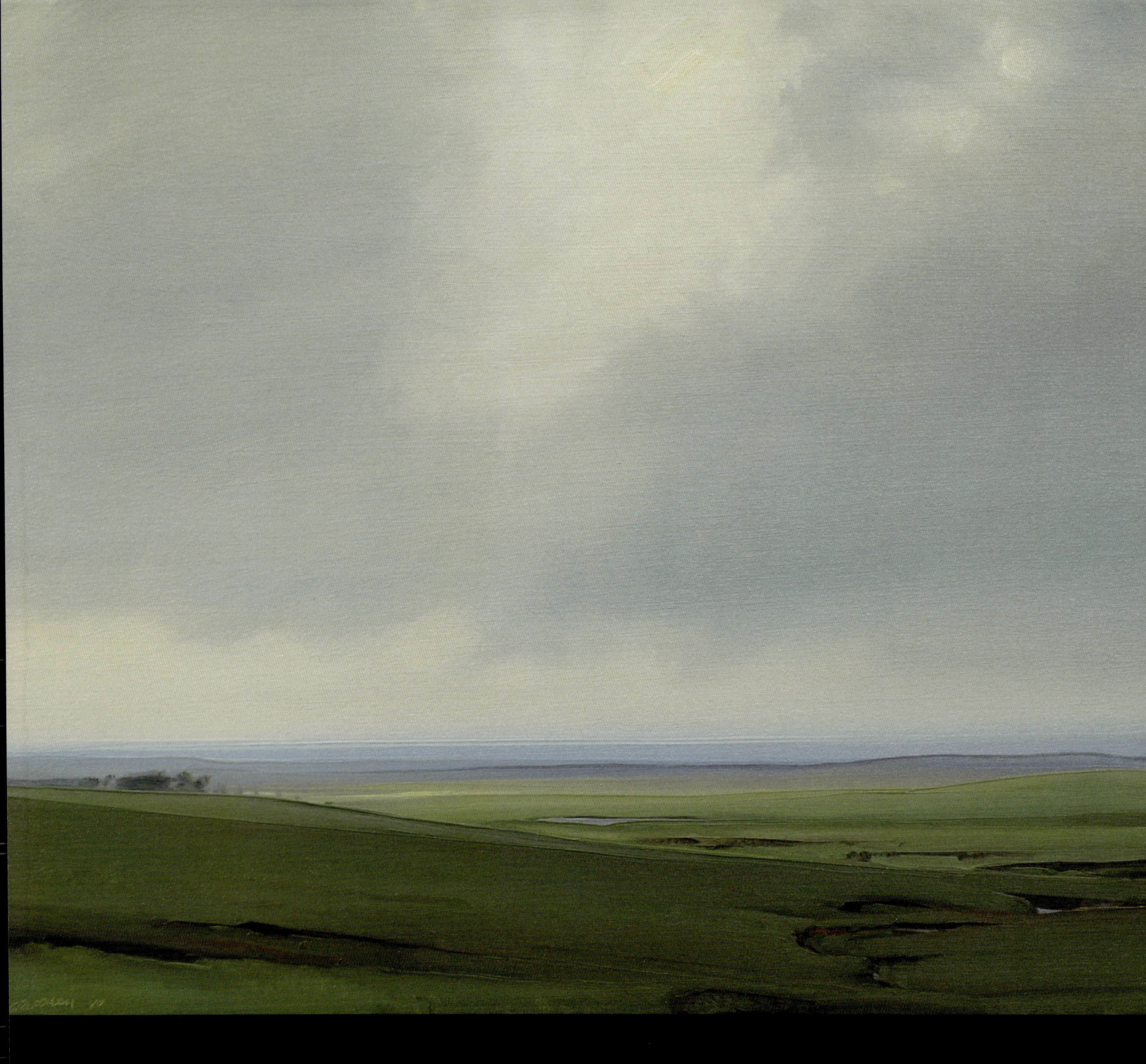

 GREEN PRAIRIE, PASSING STORMS Lisa Grossman Oil on canvas 20" × 24" (51cm × 61cm)

LISA GROSSMAN

Kansas-based painter and printmaker Lisa Grossman's work focuses on the grasslands, open spaces and prairies of eastern Kansas and the Kansas River valley. Originally from Pennsylvania, Grossman moved to Missouri to work as an illustrator at Hallmark. She began plein air painting in earnest when she discovered the tallgrass prairies of east-central Kansas. "My initial encounter with the grasslands was exhilarating," Grossman says. She left Hallmark in 1995 to pursue painting full time. Of her wide-open surroundings, she says, "The space allows room for breathing and slowing down, reflection and deeper thinking, but also a sense of vulnerability, humility, a healthy sense of our smallness on this planet—a more appropriate scale of human to planet."

What inspired this painting?

Since I first set eyes on the Flint Hills tallgrass prairies of east-central Kansas I've been deeply moved by their quiet drama. Prairies lack the obvious grandeur of mountain ranges, red rock canyons or the ocean. It's a quieter, more subtle beauty that comes to some slowly, but it is undeniably powerful. I developed a passion for the prairie that's fueled my imagination and sustained my vocation for twenty-some years now. Until I encountered these grasslands, I didn't realize I hadn't been seeing the horizon. There's a feeling of timelessness here—a strength and resilience, an enduring quality. There's an outer immensity that encourages an inner immensity—an expansion of the senses, a heightening of awareness, an elevated state of being.

Is your painting inspired by spirituality? How is that seen in your art?

Being engaged in the process of plein air painting can produce in me a sense of connection with *all that is*—origins, life processes, the ongoing evolutionary adventure, the awakening of new life around me.

Do you paint en plein air?

Plein air painting, for me, is about the firsthand experience of a place. It's my ritual of positioning myself in the land, watching and waiting, being open, and sharpening my awareness. Plein air painting allows me to participate in my surroundings in an intuitive, spontaneous manner. There's a slowing down that happens where you start noticing the nearly imperceptible movements of the earth, moon and stars, and the subtle shifts of light, color and temperature. There is a unique kind of discovery inherent in the process of plein air painting. If you're not discovering something in each attempt, the work is probably lifeless. My process is trial and error, hit or miss, and doesn't always work. It's challenging, but if it works there's energy embedded in that painting that I just can't duplicate in the studio.

What's your best advice to students on painting landscapes?

A prairie painter has to be comfortable with spareness and pay closer attention. Because of less-obvious subject matter, I think the prairie landscape forces an artist to look more deeply, carefully, and be more creative—to do more with less!

ALBERT HANDELL

Albert Handell was born in Brooklyn, New York, in 1937. At an early age, a favorite activity of his was drawing with chalk on the city streets. He began formal studies of drawing and anatomy at the age of sixteen. In 1954, he enrolled at the Art Students League of New York to study drawing and anatomy with Louis Priscilla and Robert Ward Johnson, and later studied painting for two years with Frank Mason. During the early 1960s, Handell lived and traveled in Europe. In Paris, he painted independently in his own studio, working from the model at L'Ecole de la Grande Chaumiere and at the Louvre, copying the Old Masters. Presently, Handell lives and paints in Santa Fe, New Mexico, and teaches nationally and internationally. Since 1961, he has had more than thirty one-man shows and has received over seventy prizes and awards. He is a member of the Pastel Society of America Hall of Fame.

What inspired this painting?

It was the movement of the water as it flowed over and around rocks, tumbling and forever moving forward. It was the rhythm of this flow and energy of the water in contrast to its surroundings that intrigued me.

Do you prefer particular seasons or times of day?

I love the dense greens of summer and the pearly grays and mauves of winter, and the early budding of spring greens against the winter mauves and grays. And who doesn't like the rich colors of autumn?

Do you paint en plein air?

I paint en plein air with pastel or mixed-media pastel (watercolor underpainting finishing with pastel). I paint my oils in the studio. They are usually larger and take more than one session. The advantage of painting en plein air is seeing for oneself how the same subject looks in different lighting conditions. It gives me an opportunity to see very unexpected variations in lighting.

What mediums do you use and what are your main techniques?

My oil technique is to start with abandon using transparent color washes, then I pick out an area that I understand the clearest and that I can start with and practically take to finish. During this time I incorporate use of my brush with a palette knife. The end result will have a combination of very transparent color washes contrasting with opaque application of oils with the palette knife. This gives the painting beautiful textural contrast. Another contrast that I value is the contrast between detailed areas and lost areas in the same painting.

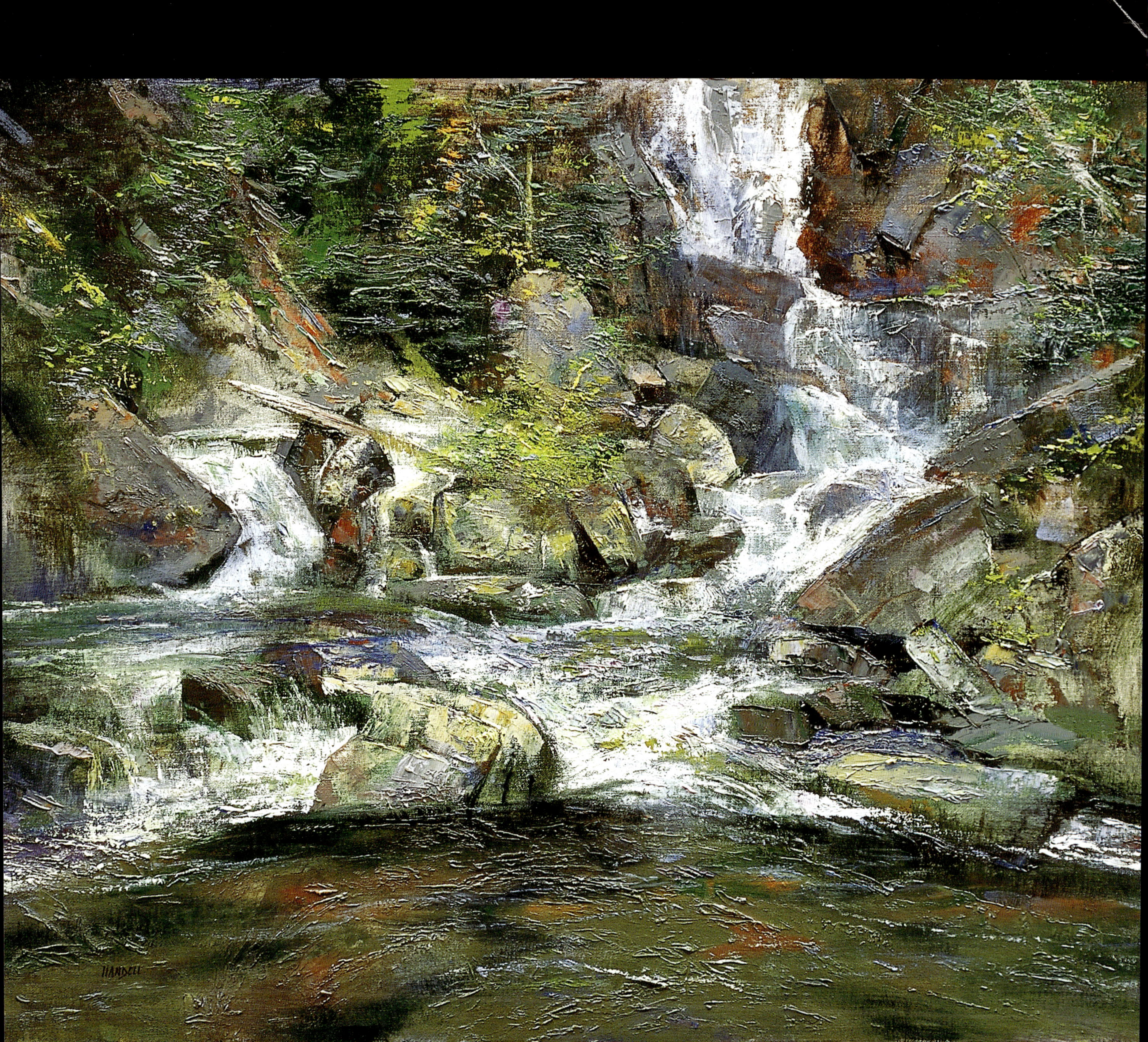
HANDELL

LIZ HAYWOOD-SULLIVAN

Having been trained as a designer, Liz Haywood-Sullivan says she was "very influenced by commercial illustration, especially the artists profiled in the illustrator's annuals of the 1970s and 1980s—also, the artists of the Brandywine School around N.C. Wyeth and the early 1900s artists of the Taos Art Colony. Their work all uses light in a very graphic way, slightly harder edged, with strong bold shapes and interesting dramatic compositions." After a career in design, Haywood-Sullivan turned to fine art and pastels in 1996 and since then has devoted herself to the medium. A signature member of the Pastel Society of America, she is also a member of the Salmagundi Club of New York and the Academic Artists Association. She conducts workshops on pastel painting and the business of art, and is dedicated to education in the arts. She lives in coastal southeastern Massachusetts with her photographer husband, Michael, in an 1890s barn converted into a house and studio.

What inspired this painting?

I was struck by the light passing through the trees and, although it was minimal due to the density of the trees, I was intrigued by how reflected light was illuminating the forest floor and the backs of the tree trunks. I love the challenge of determining the directional source of light and how the color is influenced based upon its source. For instance, the tree trunks on the left side of this painting have a bluish green cast; that's because there is a hole in the tree canopy and light is coming in from the blue sky, therefore telling you by implication that there is an opening and the sky is blue, without having to actually show it to you.

In what locations do you paint?

I paint areas that appeal to me because of the light and color palette. I love the Northeast because of the changing seasons. I love painting snow mainly because tracking light direction and color is easier to do with the landscape draped in white like a prepared canvas. Having lived in the Northeast all my life I have discovered that the very best sunsets of the year happen in November. I also love painting the Southwest because the complementary elements of the turquoise blue sky and warm orange earth tones make it hard to do a bad painting!

How do you plan your compositions?

Being originally educated as a designer, I start out my paintings with a lot of emphasis on shape and form. My compositions are taken directly from nature. Designing a painting is all about light and the abstract patterns and forms that are created as light strikes different shapes and textures. So although my paintings are realistic in appearance, they start broken down as abstract shapes in thumbnails and value studies that I do in my sketchbook.

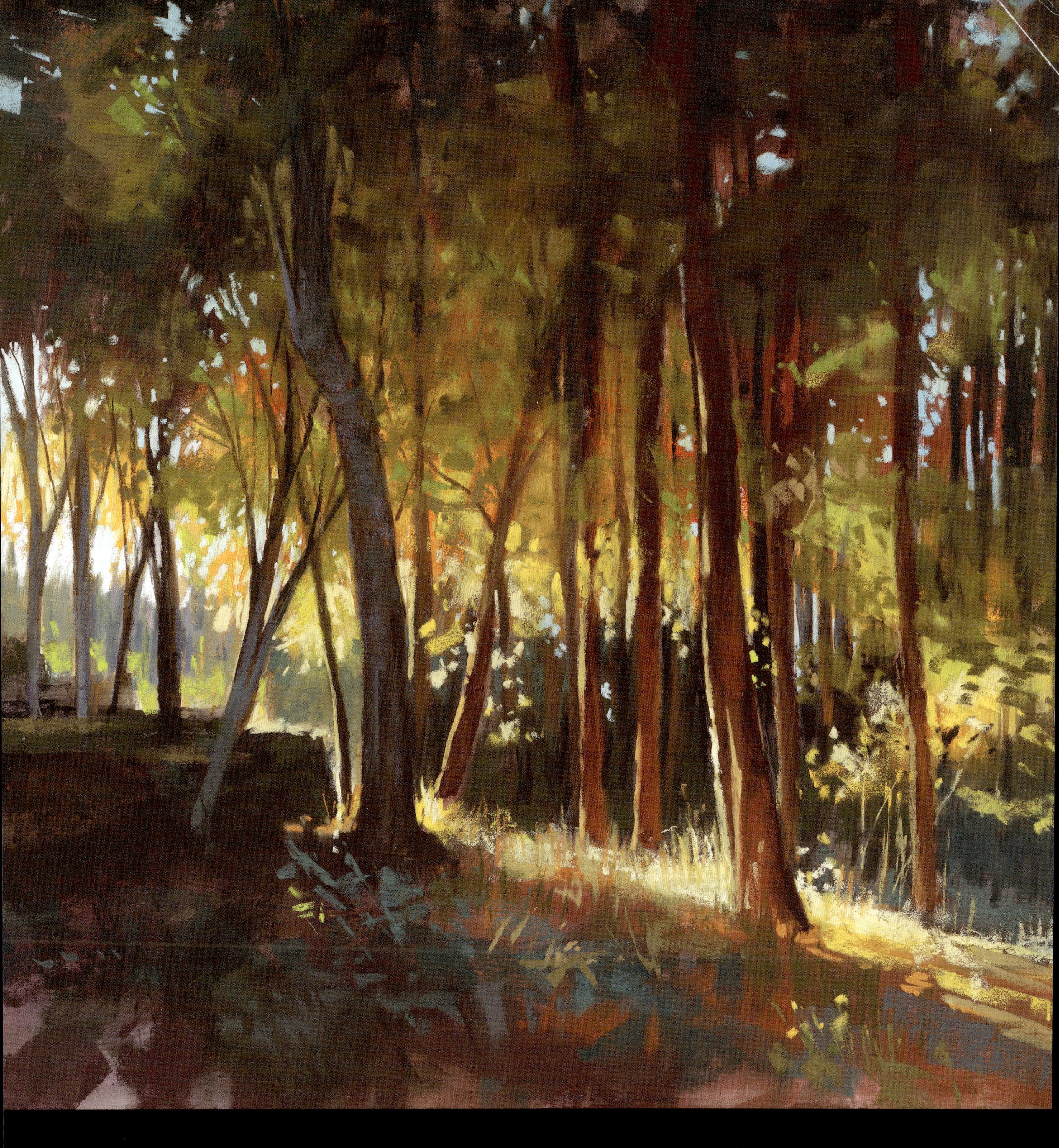

THE BRIGHT OF DAY Liz Haywood-Sullivan Soft pastels on sanded paper 16" × 16" (41cm × 41cm) Private collection, Marshfield, Massachusetts

JOYCE HICKS

Joyce Hicks works in both watercolor and oil and finds inspiration through frequent travel across the country in search of beautiful places to paint. Although Tyler, Texas, is home base, she and her husband spend the better part of each year traveling coast to coast in their RV. Her paintings are never true renditions but more about her personal response to a scene. "I'm drawn to rural areas, pastoral scenes, small country towns and seaside villages," says Hicks. "I'm entranced by sunlight and shadow and how it can transform the most ordinary scene into one capable of taking my breath away." Surprisingly, Hicks rarely paints en plein air but prefers working in her home studio where she has all her sketchbooks, notes and digital images. "With all my source material at my fingertips I can easily go back in time, recalling all that was special about the day and what made me want to record it in the first place." Largely self-taught, she has developed her own unique painting style that has garnered her awards at the American Watercolor Society's International Exhibitions and inclusion in *Splash: The Best of Watercolor* series published by North Light Books.

Q&A

What inspired this painting?

The geometric shape of the architecture and organic softness of the foreground was a pleasing combination and I particularly liked the way the rows of the field advanced me visually into the scene. It was a gray, overcast day so I simply imagined sunshine and shadow. Artistic license is wonderful!

How would you describe your painting style?

I think my work is a unique combination of styles. It is realistic because it is painted from a real place and time, and it's also abstract because I distill it into simple shapes, but mostly it is impressionistic because it is how I wish it to be and not as it actually is.

What mediums do you use and what are your main painting techniques?

I use transparent watercolor on dry, unstretched, cold-press paper. My techniques are simple: I don't use salt, liquid masking or other devices, but let the beautiful stroke of a round brush and interesting texture from a palette knife express for me what it is I wish to say.

What's your best advice to students on painting landscapes?

If you wish to paint from within, then you must train your mind's eye to see and imagine scenes as you wish them to be, not as they actually are. My paintings began winning awards when I stopped painting *things* and instead began painting *relationships* between, temperature, value, shape and color.

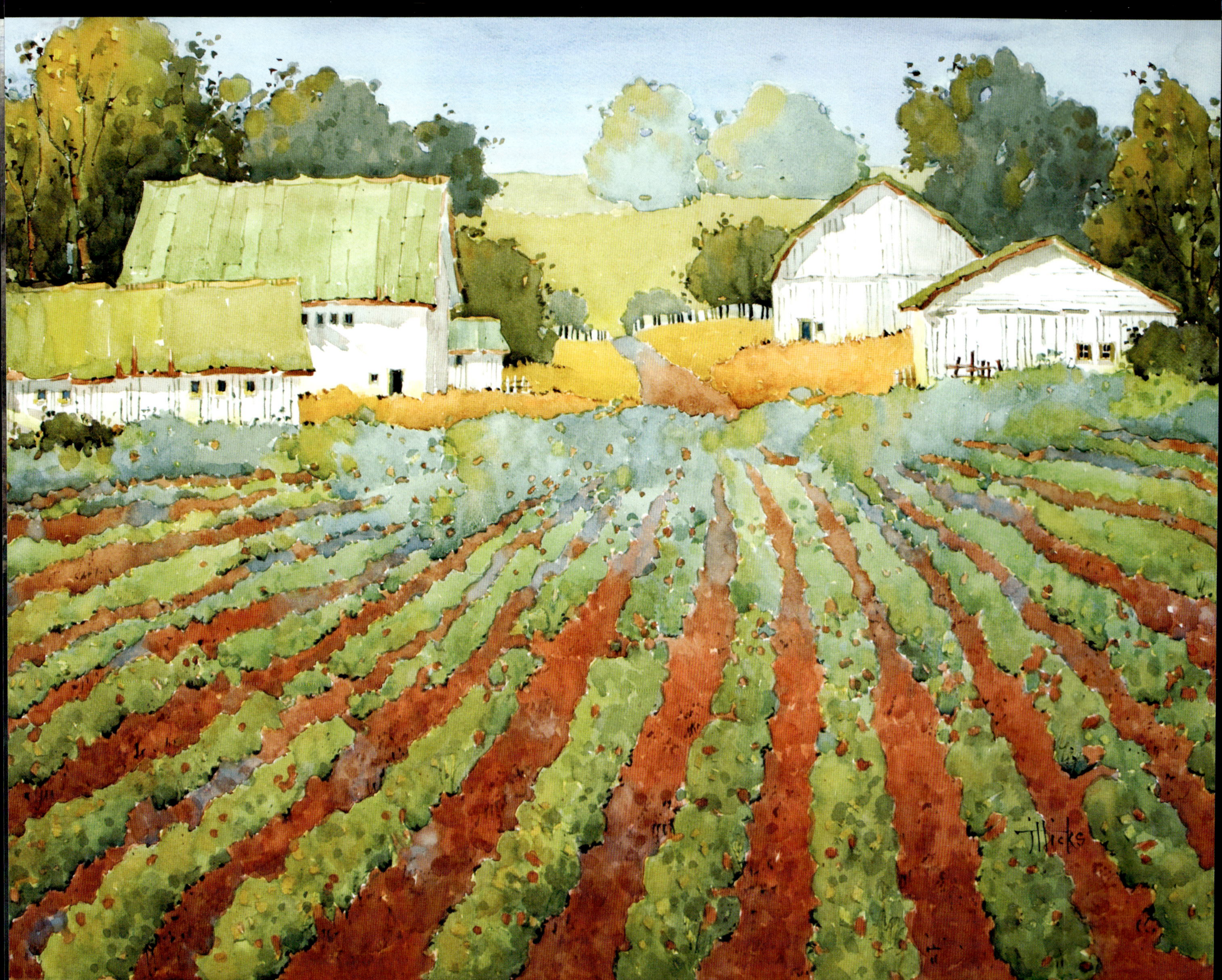
JHicks

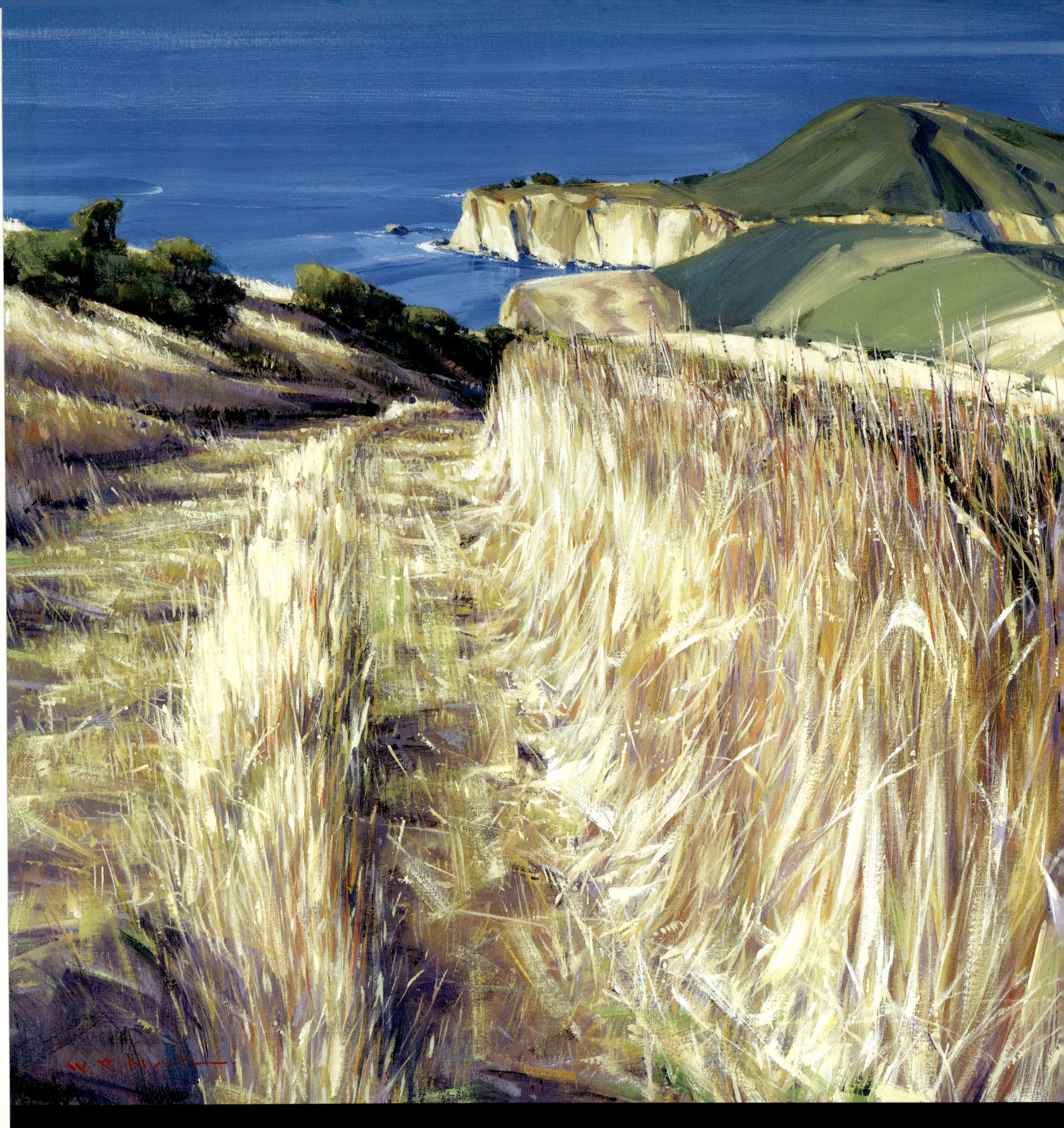

 RANCH HIGHLANDS William Hook Acrylic on canvas 36" × 36" (91cm × 91cm)

WILLIAM HOOK

William Hook (known to his friends as just "Hook") lives in two great places where landscapes almost paint themselves: Santa Fe, New Mexico and Carmel, California. With a broad brush and a colorful palette, Hook paints vast horizons and crashing surf and feels lucky to have won a few awards along the way, including the National Arts for the Parks' best landscape award and Acrylic Artist of the Year award at the National Academy of Design. He also enjoys spending time at a family cabin in Colorado where fly-fishing is a favorite pastime. In fact, he's made more than one painting from the middle of a stream. When he's not fishing, he's golfing and photographing the scenery from the far-off rough. Hook has a long family history in the visual arts: his father was a photographer and his grandmother an architect. He started painting as a child and was always encouraged to try out new art materials, which is why he still paints in acrylics today.

What inspired this painting?

I had the opportunity to paint on a ranch that towered above the Pacific Ocean. The views from these coastal hills were so dramatic that I felt this scene was mine to paint.

Do you prefer particular seasons or times of day?

It seems like I most often paint the autumn colors of the mountains and the spring colors of the coast with nearby yellow hills in the background. In either case, I enjoy the more dramatic light of mornings and evenings.

Do any historical movements, periods or artists inspire your painting?

I don't pay close attention to living artists. American Post-Impressionists and artists that were involved with the Taos Society have had the greatest influence on my thinking. Landscape painters James McNeill Whistler, John Twachtman, Victor Higgins, E. Martin Hennings, Maynard Dixon and Richard Diebenkorn come to mind when I make a painting.

Do you paint en plein air?

Acrylic paint and outdoor painting conditions are a challenge when mixed together. That being said, I paint plein air for two reasons. First, there is no substitute for experiencing natural light—it is brighter and more understandable than any other method, such as photography. Second, I prefer to paint on location where I can experience all of the ambient sounds and smells of the scenery. While painting outdoors, I also photograph the scene so that my studies and my photography can be used together in the making of a larger studio picture.

CINDY HOUSE

Before becoming a landscape artist, Cindy House began her career as an illustrator, working on bird books such as the *National Geographic Field Guide to the Birds of North America*. Today she still pursues her interest in birds by including them in many of her landscapes. House's paintings have been accepted into the prestigious Birds in Art exhibition at the Woodson Art Museum twenty-one times. "Birding, gardening, traveling and snorkeling are my primary leisure pursuits," she says. "I currently live in New Hampshire with my husband, a wildlife biologist, in an old farmhouse on forty acres of subject matter—woods, fields, streams and a pond." House is a member of the Pastel Society of America and the Society of Animal Artists.

Q&A

What inspired this painting?

Star Island is one of the nine islands that make up the Isles of Shoals off the New England coast. Years ago, I was inspired by a show of Childe Hassam's work, *An Island Garden Revisited*. The exhibition consisted of paintings of the Isles and of writer Celia Thaxter's garden on the adjacent island of Appledore. I remember standing in front of Hassam's paintings hoping someday that I, too, could paint the beauty of the Isles of Shoals.

Why is American landscape painting important today, in the 21st century?

With so much of the American landscape being destroyed or under development today, it's important for landscape painters to document the remnants of the natural world that still remain. To paint the beauty of the land, be it a national park or a quiet corner of a nearby field, captures an image for the viewer to contemplate. How big a part do scenes such as these play in their lives? Would they be willing to live without them or pass on a world without them to their children?

In what locations do you paint?

I paint in New England where I have spent the majority of my life. Having studied wildlife biology in college, knowing the flora and fauna of the subject I'm depicting is very important to me. To capture a moment in time means knowing which plants are in bloom and where they are to be found. For this reason, I paint the landscape I know and understand best.

What mediums do you use and what is your main painting technique?

I use soft pastels exclusively. By using sanded pastel paper, I can start my paintings with an underpainting of pastels fixed with Turpenoid and slowly build my painting by layering the pastels.

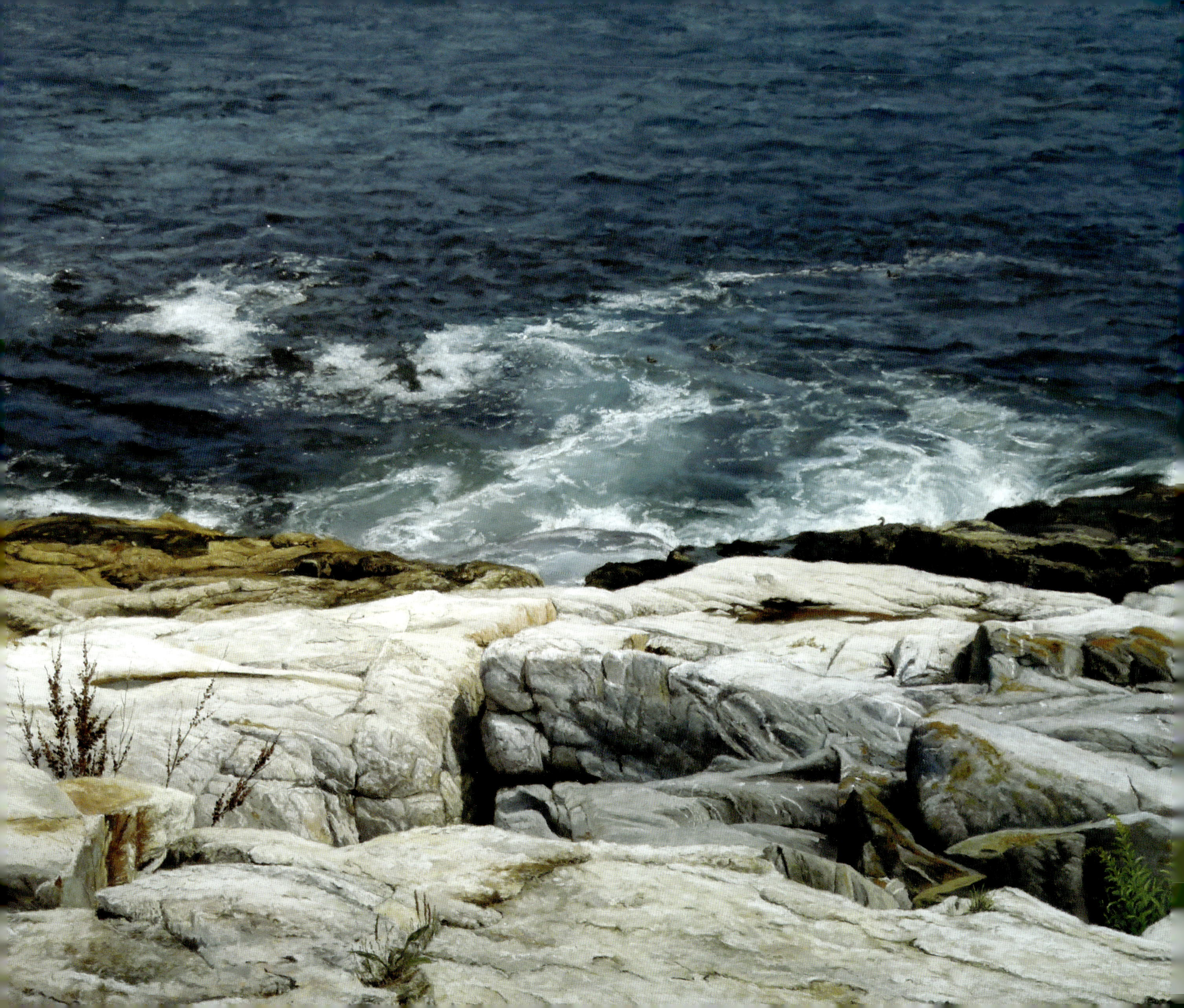

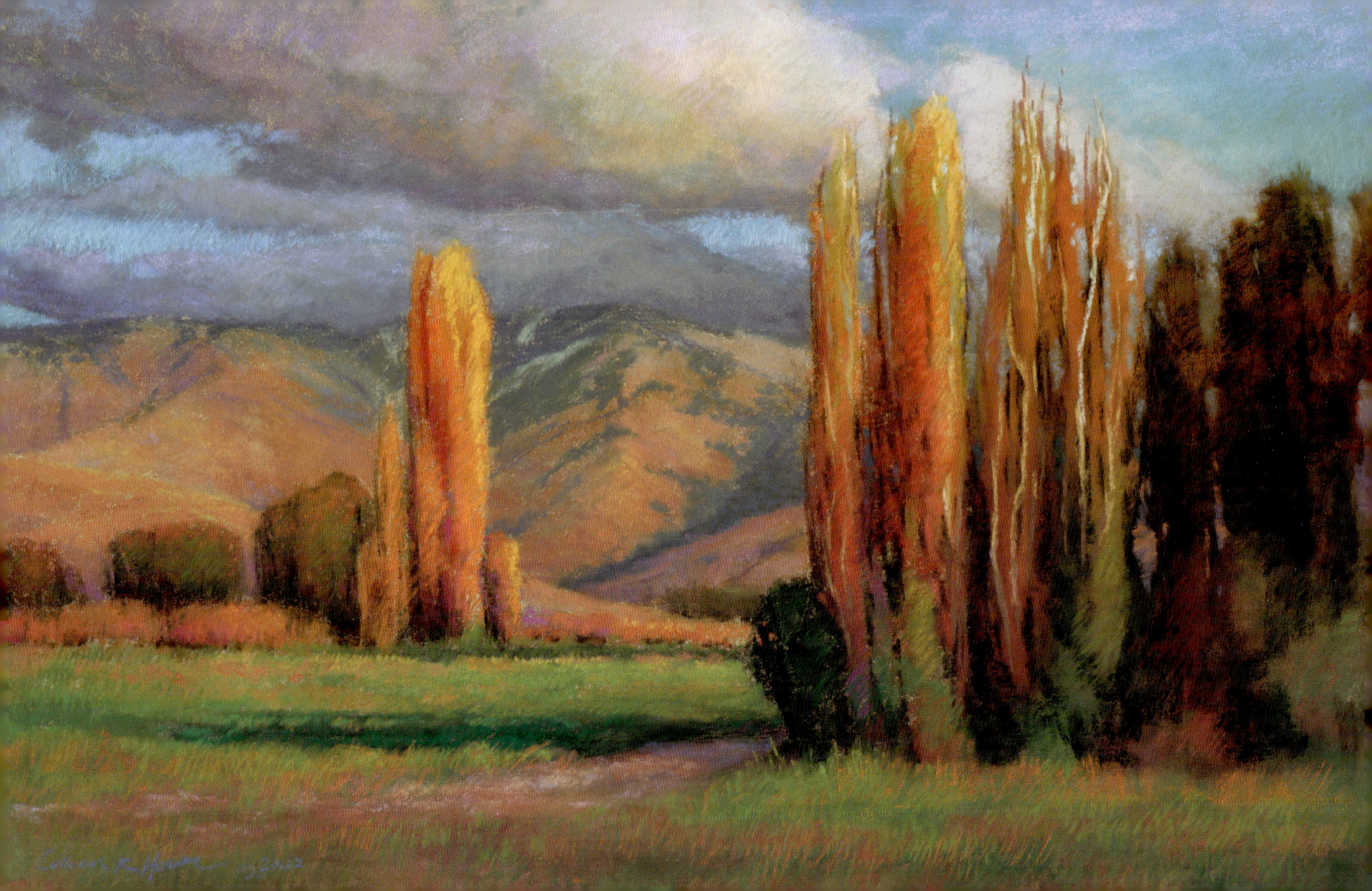

COLLEEN HOWE

Colleen Howe grew up on a cattle ranch in southwestern Montana and currently lives in northern Utah in a rural mountain valley. She loves painting, hiking, riding horses and just sitting by a nearby stream listening to the water and the birds. She does have a goal of moving to a warmer environment in winter, such as Hawaii, and is working toward that goal. Her early experiences explain her attraction to wide open places. "I particularly like to paint scenes that are very open, vast and that give me opportunity to express the natural harmony that exists with color," Howe says. "The color of light ties all the aspects of the landscape together, and whether I decide to focus on clouds or fields or trees, it is the light that becomes the underlying subject." Howe is a signature member of the Pastel Society of America and recently filmed two pastel painting videos for ArtistsNetwork.tv. She also loves to talk about and share art philosophy on her blog at colleenhowe.blogspot.com.

What inspired this painting?

The contrast of warm and cool attracted me to this scene. I had driven by several times and felt that this area should be my next painting. Late in the day, the sun was very warm on the fall color in the trees. Behind the tree groupings, early snow had fallen in the mountains, and the low clouds contributed to the cool contrast to set off the warmth of the reds and oranges in the trees. I love to paint tree groupings anyway, so to find such a perfect setting inspired me to express my passion for color and also for these types of trees: poplars and cottonwoods.

How would you describe your painting style?

I have a realistic style most of the time, but I do like to simplify and edit the entire scene so that I may exaggerate the focus on the main idea. Occasionally I will abstract a scene and flatten out the picture plane so that I can show a certain relationship between shapes, but since I am attracted to depth of field, that doesn't happen too often. When using pastel, I enjoy underpainting with a wet medium such as watercolor, which provides a transparent beginning, then I begin a careful buildup and layering of pastel color, often using optical mixing rather than actually pushing the strokes together. This particularly appeals to me during the second half of the painting. My strokes become more discernible and graphic, particularly in the center of interest.

How do you plan your compositions?

I get great pleasure from the process of planning a painting. I like to begin with a value study to simplify forms and see how shapes and contrast will appear as abstract patterns. At this stage I also consider where the principal area of interest will be and how I will lead the eye into and around the painting. When I'm satisfied with the abstract arrangement, I will consider several color studies using pastel or oil in a small format to try out obvious or unusual color combinations.

ROD S. HUBBLE

After a lifetime of drawing with almost four decades professionally, Rod S. Hubble says, "Art has become the savior of my life. I was well into my career before I realized how important this work was to me personally, and it was then I actually started to make a living with it." Hubble became a landscape painter seven years after he started painting professionally, in the high desert of New Mexico where he was raised. He had painted several landscapes of that terrain from memory; in fact, "imaginative and memory work" was his early style. Painting landscapes en plein air, he learned about color and feeling in art, describing the motion of wind in grasses, the solemnity of silence, or the passion of a rainstorm sweeping across the sky. Hubble continues, "Early in my painting life, I learned an artist can transform reality into an idealistic perfect world, so it was natural for me to become an impressionist. When I paint anything, be it from life, a photo, or even a dream memory, I make an impression of it."

Q&A

What inspired this painting?

In *Hour of Silent Offering*, I was inspired to paint a picture with a short distance, which is extended by the gradual use of blues in the background. I had been teaching my students to use this technique, although I don't encourage them to paint from imagination as I have done here. I never paint directly from imagination, but always do a pencil sketch first, then I draw the image a second time with Burnt Umber acrylic on a red-toned acrylic canvas, which imparts a pink warmth to the finished work. The acrylic dries quickly and I am ready to make my final painting in oils. In this work, I was attempting to paint solemnity and I even dreamed of the painting before; it was as if I were in prayer or meditation. One of my friends described the figure as a priestess.

In what locations do you paint?

I prefer quiet, private settings to public areas. I gravitate toward intimate settings, but I also love to paint grand and distant vistas. There is something very exciting about painting the landscape as clouds cast shadows on the land—one paints with spontaneity and the surprises that occur are really exciting. You have to paint the changes as they happen and not paint back over them as they change to something else. Painting outdoors has to happen rapidly, even when doing large works; one just uses bigger brushes and more paint on the palette. I have revisited a spot the next day to finish a large painting.

What's your best advice to students on painting landscapes?

I tell my students to work the palette as much as the painting, to use soft edges for almost everything, and to draw trees correctly. Landscape painters must understand the true anatomy of trees, as well as water, clouds and earth, and they must be able to fuse those things with light and shadow. Two or three leaves are all that a painter needs to make an impression of leaves, and a good impressionist painting will read better if it is not overly detailed. Mass supports detail, and mass also allows the painting to breathe.

HOUR OF SILENT OFFERING Rod S. Hubble Oil on linen 18" × 16" (46cm × 41cm)

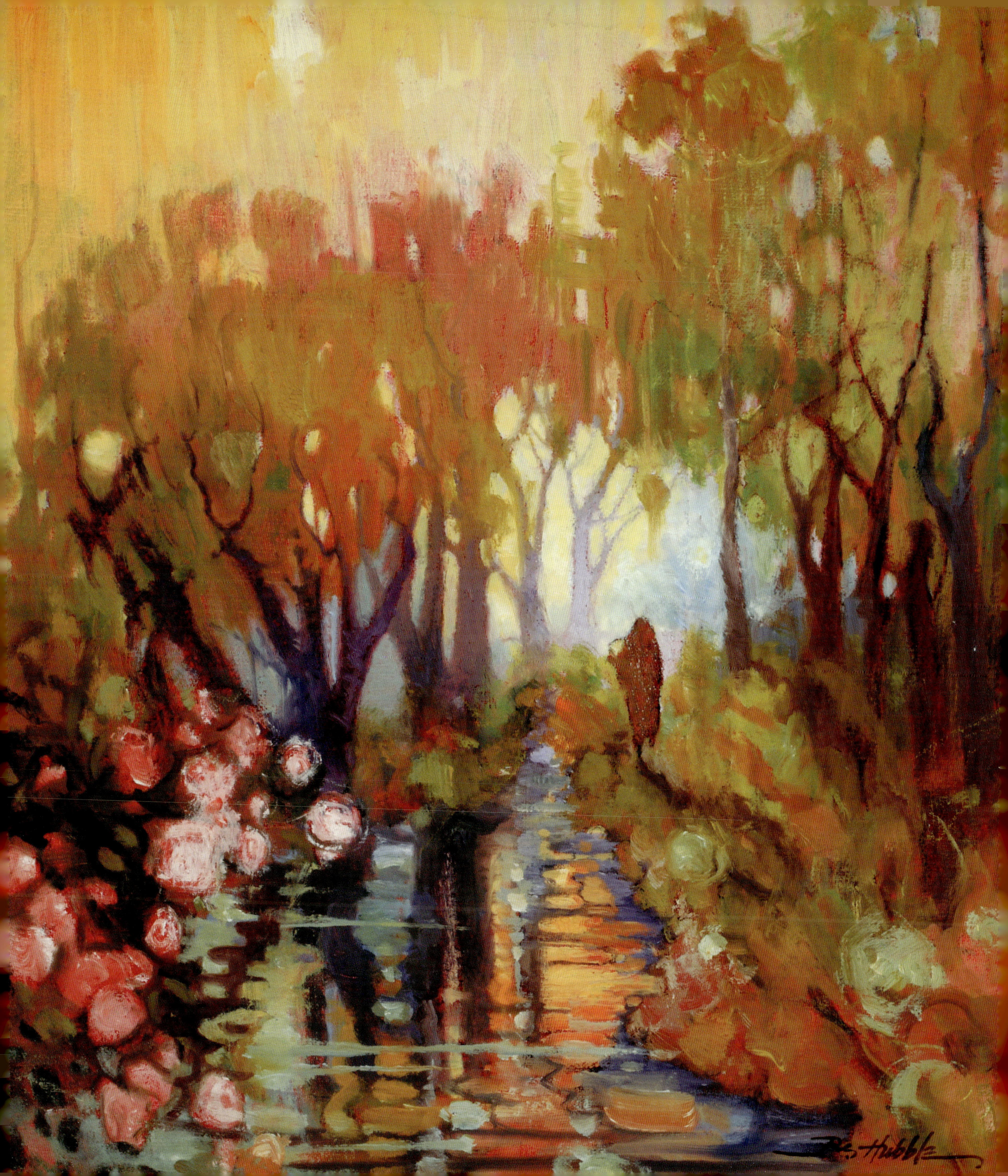

M. KATHERINE HURLEY

Cincinnati, Ohio, artist M. Katherine Hurley describes her painting style as "representational, somewhere between realism and abstraction. My hope is to capture the essence and feeling of the place rather than the detail of it." Hurley's oil and pastel paintings are often inspired by the quiet rural landscapes and farms of Ohio, where details are lost in the sheer vastness of the land's flat topography. "The landscape has always been my place of meditation and time with God," she says. "We need the beauty and sanctuary of the landscape more and more as our lives become busier and busier." Hurley keeps busy at her studio in the Pendleton Art Center in downtown Cincinnati, but also enjoys painting in her own backyard studio on summer mornings. Besides teaching workshops, Hurley has filmed three instructional videos and has been published in *The Artist's Magazine* and *The Pastel Journal*. She is a signature member of the Pastel Society of America.

Q&A

What inspired this painting?

I'm from a rural village east of Cleveland and travel back there often to visit family. I've been doing this drive for forty years and never tire of seeing the farmland and barns, especially in the early morning. This is the subject of many of my paintings.

Do you prefer particular seasons or times of day?

I love the sunrise and sunset of the day. The drama and mystery are peaking during these times no matter what the season.

What mediums do you use and what are your main painting techniques?

I use oil on canvas and pastel on paper. With both mediums, I like to start with an underpainting of orange where there is light and intensity, and purple for shadow areas. Once those big shapes are established, I start layering local color.

How do you plan your compositions?

The scene in front of me or presented in a photo isn't always the best composition. Doing thumbnail sketches gives me the opportunity to rearrange things before I start to paint.

What's your best advice to students on painting landscapes?

I advise all of my students to do black-and-white value sketches outside or from photos. This helps us see the big shapes and patterns of light and dark without getting bogged down in detail.

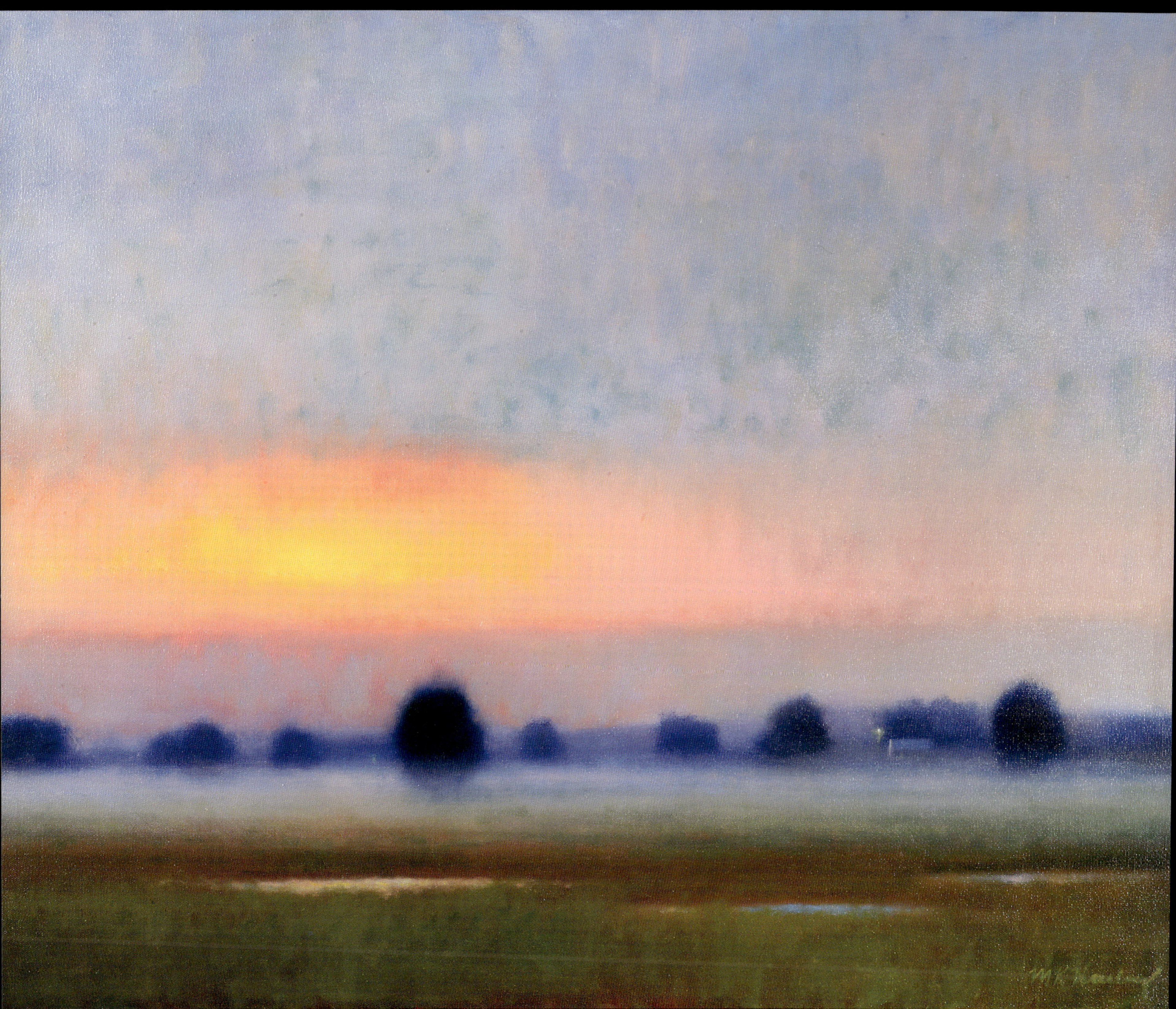

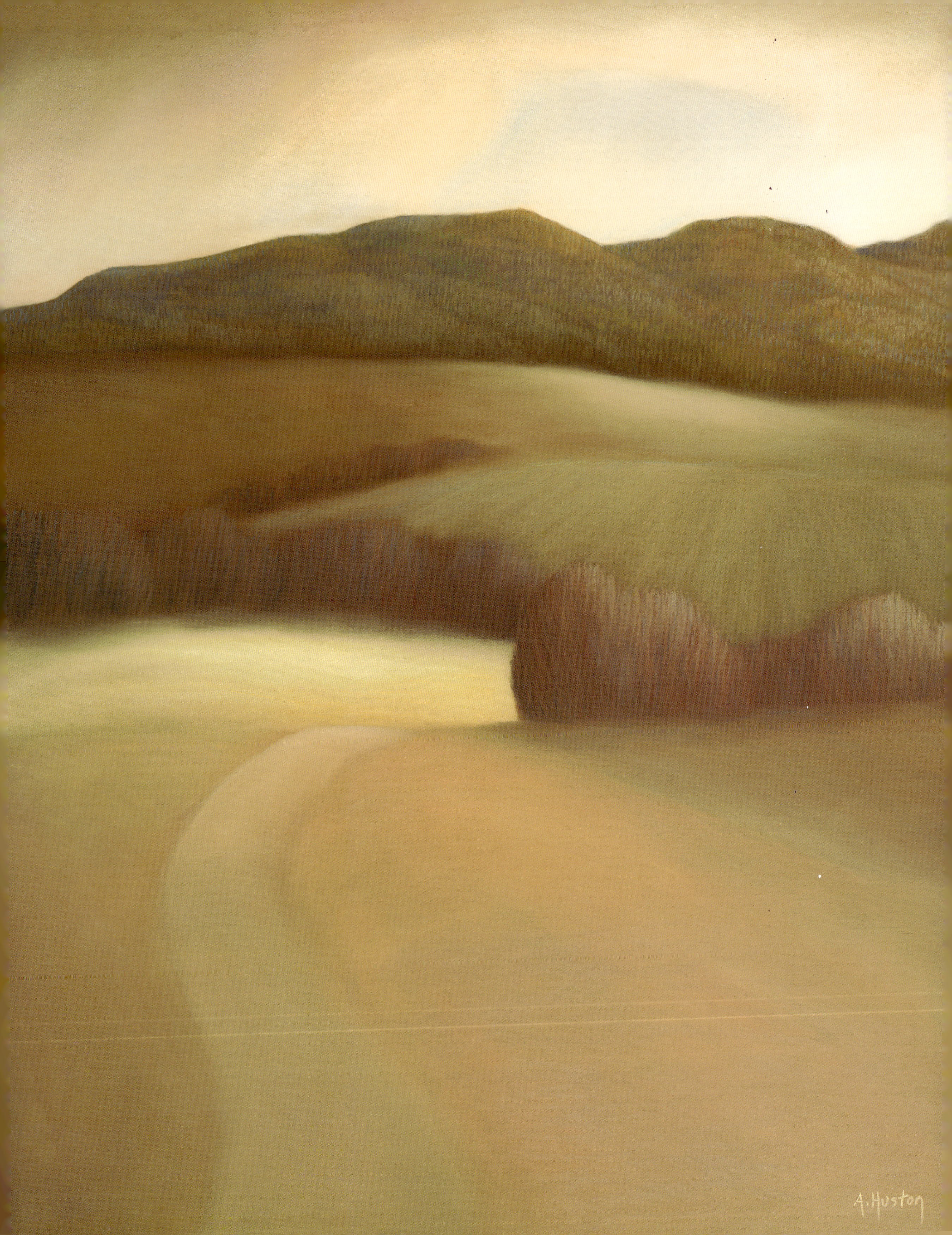
A. Huston

ANN HUSTON

Award-winning pastel artist Ann Huston is self-taught in this medium, one of the reasons her style is so unique and recognizable. Northern New Mexico is her inspiration and where she calls home. Co-owner of Studio de Colores Gallery in Taos along with her husband, artist Ed Sandoval, Huston lives in a double adobe "compound" they built in 1996 that includes a chapel, barn and chicken coop, a unique home that has appeared in many magazines and on television. When asked why this area of the country inspires her, Huston replies, "The high altitude light, the old adobes, churches and moradas, is like painting the history and culture of New Mexico. Although my paintings don't have figures in them, the presence of people can be felt in the adobes." While she does go out on location to get the sketch and to touch base with nature, she does the painting in her studio, capturing the mood and memory of the place from the day's sketch, then imparting the essence of that memory, almost dreamlike, to the painting.

What inspired this painting?

After making a detailed sketch on sanded pastel paper out on location, I come back to the studio where I eliminate most all of the detail, leaving the essence of what was really there. *Fields and Willows* is a great example: I left nothing except the fields and willow trees. It becomes a window for the viewer to walk in and out of without all the chaos, a peaceful and meditative place to go.

Is your painting inspired by spirituality? How is that seen in your art?

I paint from the inside out. I go to that place inside me that is my form of meditation, keeping in touch with who I am, keeping connected to a higher power, keeping things honest. I keep things minimal so the viewer can find their own place in the painting, and finish it with their own story. Because of this, my paintings have an enduring quality, and the viewer can change the story over time as their lives change.

What mediums do you use and what are your main techniques?

I use soft pastels, layering endlessly to achieve a depth of color, as subtle or tonal as it may be. I paint on pastel artist's sand paper because the grit can hold the layers of pastel. I don't use fixative as I don't want to flatten the color that is so carefully layered and I don't want to change the natural crystal-like pigment.

What's your best advice to students on painting landscapes?

Doing a painting is pouring your heart and soul into it, and then you have to let it go. It's a great way to learn to "let go" and apply that practice in everyday life. Everyone has a unique voice, so to students I would say, find your voice that best describes you and enjoy the process of doing it. Don't worry so much about the finished painting and how a viewer might receive it. If the painting comes from your essence, then that will be felt by the viewer.

FIELDS AND WILLOWS Ann Huston Soft pastels on sanded pastel paper 28" × 22" (71cm × 56cm)

MARGIE KUHN

With an undergraduate degree in scientific illustration, Margie Kuhn paints elements of the natural world, including the burr oak leaves in this painting, in true-to-life detail. Yes, these leaves are painted, not photographed. Kuhn says, "I collect and dry leaves, and frequently the dying leaves become more beautiful than the leaves on the trees, so I often include leaves as metaphors for beauty and/or death in my paintings." A Kansas native, Kuhn taught art at area art centers and museums, which inspired a return to school for a Master of Arts in museum education and later a Master of Fine Arts in painting. She is now teaching color theory in the design department at the University of Kansas. "My style and composition comes from my experience as a scientific illustrator, and I still look at botanical illustration for its refinement of painting technique."

What inspired this painting?

In all my work, I explore the use of icons that represent multiple ideas other than the original association. I am often puzzled by words, phrases and common ideas in contemporary culture and use these as the basis for my paintings and drawings. *Natural History*—in itself a nebulous term—has come to represent so many ideas and images that I felt compelled to examine some of the ideas behind it: beauty, death, transition and evolution. The postcards are images from the 1960s of the University of Kamsas Natural History Museum. When I found them at a garage sale, I knew I had to include them in a painting, along with burr oak leaves (a common tree in the area) and Thomas Moran's painting of the Grand Canyon.

How would you describe your painting style?

My work is realistic, trompe l'oeil, with a strong element of scientific analysis. I purposely adopted this style to make my paintings look like specimen boxes containing the actual objects. The framing is an important element, as the paintings sit behind spacers that form a shadow box frame, suggesting a collection or items in a curio cabinet.

How do you plan your compositions?

Usually, I start with an idea of the painting's concept and then look through my collection of found objects and ephemera of popular culture to find objects that might reinforce or contradict the concept. I pin my objects up on the wall and rearrange until I get a composition that interests me. Then I draw, redraw and resize. Often the original concept changes as I add and remove objects, and this evolution of the idea continues throughout the drawing and painting process; sometimes objects are added after the painting has been supposedly finished. For *Natural History* I had completed the whole painting but after looking at it for some time, I eliminated everything but the top three postcards and started with entirely new imagery for the rest of the painting.

What mediums do you use and what are your main techniques?

I use watercolor and gouache on paper, or acrylic on wood panel, with thin washes of transparent paint that eventually build up the color. I use only five or six colors—two reds, two blues, two yellows—and any additional colors that result from the layering of the transparent colors.

NATURAL HISTORY Margie Kuhn Acrylic on panel 36" × 24" (91cm × 61cm)

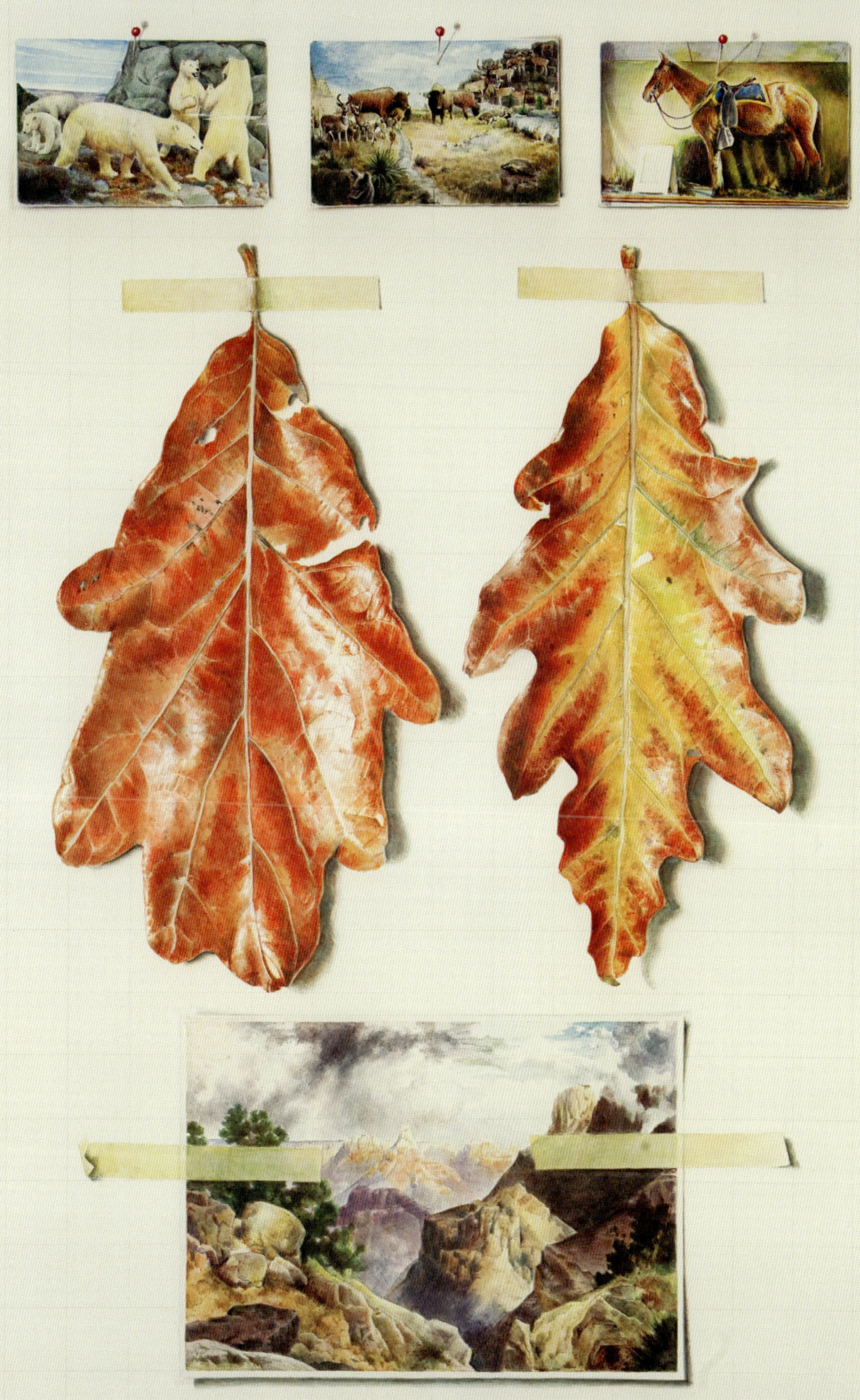

DONNA LEVINSTONE

Donna Levinstone lives in Manhattan, but her studio is in Long Island City, a place, she says, "where the sky goes on forever." She has had a lifelong love of the sky, which has been described as a "24-hour art gallery." Her earliest recollections include riding in the family's convertible and being in awe of the clouds. "To this day I get excited when I am flying in the clouds," says Levinstone. "I have recently started a skyscape pastel series of only clouds and sky. I'm a member of the Cloud Appreciation Society, which has its home base in London." With paintings in such diverse collections as the New York Historical Society, the Library of Congress and General Electric, Levinstone also donates works to various causes. A black-and-white pastel from her 9/11 series will be included in the National September 11 Memorial & Museum when it opens at Ground Zero in New York City. She is also a member of the Pastel Society of America and has been a pastelist for more than 30 years.

What inspired this painting?

My work is more concerned with the spiritual aspects of nature than an actual place. As I layer my pastel drawings with darkness and light, I explore beauty, transition and the powerful forces of nature. In *Eternal Waters*, a viewer pointed out the presence of an angel in the sky—something I was unaware of as I was drawing, yet is quite apparent in the finished painting.

What mediums do you use and what are your main techniques?

I work both in black and white and in color. When I work in black and white, I use only one black and one white pastel. I often add pastel and remove it using tissue, only to build it up again until it feels right. As I blend the pastels with my hands, it's as if I'm sculpting my imagery. My work has been described as "visual shorthand": a line will suggest a ripple in the water, a dot may be a light on the horizon, or a simple line will suggest the horizon.

How would you describe your painting style?

My drawings are an exploration of contrasts—volatility and serenity, darkness and light. Atmosphere and light play an important role in my pastel drawings. I started out painting in an impressionistic style, then I moved on to photorealism. My current style, done in pastel, represents a combination of the two. There is a semi-abstract quality to my work. I draw in my studio using inspiration from my photos and from my imagination. Even though my work is semi-abstract, it's important for me to capture the essence of what I am drawing, whether it be a reflection on the water or a light in the cloud. To paint a landscape as it is, is not as important as how it is felt.

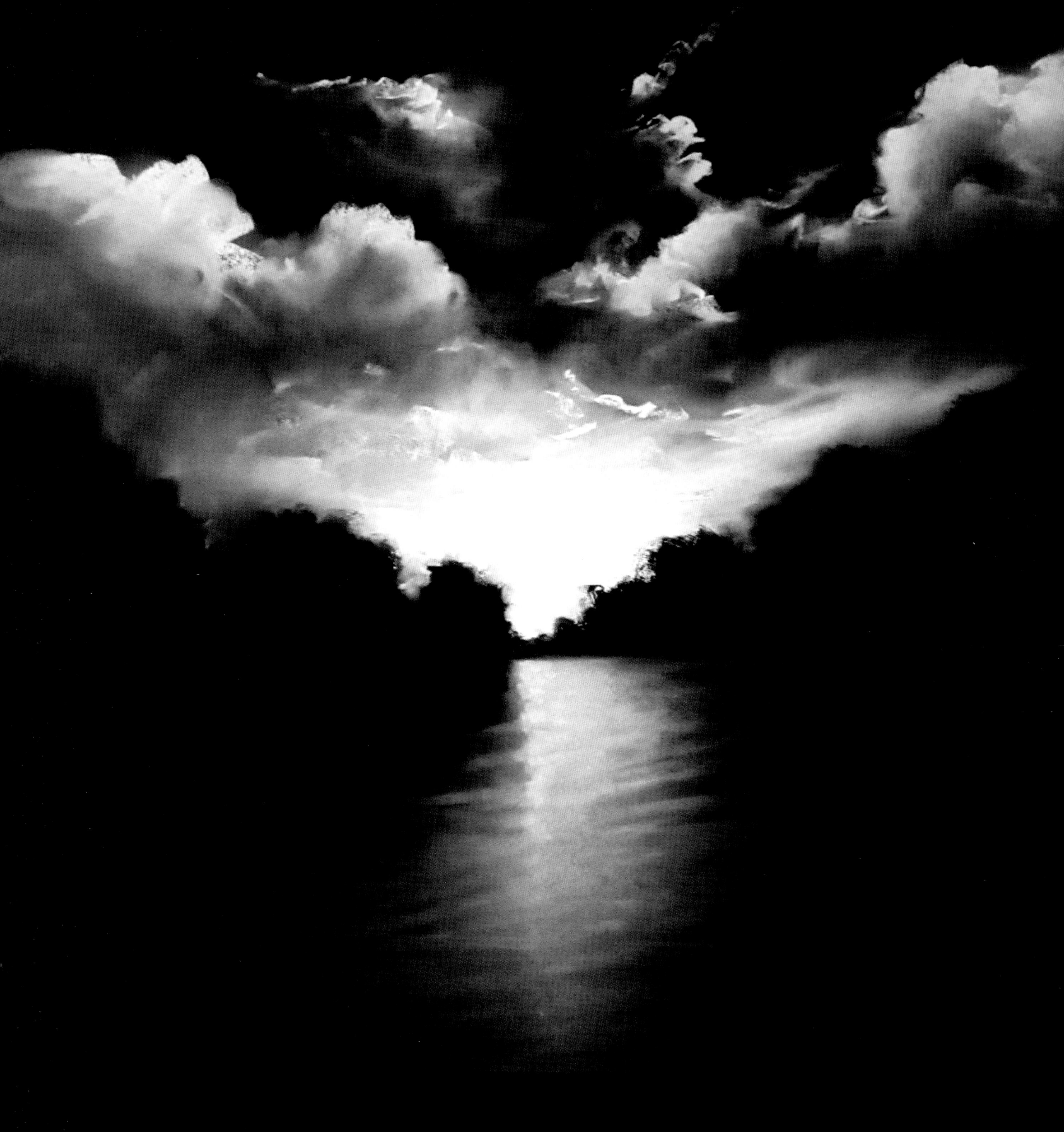

ETERNAL WATERS Donna Levinstone Black and white pastels 30" × 30" (76cm × 76cm) Private collection

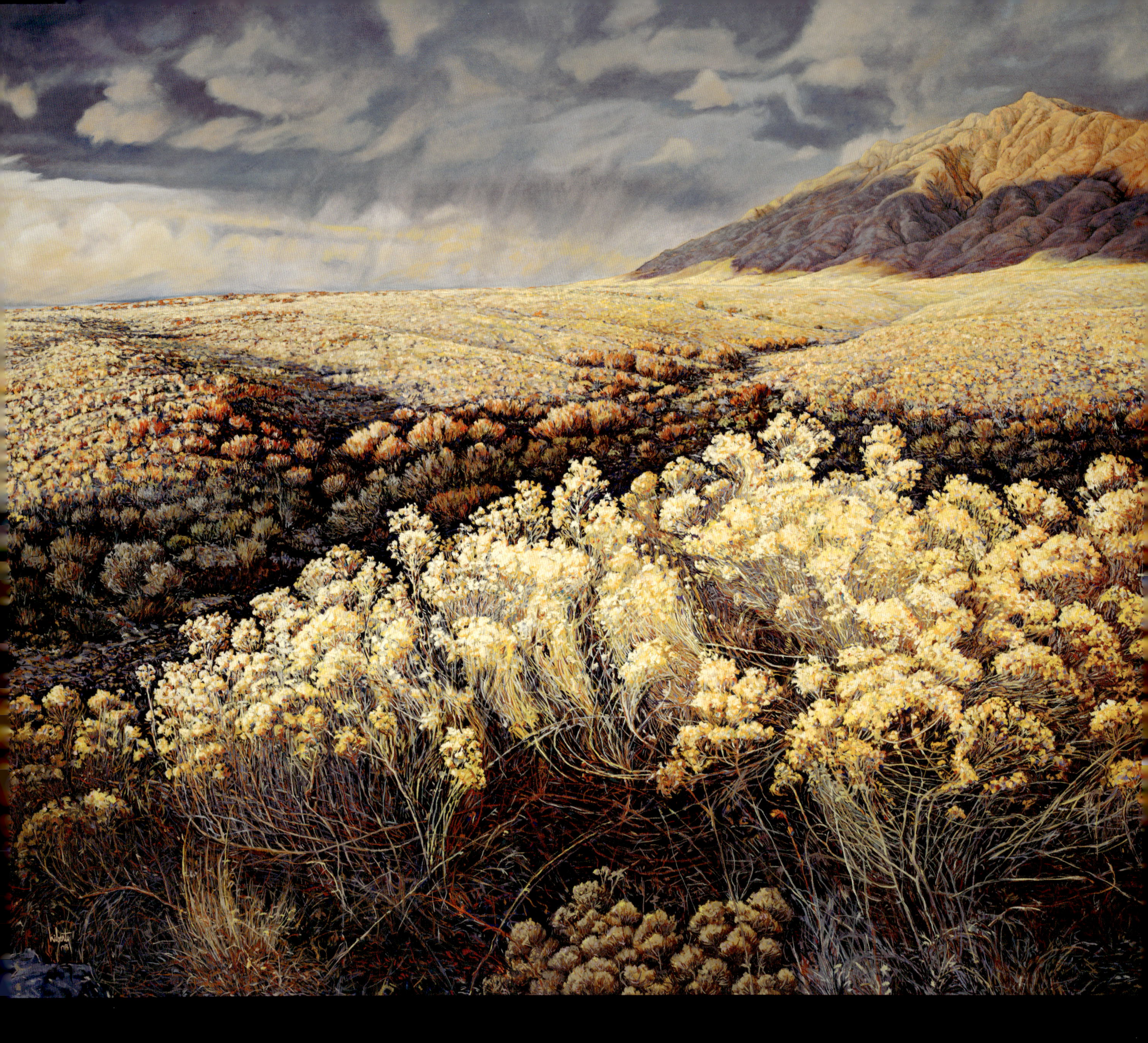

 101 VIEWS OF THE SANDIAS #9: RAIN DANCE Dennis Liberty Oil on canvas 54" x 66" (137cm x 168cm)

DENNIS LIBERTY

Dennis Liberty keeps a painter's journal and writes in it as he's painting. His love and respect for the colorful Sandia Mountains near his home just outside of Albuquerque, New Mexico, comes through not only in the extensive series of paintings he's presently creating, but also in the notes he takes every time he puts brush to canvas. "I began my series of the Sandia Mountains with *Coronado's Gold*, says Liberty. *Rain Dance* is no. 9. I plan 101 paintings of these mountains with which I've lived for over forty years. It has taken me that long to get up the guts to paint them." The view of the mountains in this painting is from the north end, a view not usually seen by those living in the city. If Liberty's artistic interpretation of these mountains reminds you of something and you're not quite sure what it is, he says, "Just like the Impressionists, with *Rain Dance* I'm continuing to take inspiration from the 19th-century Japanese woodblock artists, Hiroshige and Hokusai. These artists lived daily with the iconic image of Mt. Fuji which appears in almost all of their works."

What inspired this painting?

Exploration of color is my primary activity, my eternal fascination. In this I feel a kinship with Monet, John Singer Sargent, Jackson Pollock, Mark Rothko and Morris Louis. The Sandias provide the perfect subject to hang color on. The north end of the mountain in *Rain Dance* gives me color challenges on the land, the mountain and in the sky. My color wheel has been spinning as I seek out complementaries, secondaries, tertiaries, and analogous combinations. I love that there are no bad colors, just unworkable juxtapositions.

How would you describe your painting style?

My paintings are representational. I want viewers to be invited into the image and I want them to then explore the structure and color. I spend months painting a work like *Rain Dance*. I hope the viewer can spend years looking at it and constantly discover something new.

Is your painting inspired by spirituality?

My interest is physics, therefore light and color fascinate me. I'm entranced by how water flows and behaves—I'm captivated by how the phenomenal world works.

How do you plan your compositions?

I don't really plan them. I take a lot of photos, frame in the camera, and go from there to explore what caught my eye and interests me. I begin with a charcoal drawing on the canvas.

Do you paint en plein air? What practical advice do you have for those who would like to try it?

I do paint en plein air. Plein air painting is like being an athlete. One must adjust to the game instantly, one must commit totally, and one must accept that failure is part of the experience. Do not get fussy—just paint! Do not agonize—just paint another painting.

KIM LORDIER

Northern California artist Kim Lordier feels blessed to live where she does, south of San Francisco with open space preserves on one side and San Francisco Bay on the other. "Our terrain is vast, and we can virtually paint in the field year round," says Lordier. "What strikes me most is the quality of the lightplay on the landscape, the feeling or mood created with the light." Lordier is an artist member of the California Art Club, a signature member of the Pastel Society of America and the Laguna Plein Air Painters Association and a Distinguished Pastelist of the Pastel Society of the West Coast. "My introduction to landscape painting came about ten years ago when I saw my first exhibit of the Early California Impressionists called *Native Grandeur* that originated with The Irvine Museum and the Nature Conservancy of California," she states. "In this exhibit were paintings by Edgar Payne, Granville Redmond, Guy Rose and Franz Bischoff, to name a few. The artwork was a collective melding of the color and paint handling of the French Impressionists, and the strength of composition and tonal qualities of the Barbizon School. I continue to study the works of these artists today."

What inspired this painting?

Tender Is the Eve was created from a study done on site in the Oakland hills of California. The sun was sinking rapidly, and the Earth's shadow was climbing up the landscape. The sun was behind cloud cover for most of the day, and for the last hour of daylight, we had an incredible color display. This piece is inspired by the emotion that wells up with the close of the day and thoughts of a new beginning for tomorrow.

Why is American landscape painting important today, in the 21st century?

I strongly believe that the human psyche needs, and in some cases craves, silence from planes, trains and automobiles (computers, too). Open space and protected lands benefit all on the face of this Earth, and recording the pristine land in paint and photography is paramount in protecting our vanishing environs.

What's your best advice to students on painting landscapes?

Paint the big shapes and stay out of the details. I did not understand the strength and power of simple shapes and strong design until I started studying the paintings that inspire me and working from life. I'm still trying to work on these concepts!

Do you paint en plein air?

For many years I painted animal portraits in the studio from photographs. When I first painted outside, about ten years ago, I found what I was meant to do in life. Painting from life is peaceful, exciting and frustrating.

 TENDER IS THE EVE Kim Lordier Pastel on archival board 30" × 24" (76cm × 61cm) Private collection

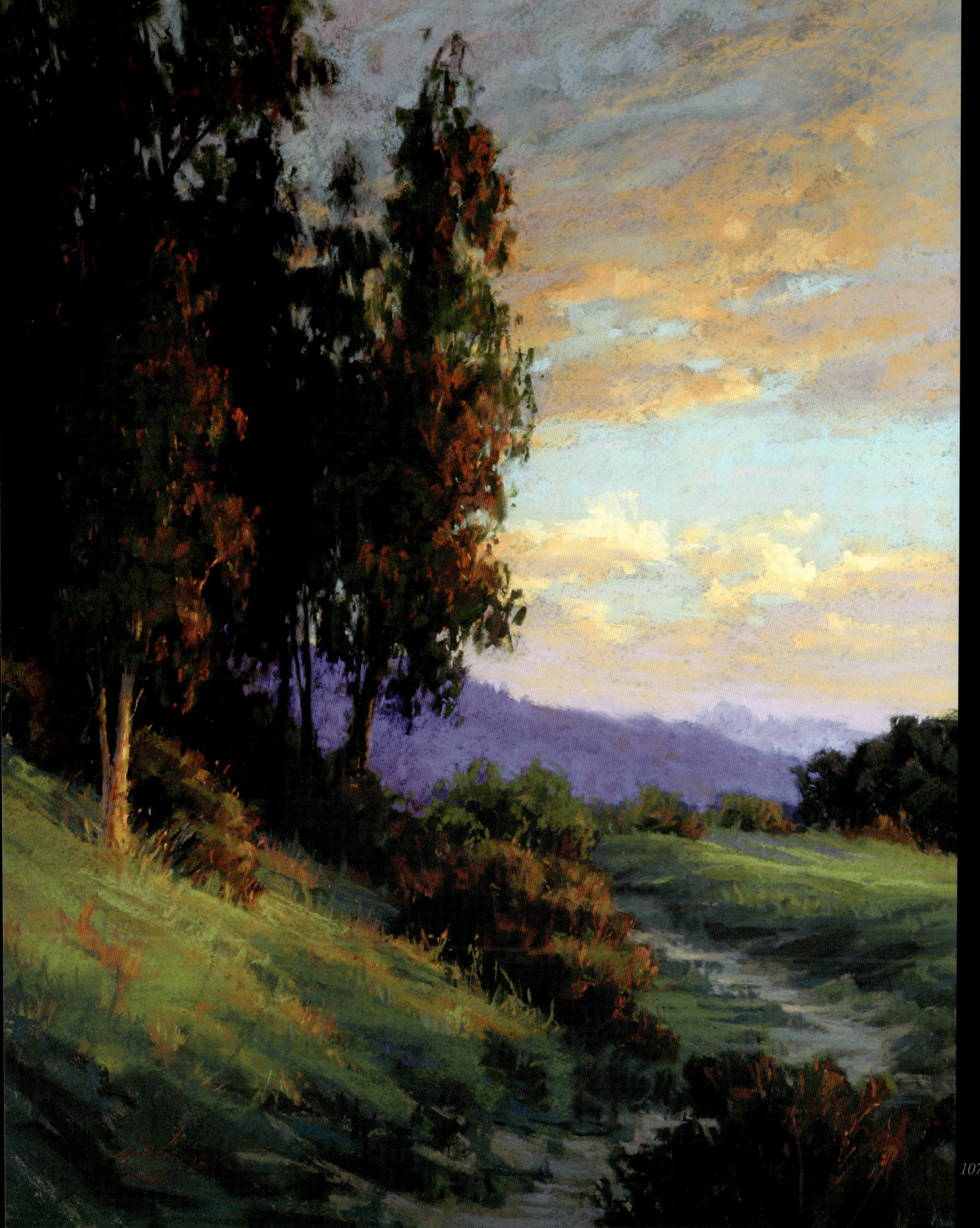

KEVIN MACPHERSON

One of the country's leading plein air painters, Kevin Macpherson is nationally recognized and collected, having attracted the attention of major art collectors including Roy Rose, the grandnephew of acclaimed California plein air painter Guy Rose. Driven by wanderlust, Macpherson is always curious to see new places and faces. New subject matter encourages fresh ideas and keeps him from getting too comfortable or relying on formulas of past success. A popular teacher and guest lecturer, Macpherson has written a classic painting instruction book, *Fill Your Oil Paintings with Light & Color* (North Light Books), which is in its ninth printing and has been translated into Chinese. His home high in the mountains near Taos offers him peace and solitude from his busy schedule. "I love to ski and Taos Mountain is a skier's paradise," says Macpherson. "I plan my trips so I can enjoy the beautiful winters of New Mexico."

What inspired this painting?

I have painted en plein air on the enchanted isle of Catalina off the coast of California since 1987. *Tree Top Vista* was a unique perspective looking down into the emerald waters of Avalon Bay. The unusual point of view makes for an interesting composition.

In what locations do you paint?

Travel has taken me to almost every state in America and over twenty countries. Recent years have found me painting in China. The people, culture and language have inspired my life in new directions. I have been studying Mandarin and painting portraits as I stay in Shanghai for four to five weeks each year. Where this will lead my art I am not sure, but I find it exciting and invigorating.

Is your painting inspired by spirituality?

Art has blessed my life and opened many unexpected doors. Teaching has been a very rewarding addition to creating art. I find real joy inspiring others to engage in the act of painting.

What does landscape painting teach us about life and art?

My art is a reflection of what I do, where I go, what I see and how I react to my life. My home turf in the mountains of Taos, New Mexico, has fueled my series, *Reflections on a Pond*, an intimate look at a small pond beside my home. Three hundred sixty-eight paintings of the same view go way beyond the mere pictorial and reveal deeper insights into my work and myself. *Reflections on a Pond* is an example of the variety of nature found when I'm painting one view in all seasons, all times of day and all kinds of weather, light and atmospheric opportunities. Accepting nature's offerings with endless compositional arrangements makes the artist's job easier. I could not invent all the compositions nature shows me. I just have to be receptive.

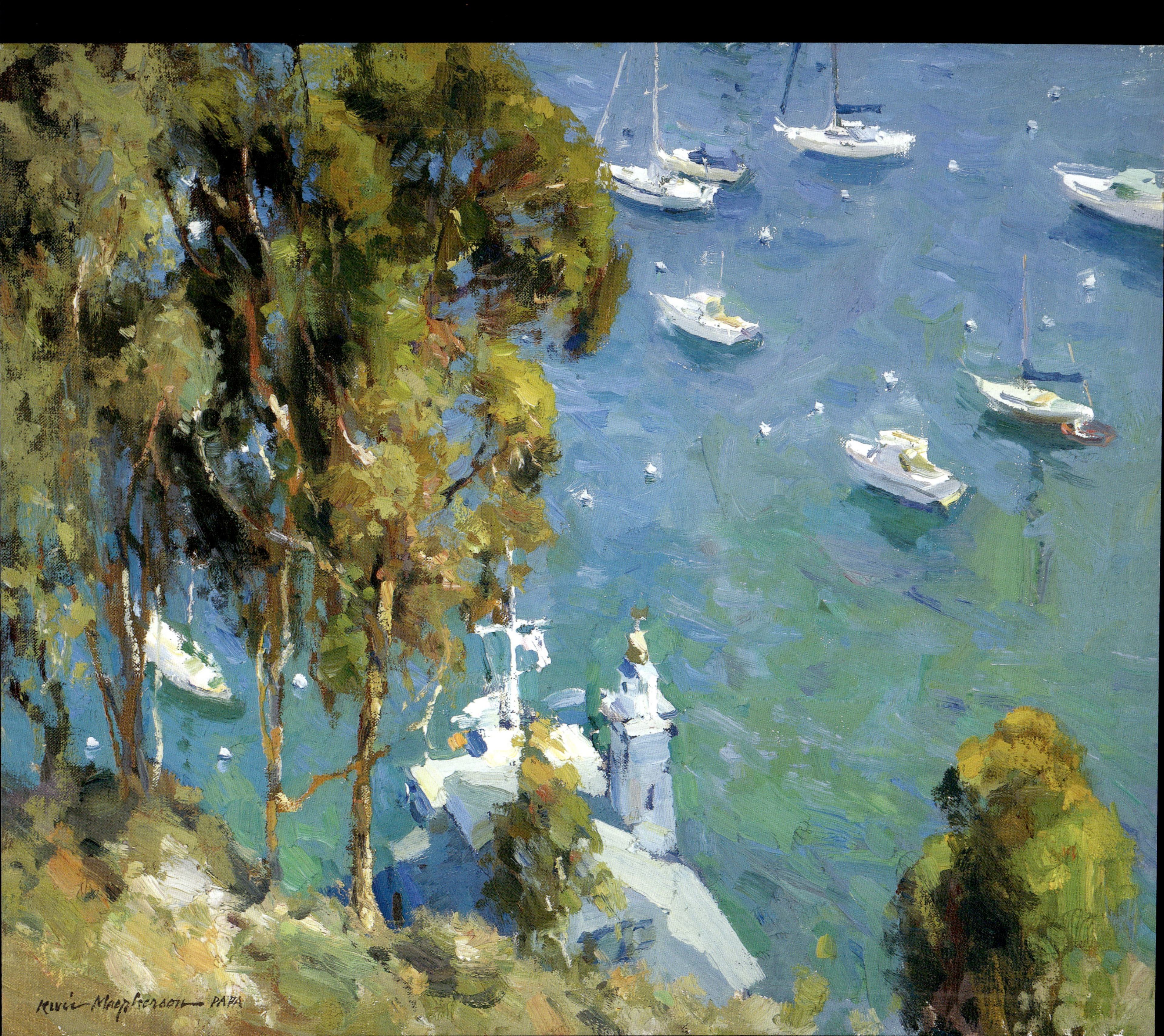

STANLEY MALTZMAN

New York State artist Stanley Maltzman is a highly acclaimed landscape painter as well as an accomplished author and educator. His skill in drawing and painting the elements of nature, from forests of tall trees down to the tiniest acorn, are a source of inspiration to the many students who have attended his classes at the Hudson River Valley Art Workshops in Greenville, New York. He is also the author of two successful art instruction books, *Drawing Nature* and *Drawing Trees Step by Step*, both published by North Light. Maltzman enjoys working in several mediums, primarily pastels, with drawing a close second, and is also proficient in watercolor, oil, lithography and etching. His art stems from nature, and his love of working outdoors has labeled him a plein air painter. He says, "There's a sense of communion with nature that is captured by working in the fields or woods whare you can touch, smell and observe the beauty around you—a one-on-one communion, an experience that just cannot be achieved indoors."

Q&A

What inspired this painting?

Autumn is a time of year that has always inspired me, and the year this painting was made was no exception—as you can see, the woods were ablaze with color! As an artist I take what's given to me and create a picture, and *Autumn Palette* is the result of that inspiration.

In what locations do you paint?

Living in the beautiful Hudson River Valley region, surrounded by easily accessible streams, woods and the famous Catskill Mountains greeting me all day, every day, I naturally lean toward the landscape. I never have to travel far to find something that appeals to my pencils or paints. It's an area rich in art history made famous by Thomas Cole, Frederic Church and many other fine artists, thus giving title to the "Hudson River school" of art.

How do you plan your compositions?

I usually walk around the area before starting my thumbnails. When these are done, and my composition and values are satisfactory, I then select a sheet of four-ply museum board and start my painting. I know I may not finish, but my sketches, color notes and value studies will give me enough information to finish up in the studio.

What mediums do you use and what is your main painting technique?

I find pastels more fun for me at this time of my life. I will work with layering and underpainting, but mostly like to use scumbling, which allows me to overlay with a thin or an impasto application, then spray and scumble again. I get very interesting effects and colors with this technique.

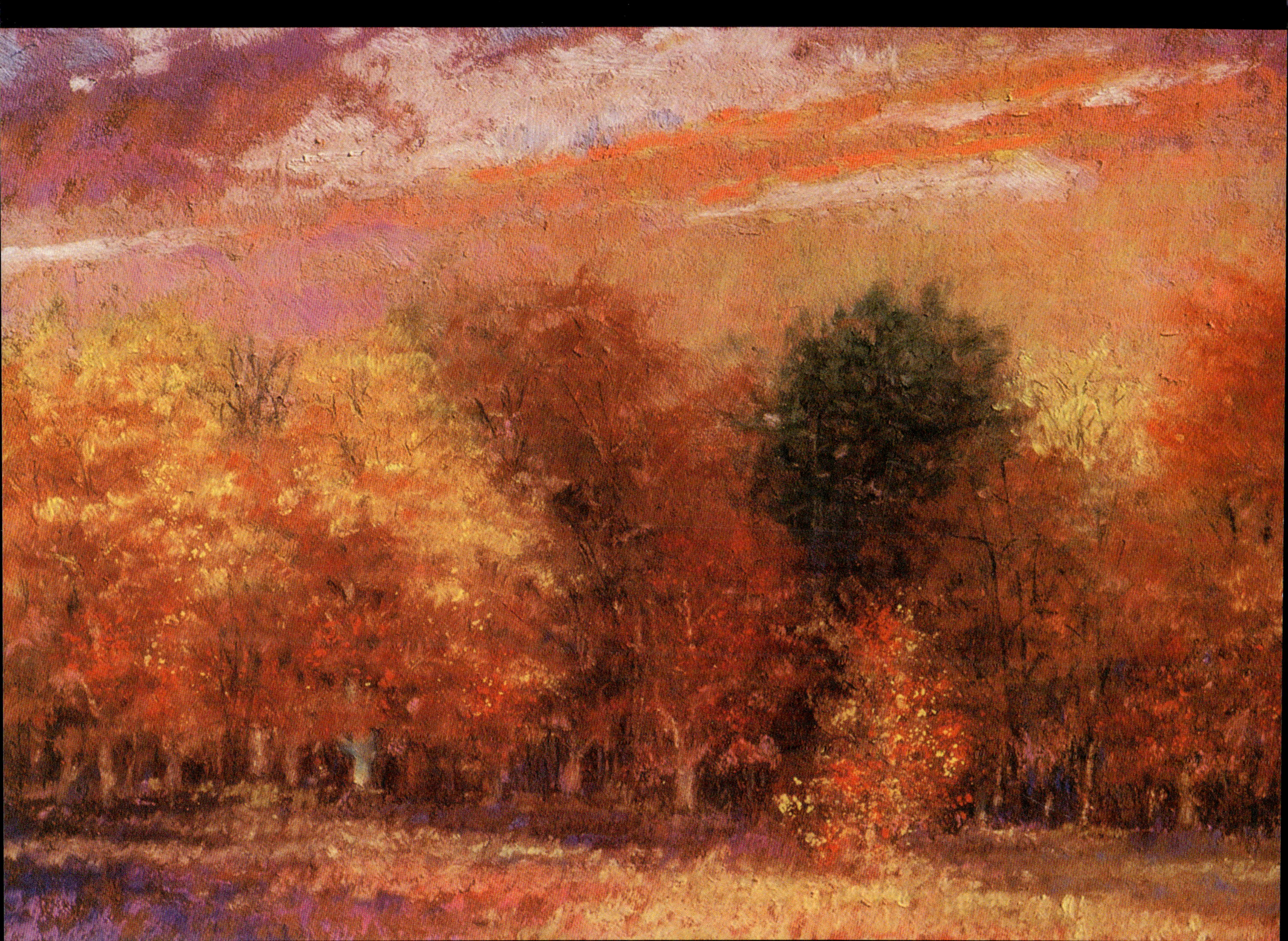

RICHARD McDANIEL

Other artists think of Richard McDaniel as a respected painter who plays music when he's not at the easel. To the musicians, however, he is a professional singer/songwriter/guitarist who also paints when he's not on stage. There is no conflict in this (other than time), for both are extensions of the same creative pulse. Many have called McDaniel a Renaissance man, for he has devoted his life to intellectual and artistic inquiry. Five of his books have been published; his artwork is included in fifteen books by other authors; he has taught drawing and painting for nearly thirty years; recorded music and performed in front of thousands; designed and built studios; and is a prolific painter with works in collections throughout the country. He hasn't much time for hobbies, although he finds hiking good for the soul and enjoys a wicked game of ping-pong or a spirited croquet match.

What inspired this painting?

The bridge at Antioch has fascinated me for several years for a variety of reasons. Its structure is minimal in design and interacts well with the clutter of factory buildings on the far shore. The bridge is situated near the Sacramento/San Joaquin River Delta, where California's two longest rivers merge before flowing into San Francisco Bay. In the 1990s I completed a series of paintings depicting the Sacramento River but did not include this scene, for it was difficult for me to access the viewpoint I preferred. I wanted to stand at a point where the tall smokestack was in a good position relative to the bridge and to the left of Mt. Diablo. A few years ago I began a series of sixty paintings of the San Joaquin River, and this time I talked my way onto private property to make my drawings and color sketches. One morning as I visited the site, a haze added just the mysterious atmosphere I craved. As the morning sun burned through the mist, the scene became visible, yet simple, with most of the clarity in the foreground, and reducing the mountain to a vague silhouette. I restricted the color range and concentrated on the simple geometry of the bridge in contrast with the organic quality of the nearby grasses.

How would you describe your painting style?

I am an abstractionist at heart. I started as a nonrepresentational painter and I always consider the basic elements of composition and color dynamics before recording any literal description of a scene. Even when my paintings seem realistic, the subject of a painting is secondary to the process of solving visual problems—adjusting the interplay of shapes and spatial intervals.

How do you plan your compositions?

Some compositions suggest themselves from the very start, and for this I am grateful. More often the design develops gradually. Many times I have a general idea and the composition only becomes clear as I develop the painting. I try to stay as loose as possible for as long as possible so that I can improvise. It's important to be able to "read" the painting as it develops, for the painting always tells me what to do. I certainly believe the wisdom in having a basic plan, but it is equally important to recognize alternate solutions that arise unexpectedly.

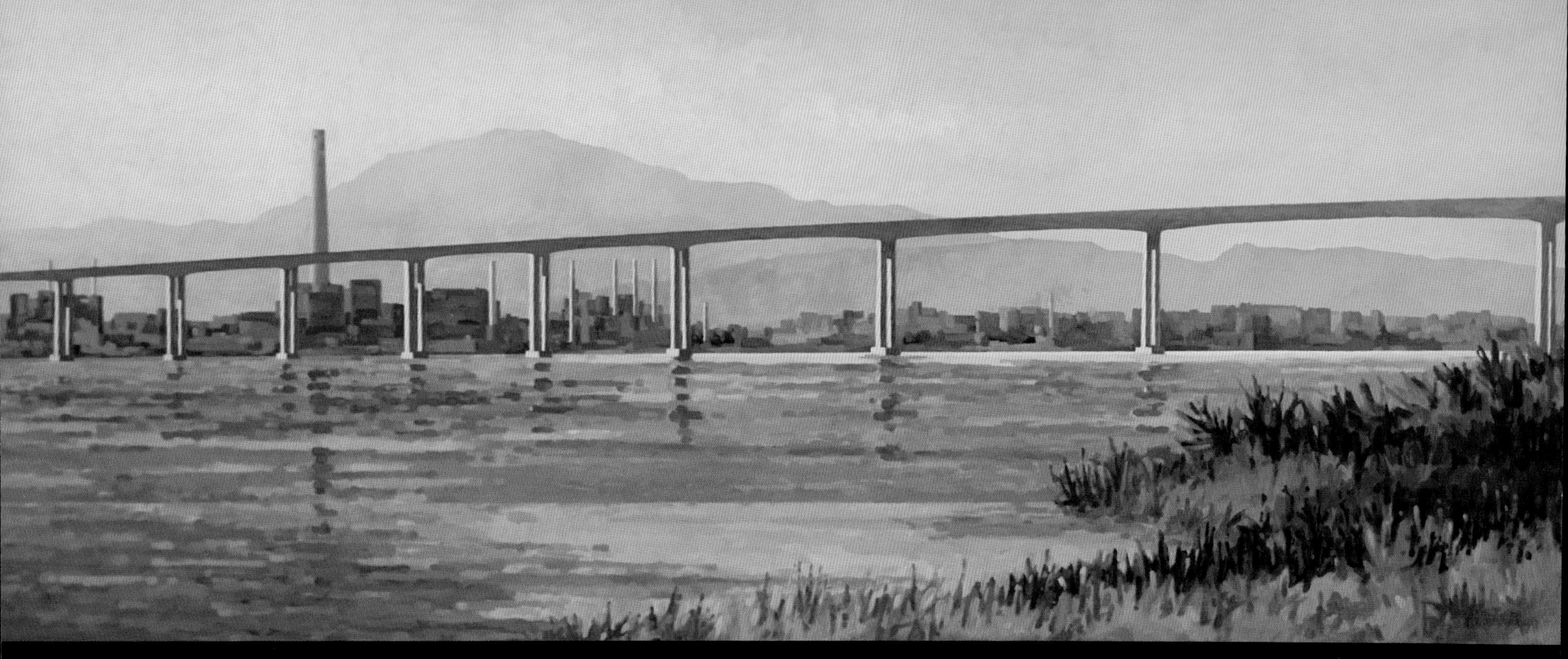

RICHARD McKINLEY

Born in the Rogue Valley of Oregon, Richard McKinley spent most of his youth growing up with the rivers and mountains that form this special place and he has been inspired by it ever since. "Winter in Oregon provides ample studio time for disciplined study and resolve," says McKinley, "but when spring arrives, I find myself eager to pack up my painting equipment. I want to plant my feet back in the cathedral of nature." A professional artist for more than thirty-five years, McKinley is a signature member and 2010 Hall of Fame inductee of the Pastel Society of America. Widely published in books and magazines, he is the author of *Pastel Pointers*, an instructional book published by North Light, and writes a weekly blog for *The Pastel Journal* on ArtistsNetwork.com.

Q&A

What inspired this painting?

I frequently visit this location in central Oregon. On this particular day the sky was overcast, which accentuated the richness of the color and I was intrigued by the textural nature of the trees, which created a perfect foil for the illuminated meadow behind. Texture, rhythm and color saturation were the main attractions. The added element of the path and wildflowers strengthened the concept.

In what locations do you paint?

What attracts me to a landscape are elements of design versus subject matter. These elements can be found in almost any locale. It is not the spectacular grand scene but more often the mundane that inspires. Remote, quiet locations are of special appeal. The high desert of Oregon and New Mexico, the out-of-the-way cliffs of the Pacific coastline, and the disappearing pastoral fields and trees of the American countryside are my favorites.

Do you paint en plein air? What practical advice do you have for those who would like to try it?

I love to paint en plein air. Having a tactile relationship with the subject is instrumental in creating a heightened sensitivity, even if it is just spending time sketching or in quiet observation. If you are new to working outdoors, be kind to yourself. It's very different from working with photo reference. Don't start out with inflated aspirations of creating your best masterpiece; instead, begin with simple mechanical field studies. Realize that it is not about finishing. It is about gaining landscape sensitivity that will affect all of your landscape work, whether in studio or on location.

Be aware of your surroundings. On one plein air adventure, I had my pastel palette open in front of my easel and kept noticing that whenever I stepped back to see how the painting looked from a distance, there seemed to be fewer sticks of pastel in the palette. Thinking I was losing my mind, I decided to carefully walk backwards, keeping an eye on my setup. As I did, a large bird swooped down from a nearby tree and picked up a pastel stick from the palette and returned to his perch. While I may have lost a few precious pastel sticks, that bird had adorned his nest with some of the most colorful decorations in the forest.

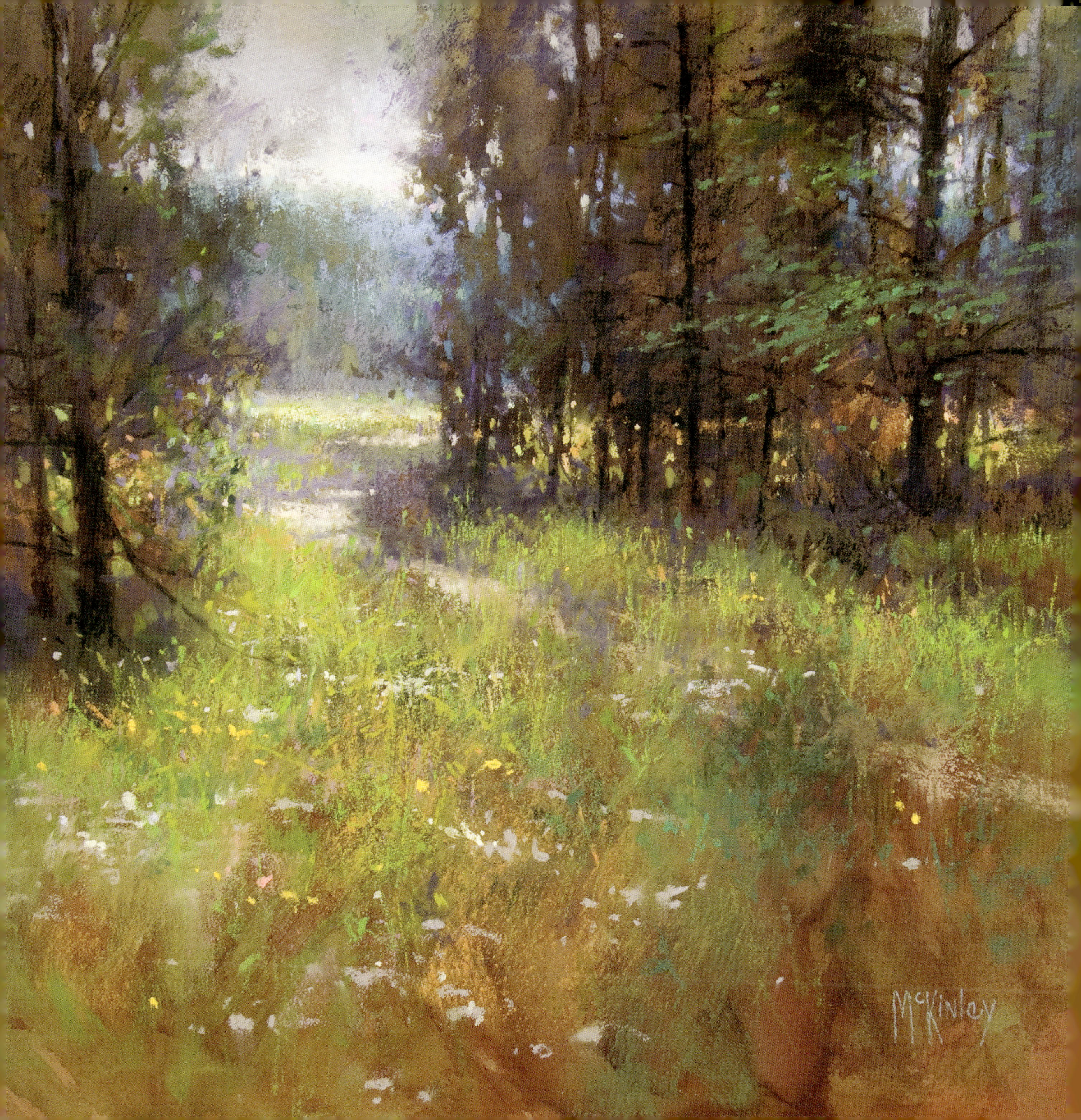
McKinley

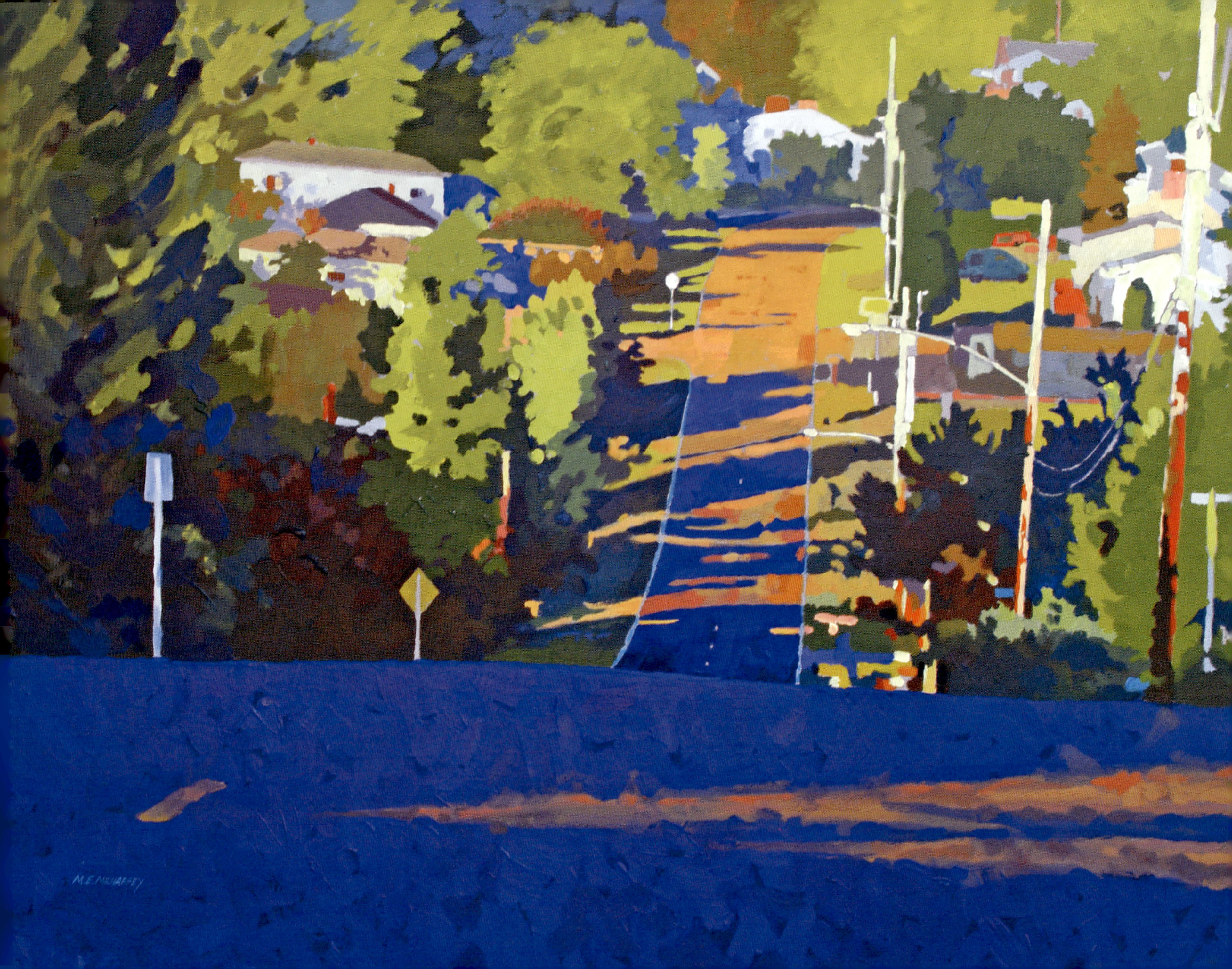

MARK MEHAFFEY

Mark Mehaffey is a retired public school art instructor who believes our art future is with the young, and he is dedicated to building that vision. To his students, he says, "Think about shapes, not things. Trees, clouds, buildings, people, lakes, mountains are all shapes that we get to arrange. Often the best composition is not the one in front of us, but the one we design." Mehaffey paints in both watercolor and acrylic, and uses a variety of surfaces with both mediums, ranging from paper and board to canvas and Yupo. A signature member of the American Watercolor Society and the National Watercolor Society among many others, Mehaffey has won major awards in juried exhibitions across the country, has published a book on watercolor, and recently filmed two painting videos for ArtistsNetwork.tv. He describes painting as "the hardest, most mentally engaging, frustratingly fun activity there is . . . exactly like life!"

What inspired this painting?

I was teaching a painting workshop on Whidbey Island, Washington, and would walk back and forth from where I was staying to the teaching venue. Every afternoon the warm sunlight would rake across the road home. The long shadows were particularly interesting and beautiful and had to be painted.

Do you prefer particular seasons or times of day?

Summer is the most difficult season—at least here in Michigan it is. Lots and lots of green! It becomes about subtle temperature variations and how the atmosphere affects colors as they recede into the distance. Spring has bright greens against still-visible structures, winter is all about dramatic light and shadow, and fall has those gorgeous yellows, oranges and reds.

How do you plan your compositions?

Everything gets distilled in my sketchbook. I simplify, arrange the shapes and assign values to all shapes based on the focal point. I keep these painting plans small—postcard size, but they are accurate renditions of how I want the painting to look. If I like my plan, I paint it. If not, I do another sketch, and sometimes another until I'm satisfied with my design.

What mediums do you use and what are your main painting techniques?

I use heavy-bodied paint directly from the tube. I love that acrylics dry fast. It allows me to repaint any passage within minutes. I use both wet blending (you must act quickly!) and scumbling for blending one value into another. When my painting is done, I apply two layers of spray gloss varnish to protect the paint and to pull everything together.

JAY MOORE

Jay Moore has become well known for his tranquil landscapes that epitomize the beauty and grandeur of the West. His work is in the permanent collections of the Denver Art Museum and the Colorado Springs Pioneer Museum. Moore grew up in the foothills of the Rocky Mountains and makes his home there today. "As a Colorado native, I have seen much of the state," he says. "In fact, in my studio I have a large map of Colorado with red pins indicating places I have painted at least once. At last count there were over 300 pins." Moore loves the wilderness and backcountry and travels widely in search of beauty to such places as Alaska, Hawaii, Canada and the mountain states west to California. Family road trips, hiking, fishing and camping fill his time away from painting. He enjoys teaching and for the past several years has conducted a six-month mentorship program to help artists with real-world advice and assignments. The goal is to help them go from part-time amateurs to full-time professional artists.

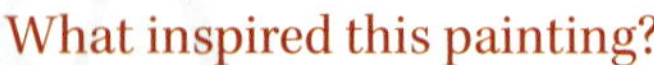

What inspired this painting?

I would like to say that I chose the subject for *Lords of the Tundra* but in this instance, the subject actually chose me. I was painting with my son and some friends on 14,000-foot-high Mt. Evans, near Denver. Usually at this altitude in December, you're battling winds and weather, but this day it was calm and sunny. We were enjoying painting the afternoon light on the mountain when these mountain goats came out of nowhere and wandered right into the foreground, as if they were on stage. Their winter coats were perfectly white as if they had just been shampooed. The late afternoon light gave them a golden halo effect. I turned to the others who had only been out painting a couple of times and said, "This just does not happen!" We started taking pictures and painting as fast as we could. I knew this good fortune would eventually result in a large-scale painting that included the goats.

Do you prefer particular seasons or times of day?

It's safe to say that every artist prefers the early morning or late afternoon light due to the dramatic shadows and rich colors. However, I have always painted on location from dawn to dusk, going from one small canvas to the next and taking only short breaks in between. The light, atmosphere, clouds, shadows and colors are all constantly changing and I find each phase of the day interesting and challenging. I plan a day painting outdoors according to what view looks best at that time of day. For instance, the mountain peak will look best at first light, the river in the valley is best at mid-morning, the barn in the afternoon, and the meadow in the evening.

What's your best advice to students on painting landscapes?

If you want to try painting outdoors, get good equipment and supplies so you don't have to struggle with technical problems and can concentrate on painting. Practice mixing colors so you can get what you want quickly. Don't get too dependent on photographic reference. All the best artists I know paint very well from life because they have spent countless hours and years practicing.

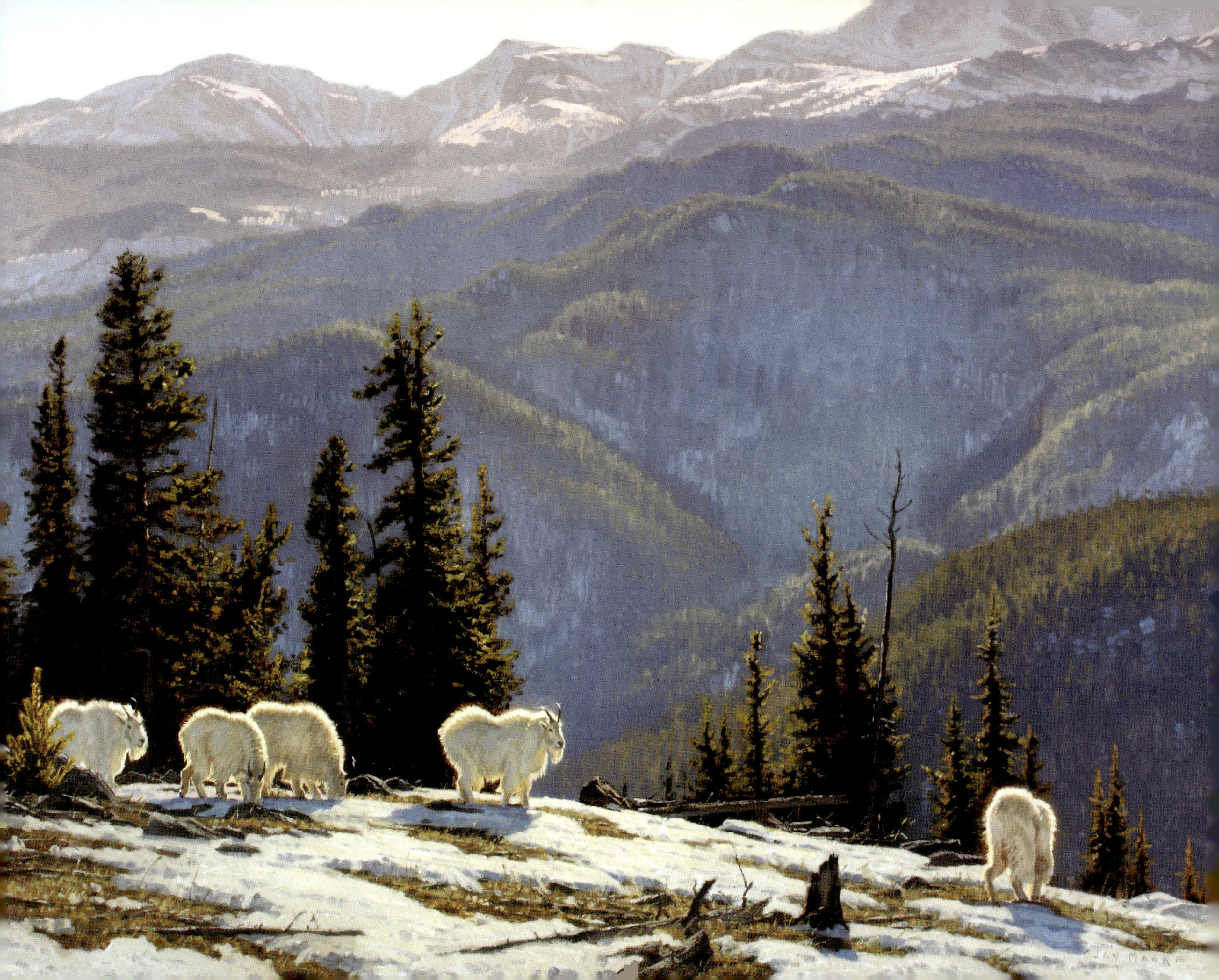
JAY MOORE

ELIZABETH MOWRY

Longtime painter and author Elizabeth Mowry understands with every part of her being that, as an artist, she stands on the shoulders of giants. She has learned from and drawn powerful inspiration from the likes of George Inness, now considered the "father of American landscape," Isaac Levitan, the 19th-century Russian landscape painter, and John F. Carlson, whom she remembers meeting when she was five years old in Woodstock, New York. Mowry is the author of four books: *Paint the Changing Seasons in Pastel, The Pastelist's Year, The Poetic Landscape*, and *Landscape Meditations*. She has received more than forty national and international awards for her landscape paintings, and was the 2009 Hall of Fame honoree in the Pastel Society of America. Mowry now lives in Colorado and finds fresh inspiration in a landscape very different from her former home in upstate New York.

How would you describe your painting style?

Reviewers and critics back East where I lived until five years ago were the first to consistently describe my work as "poetic." I realized that I was not painting nature how it was, but rather how I thought it could be. Briefly, "poetic landscape" embraces the most common natural elements familiar to all people, but much of it is introspective as opposed to site-specific. It's a reminder of the importance of tranquility, and its strength emerges from what is left unexpressed because it always falls just short of closure.

Is your painting inspired by spirituality? How is that seen in your art?

The paintings that have evolved in my recent work are about solitude and also about closure, a change brought about over time by reflection. Other recent work is about mortality but without sadness; spirituality without the noisy pursuit of it; and a gentle, overall joy, through painting, that comes from the exploration of beauty, sometimes even tragedy.

Do you prefer particular seasons or times of day?

Although I admire paintings that depict strong contrasts of sunlight and shadow, my honest preferences for my own paintings lean toward overcast, quiet light that allows me to access something deeper within the composition. I like when I feel that I've been able to tap into some bit of mystery that exists, but which I purposely try not to paint. So in essence, closure is not depicted, but one feels that it is near.

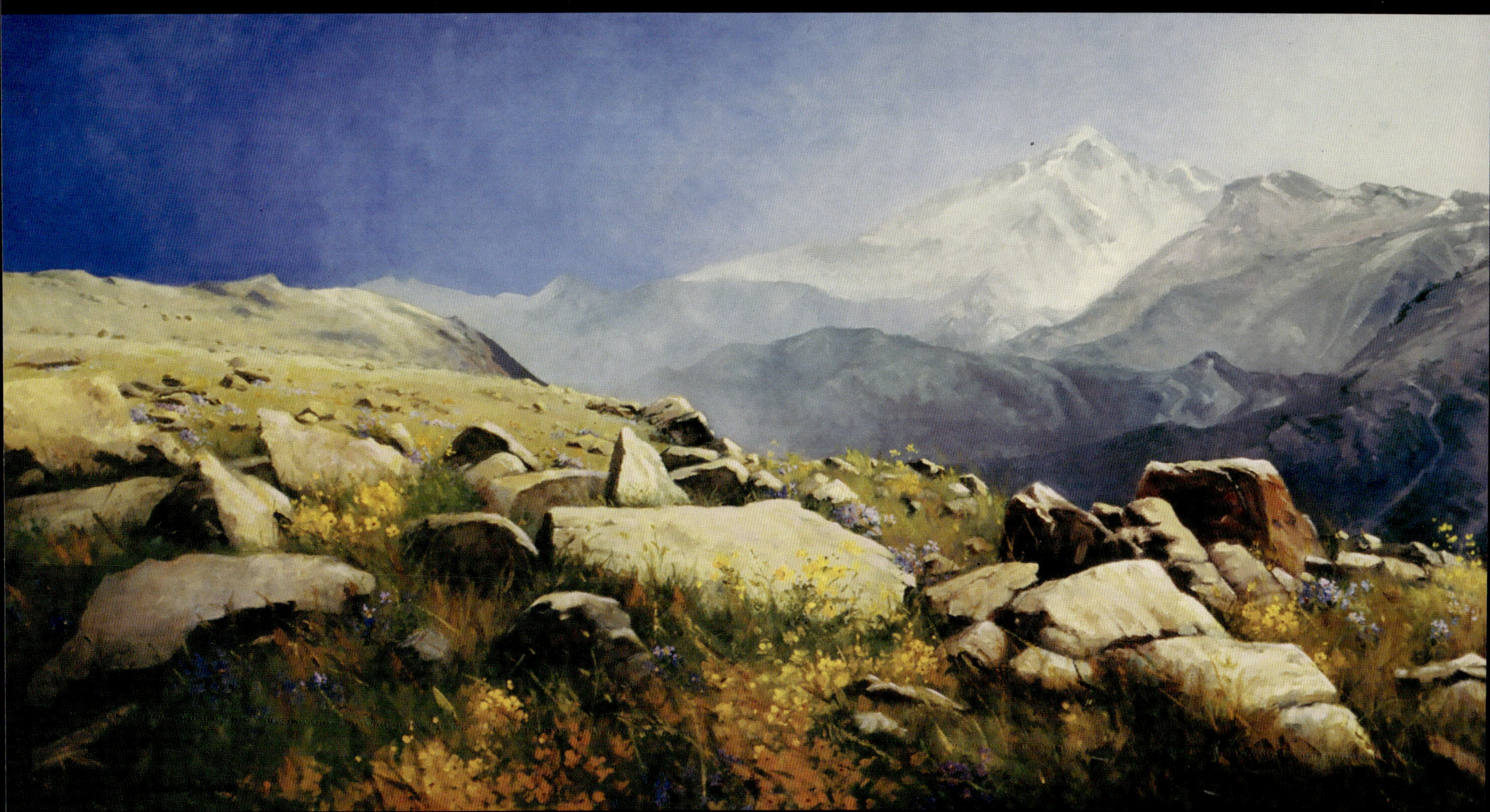

PAUL MURRAY

Paul Murray had a graphic design business for twenty-six years and painted part-time. That all changed in 2001 when he won best of show in the International Association of Pastel Societies biennial exhibit. It was then that he decided to paint full-time. Murray lives and works just south of Santa Fe because "the light in northern New Mexico is just fabulous. There is no other light like it anywhere else in America." Besides painting, he likes adventure. "Some friends and I have ridden our bicycles across the U.S. My brother and I have hiked the Grand Canyon twice. Last year I was an artist-in-residence at the North Rim of the Grand Canyon for three weeks. I got to explore everything!" When asked how he would describe his painting style, Murray replies, "I can't avoid being described as 'realistic.' I like the challenge of representational painting. It's my form of discovery. Most of my paintings are not done so I can make some sort of statement. They are my attempt to understand what's there. They're more like questions than answers."

What inspired this painting?

Very early in the morning is one of my favorite times of day. It's such an optimistic time; a full and wonderful day lies ahead. Also, early morning virga is such a rare thing so the imagery itself was very appealing. "Virga" is rain that never reaches the ground. When it's really dry, like here in the desert, rain can evaporate during its journey from the clouds to the ground. At sunrise or sunset when the light is just right, these curtains of rain, or virga, can look spectacular.

What mediums do you use and what are your main techniques?

More and more I'm moving towards large paintings done in oil. It is so flexible and subtle. I do a lot of glazing for atmospheric effects and subtlety of light.

Do any historical movements, periods or artists inspire your painting?

I'm not tied to any particular period or movement. I'm most interested in whether something works or not. Oddly enough, my favorite painter is Mark Rothko.

How do you plan your compositions?

Generally, in some shape or form, I use the rule of thirds. My instincts take me there. I do really appreciate broken symmetry and use that way of composing, but this is rare and hard to do without it looking trite or clichéd.

Why is American landscape painting important today, in the 21st century?

There is so much powerful metaphor in landscape painting. It is literally and figuratively the foundation of our civilization. It is so much a part of who we are. In this hyper-electronic digital age where visually anything is possible, we are removing ourselves from reality. We view progress for its own sake without having any concern for where it will take us. We can't make useful progress unless we are aware of where we come from, our roots. Landscape painting does that.

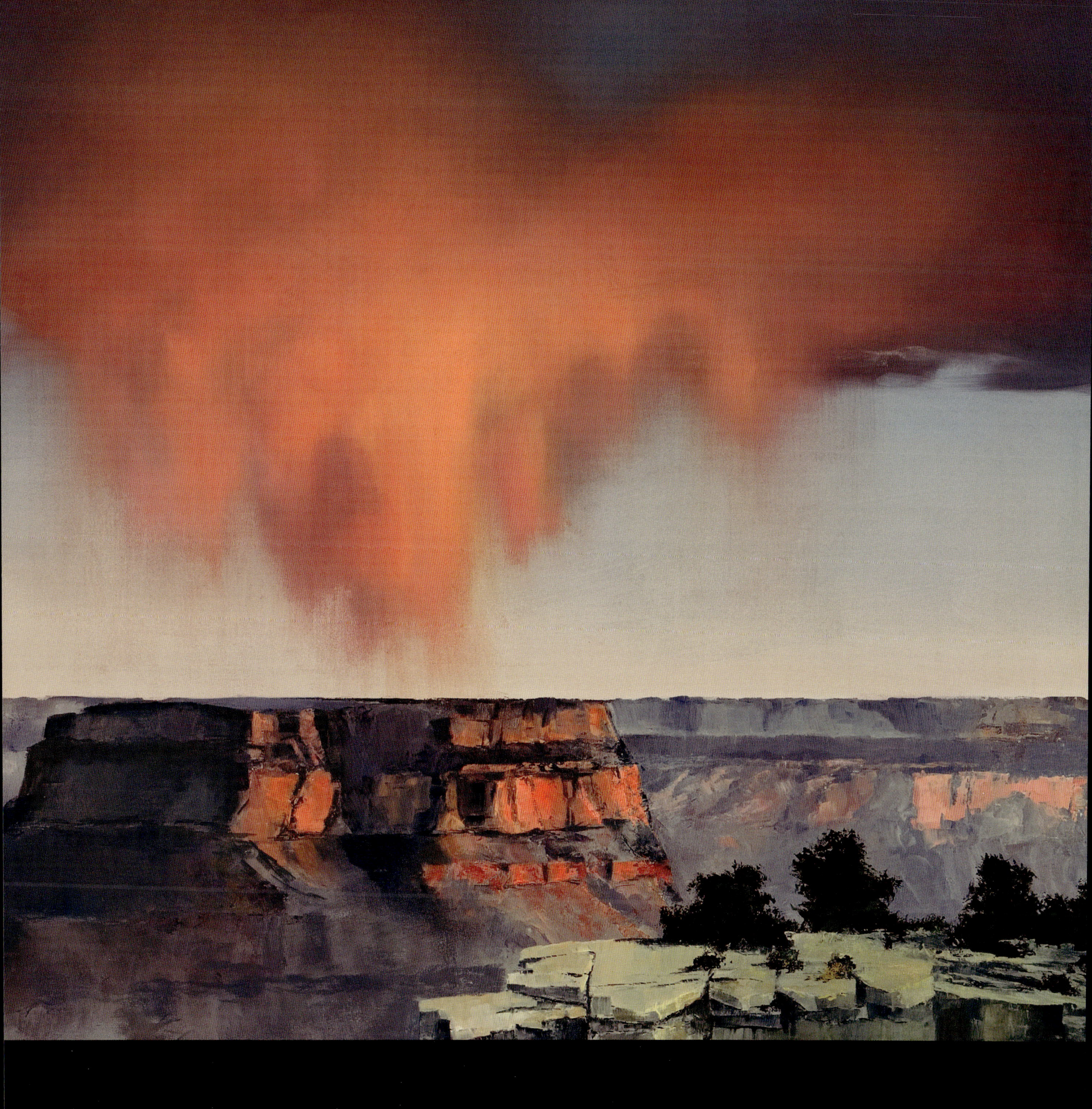

MORNING VIRGA Paul Murray Oil on coarse linen mounted on board 36" × 36" (91cm × 91cm)

P. A. NISBET

Peter Allen Nisbet has been a student of fine art for thirty-eight years. In 1970 he received a degree from the University of North Carolina followed by a commission in the United States Navy. He served as a line officer at sea with a ten-month tour of duty in Vietnam. During that time he was personally appointed by the Secretary of the Navy to serve as Director of Art Services for the Navy's Office of Information. Following military service he began a commercial art business, providing graphic design and illustration for over twenty-five national organizations. In 1980 he moved to the Southwest and began painting landscapes. "Clearly, I am strongly influenced by the work of J.M.W. Turner," says Nisbet. "I have also appreciated the work of the American Luminist and Tonalist painters, and I see myself as squarely in the camp of the American landscape tradition." Among many other awards and achievements, Nisbet recently won the Farney Award for Best Painting in 2008 and 2009 in the Quest for the West exhibit at the Eiteljorg Museum in Indianapolis. When he's not painting, he's teaching workshops and traveling to California to study ocean waves.

What inspired this painting?

I have been an avid student of clouds for more than three decades. My first attempt to paint thunderstorms in 1975 resulted in failure, and I learned very quickly that clouds were extremely difficult to portray in paint. I kept at it for all these years and am still amazed by the things I witness in the sky. In the painting *Colossus*, a grand theme emerges from the dust of the southern New Mexico desert. It is stupendous in size and power, and I make it my business to search for events like this every summer. The finished painting was done from a grisaille underpainting and was completed using layers of colors applied transparently, one over the other.

Why is American landscape painting important today, in the 21st century?

Artists who spend time in nature quickly come to an understanding that what they are witnessing in the landscape are actually transcendent moments; landscape painting weaves a kind of connective tissue to the art of the past and those souls who were pursuing the light centuries ago. There are moral tales and human dramas playing out, all the time, under the great dome of the sky.

In what locations do you paint?

I'm a student of what I would call "exploration art." By this I mean it has been my goal to explore distant locales in pursuit of light in the landscape. I have painted in places as remote as the South Pole. Once you get that far you realize that unless you leave the planet there is really no farther place on Earth to go. For sheer majesty and drama nothing matches the Southwest. I'm particularly fond of the deserts and canyons of Arizona.

What's your best advice to students on painting landscapes?

Get out there and walk the land. Observe critically the effects of light and shadow on all landforms and in all kinds of weather. Paint outside and bring your work back to the studio, set it aside and allow your dreams and visions to seep into the event. Remember what you saw, but also embellish those things that provoke your spirit. Your work should embody your beliefs and it should be unique only to you.

COLOSSUS P. A. Nisbet Oil on canvas 48" × 36" (122cm × 91cm)

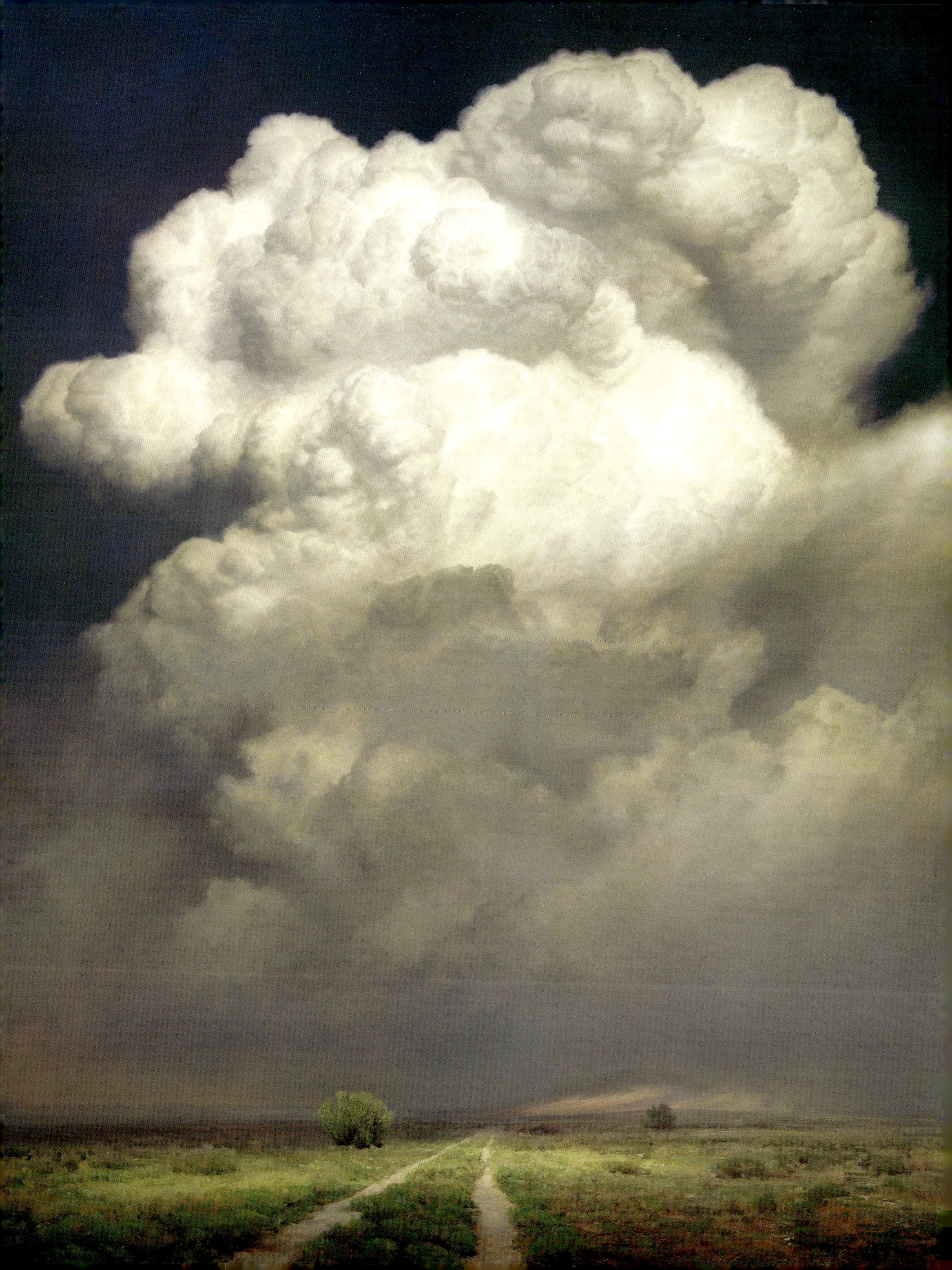

BRUCE PEIL

Athens, Texas, artist Bruce Peil is the co-founder of the Outdoor Painters Society and is a signature member of the Oil Painters of America. He and his wife, Stacey, have an artist's retreat at his Texas home and studio where he teaches workshops. Their property was formerly the site of an old dairy where Bruce converted the 900-square-foot milk house into his studio and classroom. As a teacher, Peil advises his students who want to paint landscapes to "understand that the same principles apply whether you are painting a landscape, a still life, the figure, or whatever. It is all just light hitting a shape. You don't change your way of thinking about the subject depending on what the subject is. You use the same thought process and look for the same things no matter what the subject is. The most important thing is that you observe your subject matter from life. That's where the truth is."

What inspired this painting?

I was drawn to this scene mainly because of the contrast between the light and shadow areas and the movement of the water. The dark figure standing in front of the sunlit water adds to the contrast and gives a sense of scale. Fall and winter are the most exciting times of year to me as far as subject matter is concerned. The locations I like most to paint are extremely varied. It doesn't have to be an overly dramatic scene to attract my attention.

Do you paint en plein air? What practical advice do you have for those who would like to try it?

I have learned nearly as much from painting on location as I have from the people I have studied with. My best advice to people wanting to paint on location would be: 1) Don't go until you have a command of your palette and you are able to mix the colors and values you see in front of you. Mother Nature won't wait for you to learn how to mix color. 2) Work smarter, not harder. Travel light. A good painting does not come from how many art supplies you take with you. If you have to carry your stuff in a cart, you have too much stuff. All your effort and focus needs to be on the subject matter, not on trying to wrangle your equipment and the time and effort it takes to get ready to paint. Remember, you have to pack all that stuff up again to move to the next location. 3) When in doubt, paint what you see, not what you think you know.

What mediums do you use and what are your main techniques?

I paint primarily in oils. I have done pastels in the past but oil is my preferred medium. I build a painting in much the same way a house is built. First the underlying foundation is laid, upon which everything else is built. Then as each shape is refined, I focus on laying paint on top of paint, not mushing it into what is underneath. I mix what I see on the palette; I do not mix the colors on the canvas. Afterwards there is a drying period when I work back into some areas to clean up edges and make final adjustments.

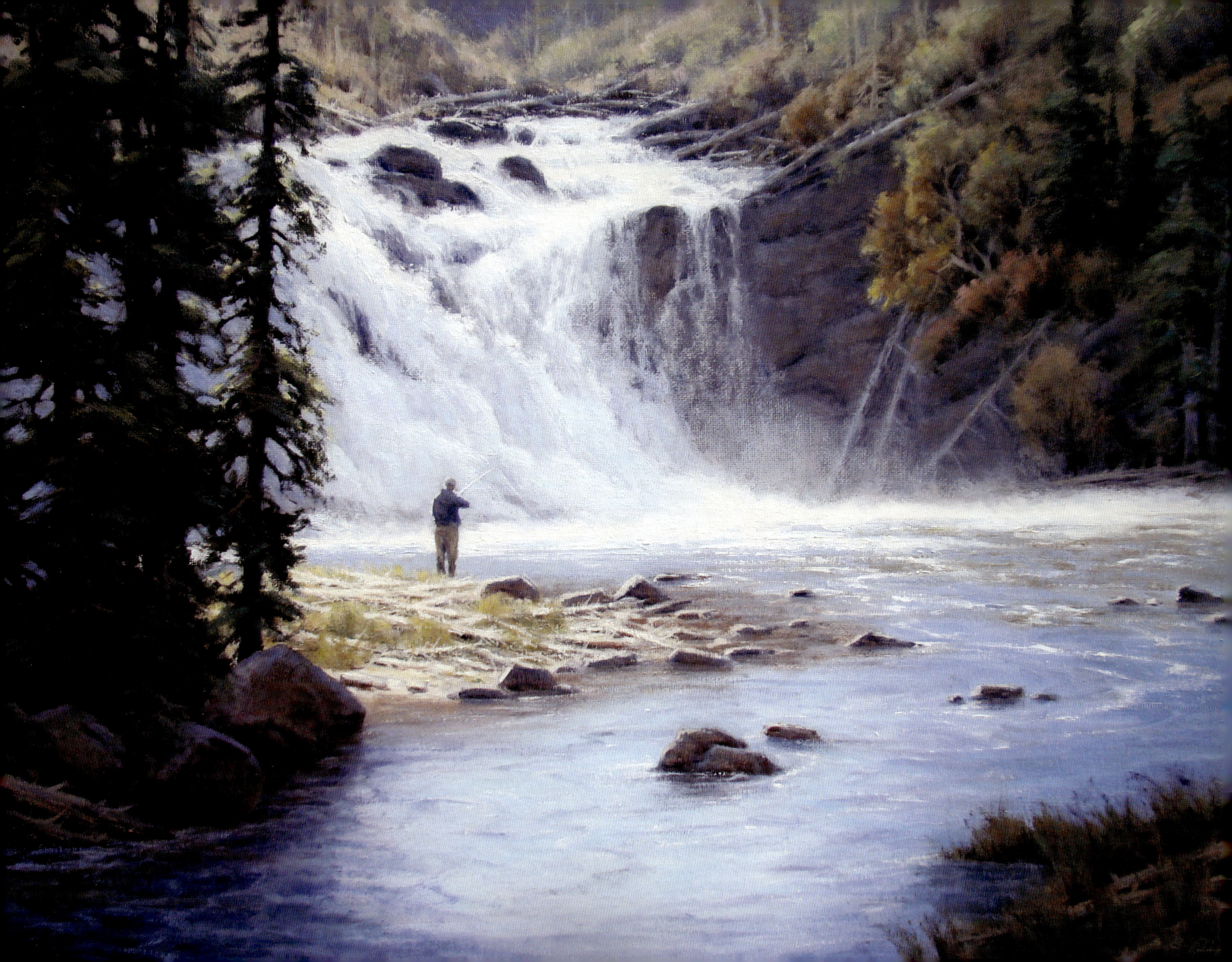

TOM PERKINSON

Tom Perkinson lives and works in New Mexico because he has become enchanted by the "Land of Enchantment." Born in Indiana, he was raised in the countryside and developed an early love for the natural landscape. After studying art at the John Herron Art Institute in Indianapolis, he received his Master of Fine Arts degree at the University of New Mexico, where he taught art for two years. In 1970, he committed his life to painting full time. Even though he lives in the spectacular landscape of New Mexico, all of his work originates in the studio. "I do not paint en plein air or make sketches, and I hardly ever work from photographs," Perkinson says. "I consider myself a regional painter. As I travel around the state, I somehow retain interesting images and scenes in my mind. When I start a new painting, these images and scenes that inspired me begin to reappear in the work." Perkinson's paintings are in many private and public collections, including the Museum of New Mexico in Santa Fe, the University Art Museum in Albuquerque, and the Eiteljorg Museum in Indianapolis. He has come full circle.

What inspired this painting?

Here in New Mexico, late afternoons and sunsets offer up a dramatic, quickly changing variety of colors, shapes and values. In *Rainstorm on the Mesas*, I attempted to create a sunset that includes all of the elements of sunsets that have inspired me in the past, along with that elusive, calm feeling that seems to settle over the landscape as the sun sets. Since I paint intuitively and do not use photos and sketches, I can paint what I want to see.

How do you plan your compositions?

I let it evolve and keep my eyes open for an interesting, uncontrived composition to appear. Initially I lay down abstract images of different shapes, sizes and values, and search for a structure. When I find a composition I can work with, I continue with the subject matter of the painting. But I like to keep my options open as the painting evolves.

What mediums do you use and what are your main painting techniques?

I paint with watercolor, pastel, acrylic and oils. For the last couple of years, I have been experimenting with watercolor and mixed media. I use 300-lb. (640gsm) archival rag-board cold-press watercolor paper. I start by taping the paper along the edges to a firm board to keep it laying flat. I then randomly lay down some washes and shapes of different values and sizes with liquid watercolor. At this time I play the lights and darks against one another to create an abstract structure. Sometimes I place clear water on the paper and introduce the liquid watercolor to the pure water wash, then watch the beautiful uncontrived things that happen. I begin to look for a landscape. Once this part of the painting is dry, I can start adding colored pencil and pastel. Also, I can use fine sandpaper to remove an area of paint if I want to. I have found that this practice of addition and subtraction, which happens early in every painting, adds interest, richness, a sense of history and a certain mystery to the completed painting.

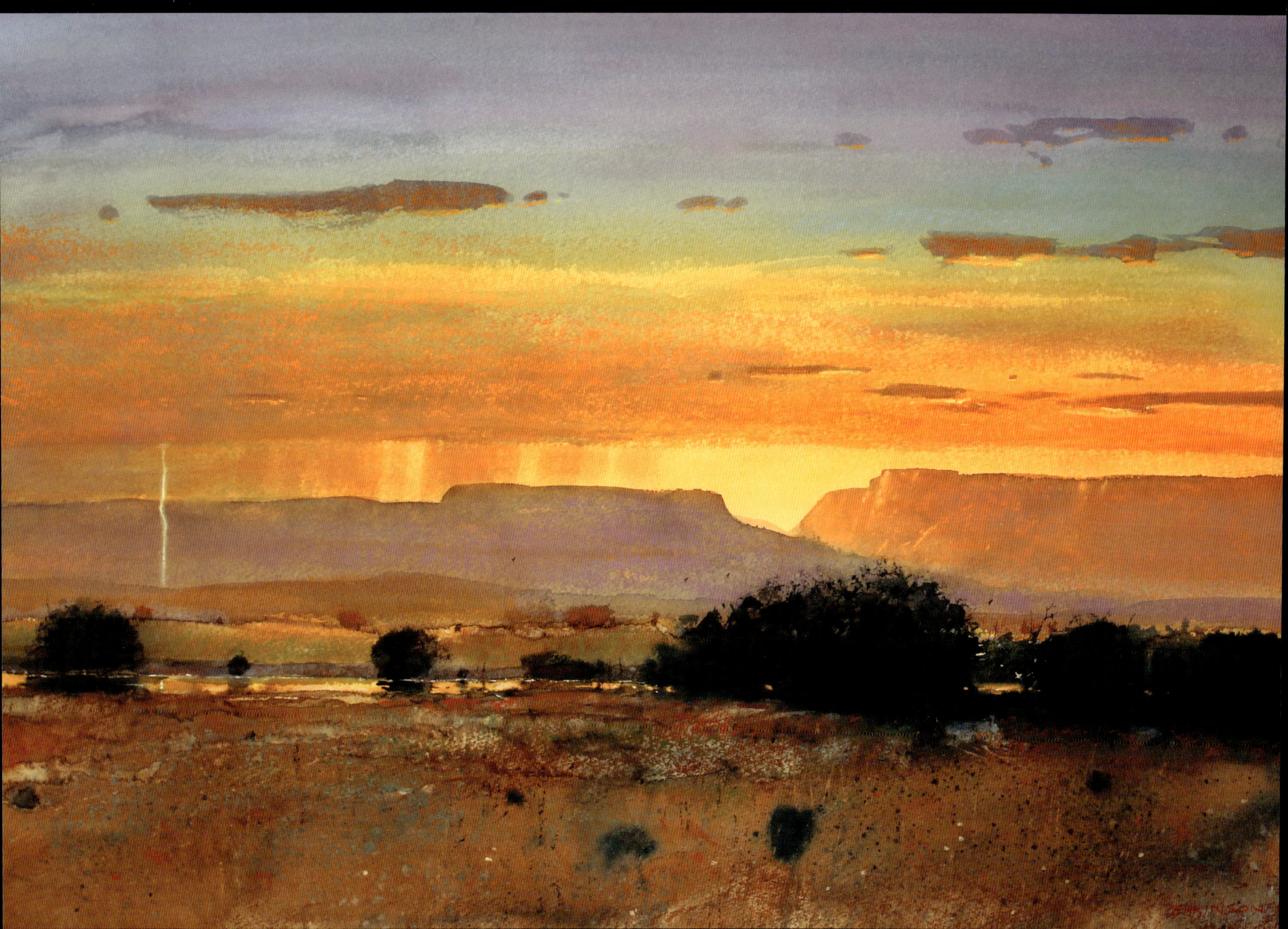

ANDREW PETERS

Early in his career, Andrew Peters made an epic journey across Africa, drawing and painting game animals and indigenous peoples in fourteen countries. The journey was inspired by Karl Bodmer who painted the American frontier in 1833. Thrilled by creating art from life in remote places, Peters traveled through South America and lived in Cusco, Peru. He has also lived and studied in Florence, Italy, and has painted in Ireland, Morocco, Spain and Romania. During the decade he lived in Santa Fe, Peters painted landscapes of northern New Mexico, pursuing the traditions of the Taos Founders. His plein air paintings faithfully capture light and beauty from life and are key to the veracity and integrity of his richly imbued larger works. "A painting should read like a window onto a place," he says, "luminous and fresh. Light, not line, determines form." Peters resides in the Loess Hills of Iowa, overlooking the Missouri River. He is an ardent conservationist and keen naturalist and spends much of his time roaming forests, prairies and marshes. He loves fly fishing, canoeing and horsepacking into remote wilderness.

What inspired this painting?

An alpine lake at timberline is a potent symbol of unspoiled wilderness. In this painting, the sparkling waters of the loch lead us gently toward the towering granite Sharkstooth peak and the glaciers beyond. Photographs simply do not convey the enormity of such places. As an artist, I'm able to draw and paint the scene en plein air and record the proper relationships, as human eyes and emotions perceive it.

How do you plan your compositions?

I find my compositions in nature. Each painting begins by traveling backroads or hiking wild places looking for a good arrangement of natural elements in any kind of light. There is always a thrilling moment when discovering a scene so beautiful and perfectly composed that it must be painted. Then, I set up a field easel on a tripod and carefully draw these elements in proper perspective. I am completely faithful to the natural composition when painting en plein air. As a naturalist I understand that landforms, trees and skies have scientific reasons for being arranged as they are. They are inextricably linked by ecology. Back in the studio, I am more at liberty to let artistic judgment overrule nature in composition and often move elements for the better.

Do you paint en plein air? What practical advice do you have for those who would like to try it?

I do paint en plein air and highly recommend it. It is by turns exasperating, thrilling and confounding, but always a kind of satisfaction comes from it. You will see things in nature others will miss. You will spend time looking at far horizons and not looking at electronic and digital devices. Each plein air painting you create—no matter how clumsy or crude—will be a better postcard memento of your day than any photo could be.

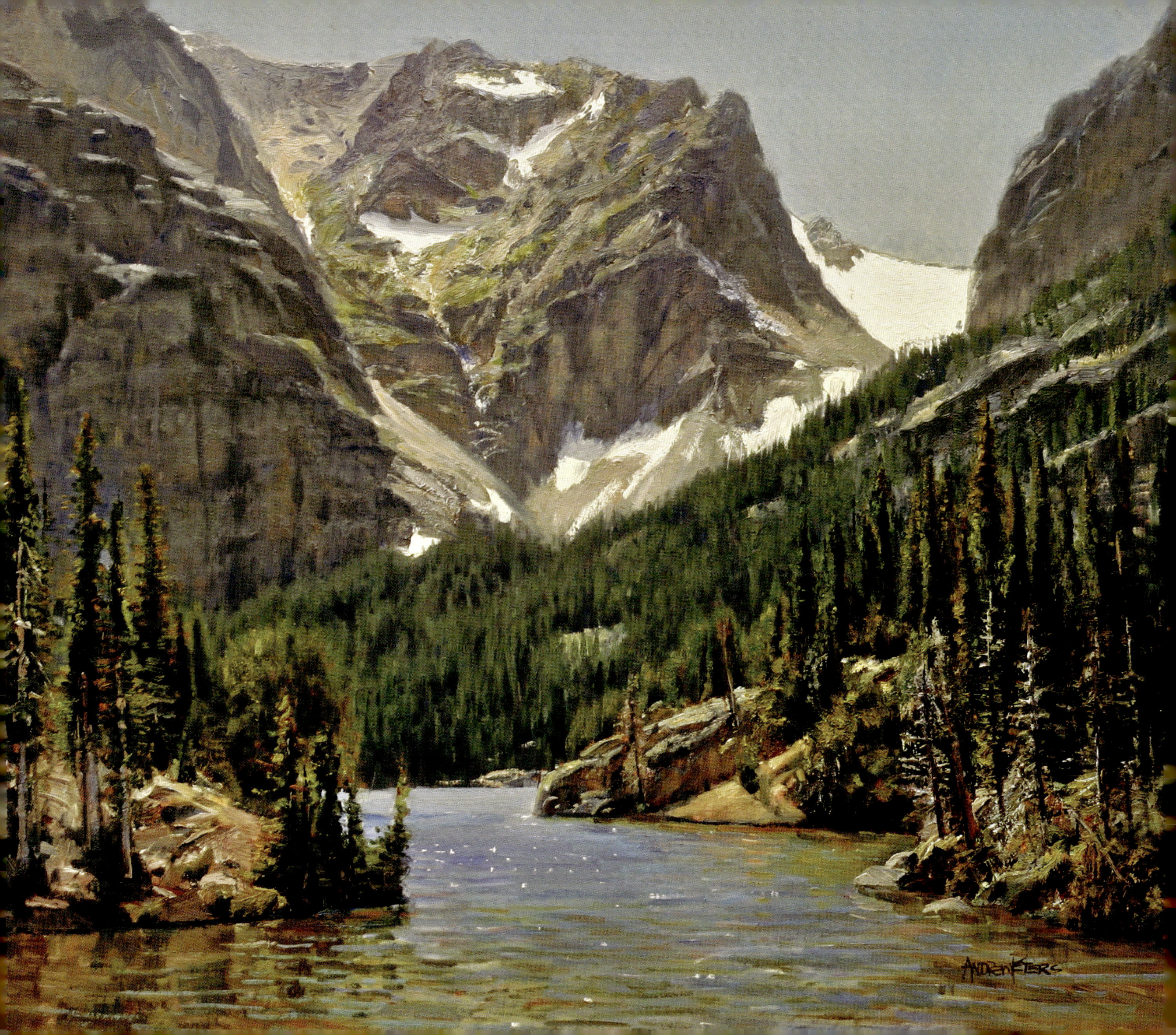

JULIE GILBERT POLLARD

Phoenix artist, Julie Gilbert Pollard, paints in oil and watercolor in a fluid, painterly manner. Her painting style, while representational, is colored with her own personal concept of reality. "The eye may see as a camera sees," says Pollard, "but the mind's eye sees an altered, imagined image, what it wants and hopes to see. It's that illusive image along with a heightened sense of 'realness' that I try to express in my paintings." Pollard is the author of *Brilliant Color* for North Light and recently filmed two watercolor DVDs for ArtistsNetwork.tv. She has taught watercolor and oil painting using her innovative techniques since 1987, and currently conducts classes and workshops in many venues including the Scottsdale Artists' School and La Romita School of Art in Umbria, Italy. Her best advice to students on painting landscapes? "Learn to translate the confusion you see before you to large simple shapes, rather than attempting to duplicate the detail. That's the first step to capturing the essence of a landscape."

What inspired this painting?

Quite simply, because I love the look, feel, colors, sound and smell of a creek, especially in the fall with the brilliant leaves floating down, catching the light, then getting caught in the current to be set upon their downstream journey. Moving water is fascinating to watch, confusing to draw and paint until you learn how to capture its essential components. Perhaps the challenge is part of its charm!

In what locations do you paint?

For some reason, I'm drawn to rocks, water, flowers and foliage. I'm especially attracted to "waterscapes" more than to any other subject.

How do you plan your compositions?

I look for a design formed by the shapes and value patterns in the scene. Without a workable design, the most beautiful scene won't make a good painting. A picture might be "pretty" but if the design is weak, the painting has no power to hold the viewer's attention. Asymmetry, being much more interesting than symmetry, is paramount!

Do you paint en plein air? What practical advice do you have for those who would like to try it?

I have had so many people tell me they fear they aren't good enough yet to paint en plein air. And it can, indeed, be a very daunting thing to attempt. My advice: 1) Adjust your expectations. Don't expect to paint a masterpiece. Realize there is a learning curve and treat each expedition as a learning experience. 2) Allow yourself to have fun—just enjoy being in the open air and messing about with the beautiful colors on your canvas. 3) Enjoy all the cool equipment and supplies—these are your toys! 4) But keep the toys to a minimum. 5) Some direction from an instructor can smooth the way . . . and practice!

REFLECTIONS IN GOLD Julie Gilbert Pollard Watercolor on canvas 20" × 16" (51cm × 41cm)

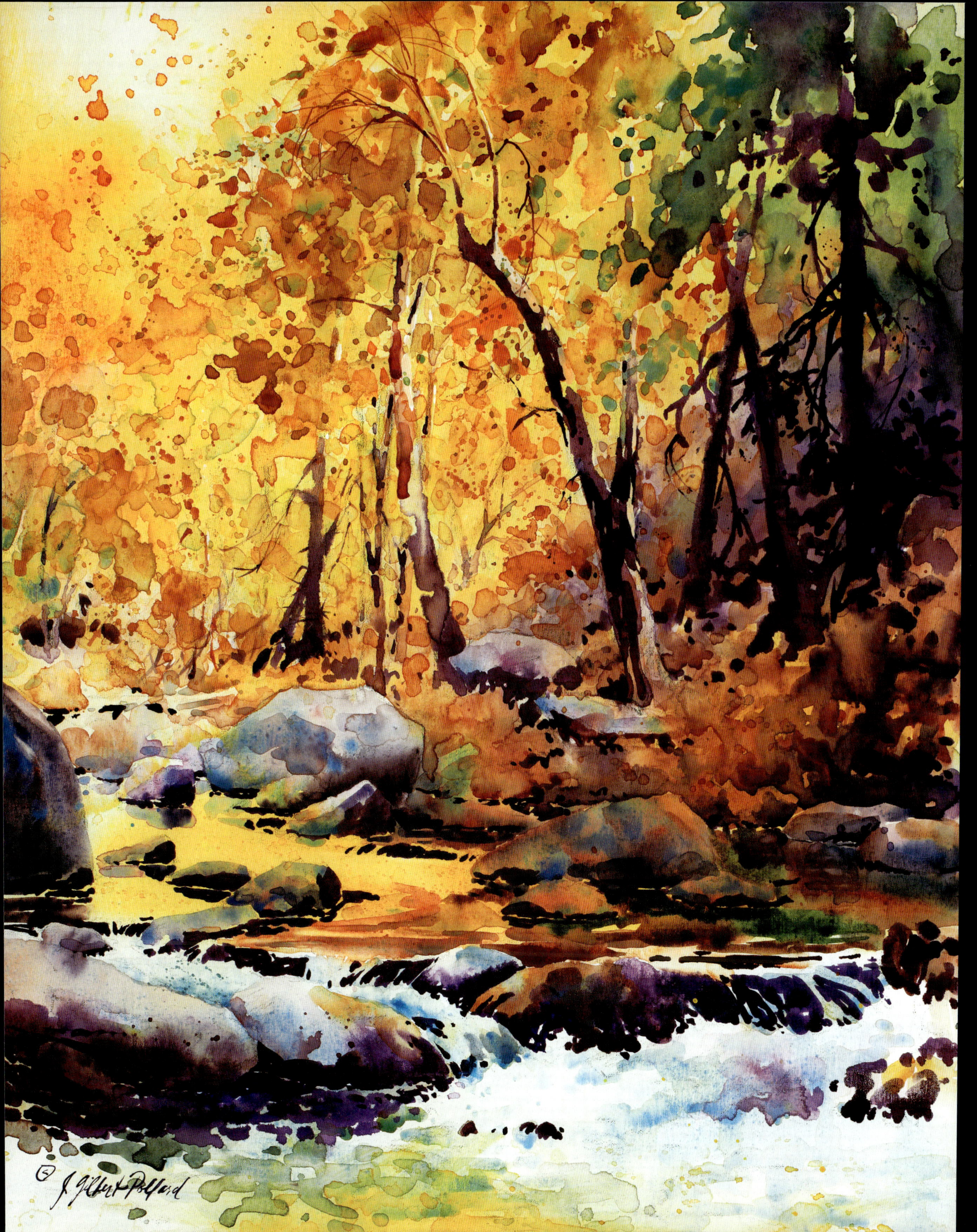
© J. Gilbert Pollard

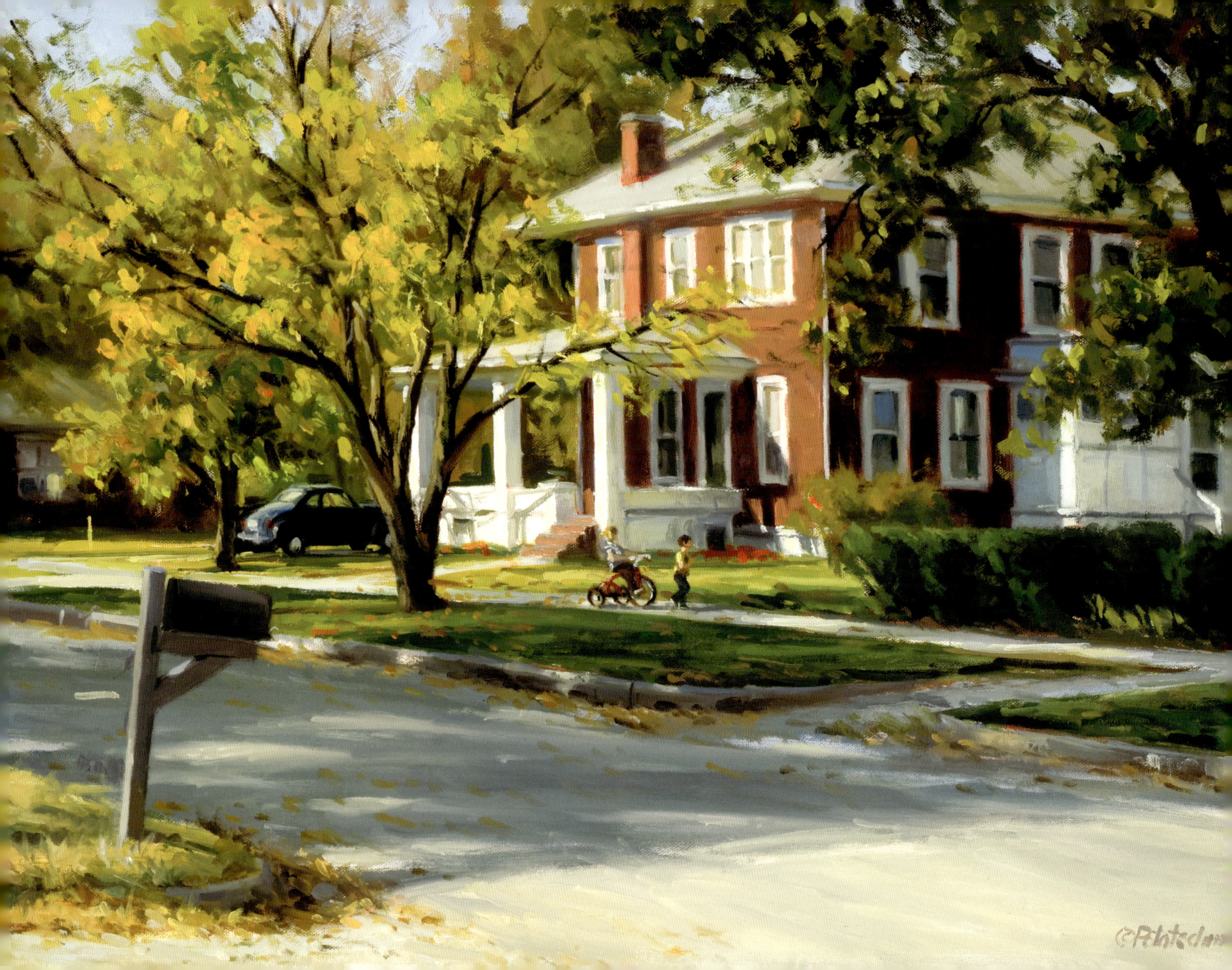

JOHN POTOTSCHNIK

John Pototschnik (Poe-toe-sh-nick) was born in St. Ives, Cornwall, England but grew up in Wichita, Kansas. He received his art training at Wichita State University in advertising design, followed by instruction in illustration and design at Art Center College of Design in Los Angeles. Most recently he has studied human anatomy at the Lyme Academy College of Fine Arts in Old Lyme, Connecticut. Pototschnik is a signature member of the Oil Painters of America and the Outdoor Painters Society. He now resides in Wylie, Texas, with his wife, Marcia. "My artistic influences are diverse," he says, "ranging from the Barbizon painters of Corot, Daubigny and Millet to American tonalist George Inness. I believe all I need to know of the principles of art are to be found in the works of the masters. My paintings are not flamboyant, mysterious, trendy or shocking but I am interested in depicting the truth about life, as I see it, in a naturalistic way, free of frills and bravado. I enjoy depicting simple, common, everyday life and its objects as things of beauty and worth."

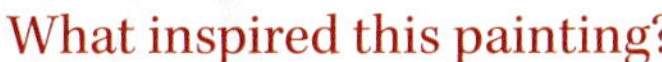

What inspired this painting?

All the subjects I paint are motivated by personal experience. I paint things I know but also things that create positive emotions and memories within me. Several things appealed to me about this scene, the primary one being the house itself. I have always been attracted to structures and at one time actually considered becoming an architect. There's nothing spectacular about the house but in the warm morning light and context of the neighborhood, it created a sense of stability and safety. A little extra push from me through the addition of the family car and children happily playing, and *Only in America* was born.

In what locations do you paint?

Small towns, farms, the open rural spaces of America are my favorite locations to paint. I have an emotional connection to these subjects because they generate happy memories and are all part of my formative years. They also represent, for me, all the positive aspects of family, community, security, trust, hope, productivity, independence and freedom.

What's your best advice to students on painting landscapes?

Certainly, if one desires to be a landscape painter, they must be a student of nature and all its subtle nuances. The best way to study nature/landscape is to paint en plein air. I don't believe plein air painting is the be-all and end-all, but it certainly is a necessary beginning, becoming a lifelong habit. Really, the subject is not that important, for the principles of good painting are not dependent on the subject. A clear concept, effective composition, accurate drawing (proportion and perspective), simple value structure and supportive, harmonious color are all necessary ingredients for producing a noteworthy landscape … or cityscape, portrait or still life.

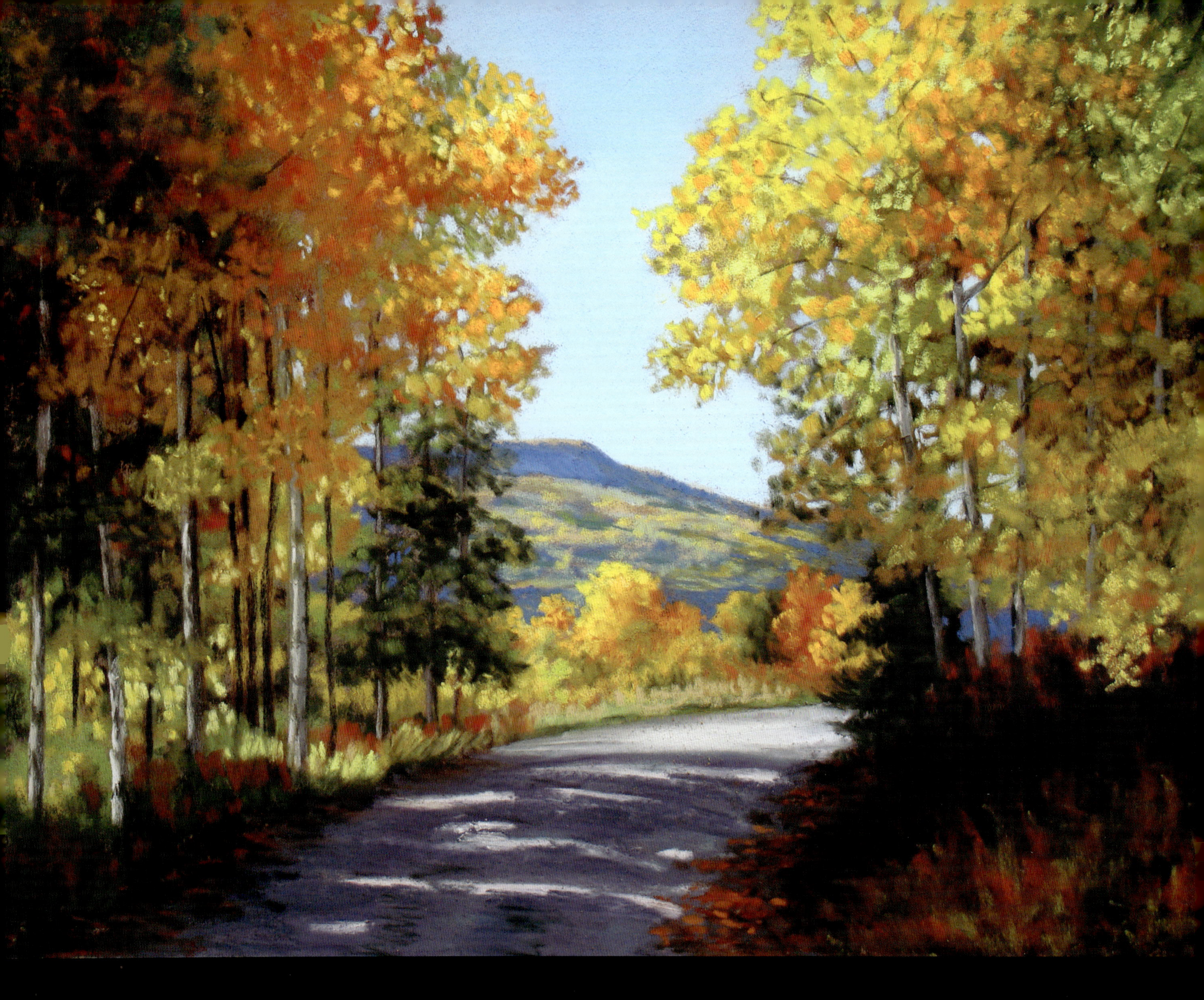

ASPEN ROAD Maggie Price Pastel 8.5" × 11" (22cm × 28cm) Collection of Chuck Lewis

MAGGIE PRICE

Maggie Price has worked in oils, acrylics and watercolor, but when she turned to pastel in the early 1990s, she found her passion, and it's been her primary medium since then. "I've painted many subjects over the years, from landscape to still life to figures," says Price. "I loved life drawing when I was in school, but the landscape speaks to me more than any other subject. I love the beauty of nature, and am constantly fascinated by light and shadow in the natural landscape. When I see a subject that takes my breath away, I want to share that beauty with others. When I'm able to come close to describing it in a painting, it makes me really happy." Price was a co-founder and former editor of *The Pastel Journal*, a national magazine for pastel artists. She now serves as a contributing editor and is on the editorial advisory boards of both *The Pastel Journal* and *The Artist's Magazine*. She is the author of *Painting with Pastels* and *Painting Sunlight & Shadow with Pastels* (both for North Light Books), as well as two instructional videos for ArtistsNetwork.com.

What inspired this painting?

I liked many things about this subject: the fall colors in the trees, the contrast of the golds against the blue of the sky, the road curving into the painting, and the mystery of the distant mountains.

In what locations do you paint?

I paint everywhere I can. I love painting the landscape near my home in New Mexico, but I also love the southern Colorado landscape, which is where this painting subject is. We have a favorite place in the mountains there that we've been visiting for over twenty years. Painting familiar places is good in that you can explore the nuances of the landscape. But I also like painting unfamiliar places.

How do you plan your compositions?

If I'm working outdoors, I'll start with a quick thumbnail sketch. If I'm working from a photo, my planning starts at the time I take the photograph. I work only from my own photos, as the first compositional decision is made through the viewfinder of the camera. From there, I move to the computer, where I experiment with cropping, resizing and moving the image around within a frame until I get the basis of a composition. Then I turn to the sketch, where I can rearrange elements to make them work better in the final design of the painting.

Do you paint en plein air? What practical advice do you have for those who would like to try it?

I do paint outdoors, and I believe it's important for a landscape painter to do so. Actually, I think both plein air and studio work are important—painting outdoors, you learn from the landscape. Indoors, in the studio, you can take time to experiment. I would advise someone getting ready to go out for the first time to just do it, but don't overdo it. Work small, and limit your paintings to about an hour or so. Don't worry about finishing a painting to the point it could be framed. Instead, think of what you can learn from it. Each painting will teach you more about the landscape than you could have imagined beforehand, and after many paintings, all of your studio work will improve because of the knowledge you've accumulated.

STEPHEN QUILLER

Living and working in the mountains of southern Colorado, artist and author Stephen Quiller likes to paint the natural world and weather of the San Juan Mountains in all four seasons. His paintings of snow-covered hillsides are especially evocative, capturing the effects of light and shadow and colors most of us are not even aware of. Quiller is a watermedia painter and in the early 1980s co-authored the first two books on the subject of watermedia and their combinations. "'Watermedia' is a term for any medium that uses water to dilute the paint," he says. "Thus I work in transparent watercolor, gouache, acrylic and casein, and have spent my life to this point working with each medium's visual qualities and handling characteristics and how they can best be used by themselves or together." A member of the American Watercolor Society and the National Watercolor Society, Quiller is a prolific author and a popular teacher, having written six books on watermedia and color, produced fourteen videos, and he continues to conduct painting workshops worldwide.

What inspired this painting?

During the winter after a day of painting, most late afternoons I cross-country ski. Because I live in a remote mountain area of Colorado I make my own trails. Some are longer and some shorter; some are steeper up and down hill while others have a flatter kick-and-glide rhythm. Although I always take a small backpack with a sketchbook, I do not go out looking for a subject but have found it best to let the subject find me. On this occasion I was skiing down a south-facing slope on the Ridge Trail. There was a strong light and shadow pattern—a flickering impression—on this aspen-lined path that grabbed me. I stopped at the bottom, took out my sketchbook and made a few lines and wrote down some notes. That was enough to inspire this work.

In what locations do you paint?

I have a home and studio by the headwaters of the Rio Grande in the mountains of southern Colorado, and many of my works come from views right here, while others come from within a ten-mile radius. My best work comes from these subjects, as I know this area deeply. Most years I also travel to a foreign country to paint. I find myself out of my comfort zone painting fishing boats, European villages and coastal scenes. My color palette shifts and I use my brushes in ways that are very different for me. I feel that these moments add to my vocabulary as a painter and make me a better artist.

Is your painting inspired by spirituality? How is that seen in your art?

Yes, very much so. I want to focus on the energy and vibration and interconnectedness of all nature's forms. And while working en plein air especially, I am communing with nature. The more time I spend with a subject, the more it reveals itself. Color, patterns and rhythm appear that at first I was unaware of. I realize that my brush and water, paint and paper, my eyes, hand, arm and body, as well as the light and sounds and nature's forces, all become part of the dance and act of the painting. It is an experience that I love. I do not think of the finished work but just enjoy this time. The rest takes care of itself.

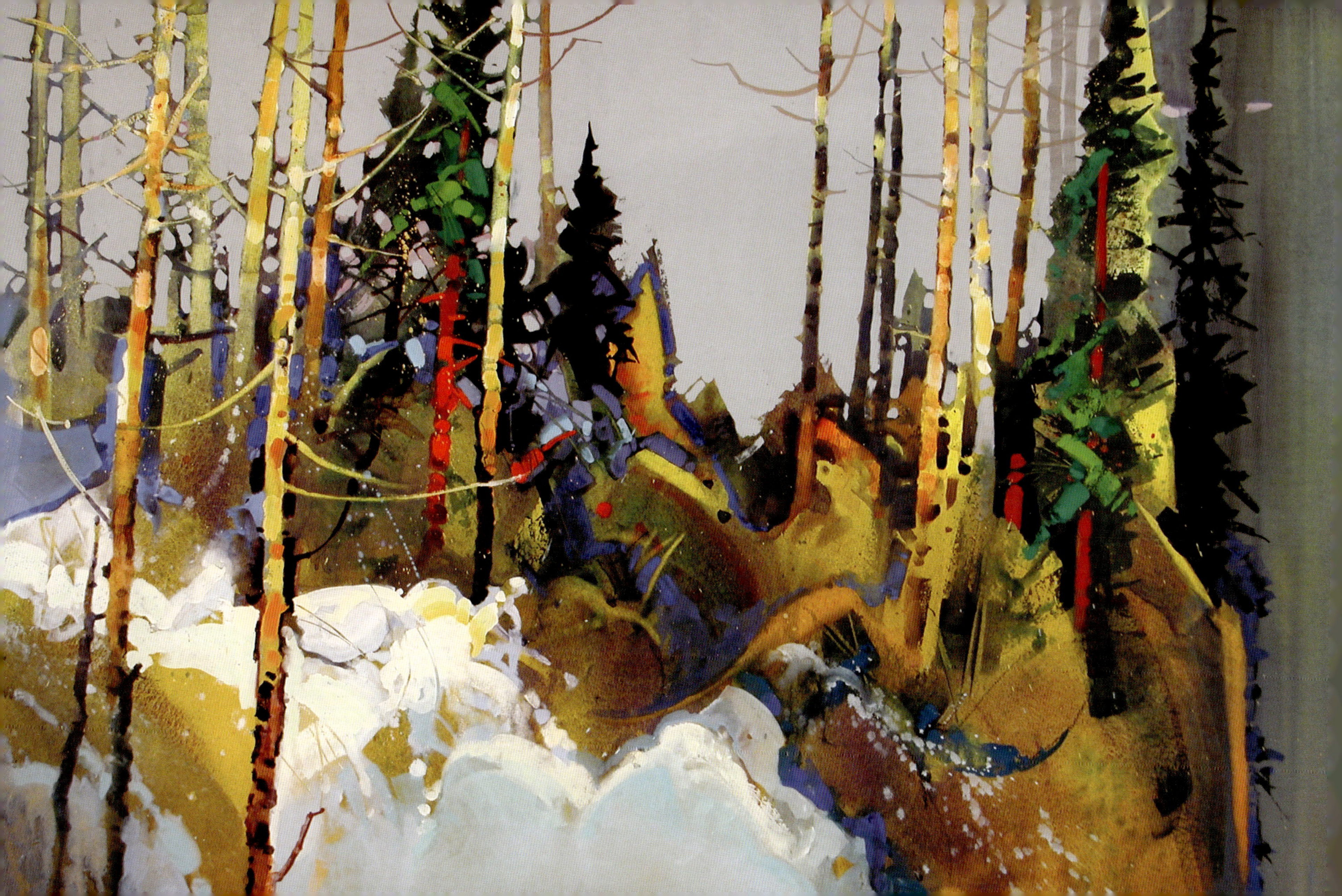

DON RANTZ

Award-winning artist Don Rantz lives and works in Prescott, Arizona, a small town with abundant natural beauty. A member of the Arizona Pastel Artists Association, Rantz absolutely loves painting and teaching others to paint. He strongly advises his students to "get outside a lot and study the effects of light in nature. Learn the differences between real light and photos. Use photos as reference, but rely on your outdoor visual experience to make your paintings come to life." In 2006, Rantz won the Ruth Richeson Award for Excellence in the Pastel 100 competition, sponsored by *The Pastel Journal*, for his piece *Desert Vista*. In 2007, another of his works, *Desert Backlight*, took second place overall in the Pastel Society of New Mexico's national show. And in 2009, his painting *Home of the Ancients* won best of show in that year's Pastel 100 competition.

What inspired this painting?

Sunset at the Grand Canyon is often a magical experience. While this piece is not an exact representation of a specific place or scene, it was compiled from my various experiences in the canyons of the West over the years.

How would you describe your painting style?

In general, I am a representational painter. I do, however, like to push the color boundaries once in a while, simplifying the compositions, shapes and colors, playing with exaggerated color harmonies to produce more visually exciting pieces than can be found in nature. *Canyon Color* is one such piece. People respond very positively to these color pieces.

What mediums do you use, and what are your main painting techniques?

I use pastel on Wallis paper, with an underpainting of pastel dissolved on the paper with denatured alcohol. I strive for lots of atmospheric layers, with foreground elements placed to lead the viewer to my chosen center of interest

Do you paint en plein air? What practical advice do you have for those who would like to try it?

Whenever time and weather allow, I go out and sketch or paint. The first three years I worked in pastel, all I did was paint en plein air. It is essential to have a realistic visual vocabulary to be a truthful landscape painter, and without spending a great deal of time painting in the field, your studio paintings from other reference will not have an authentic feel to them. My advice is to keep it simple. Use a limited palette, move quickly with confidence, and ignore any detail that is not directly concerned with your center of interest.

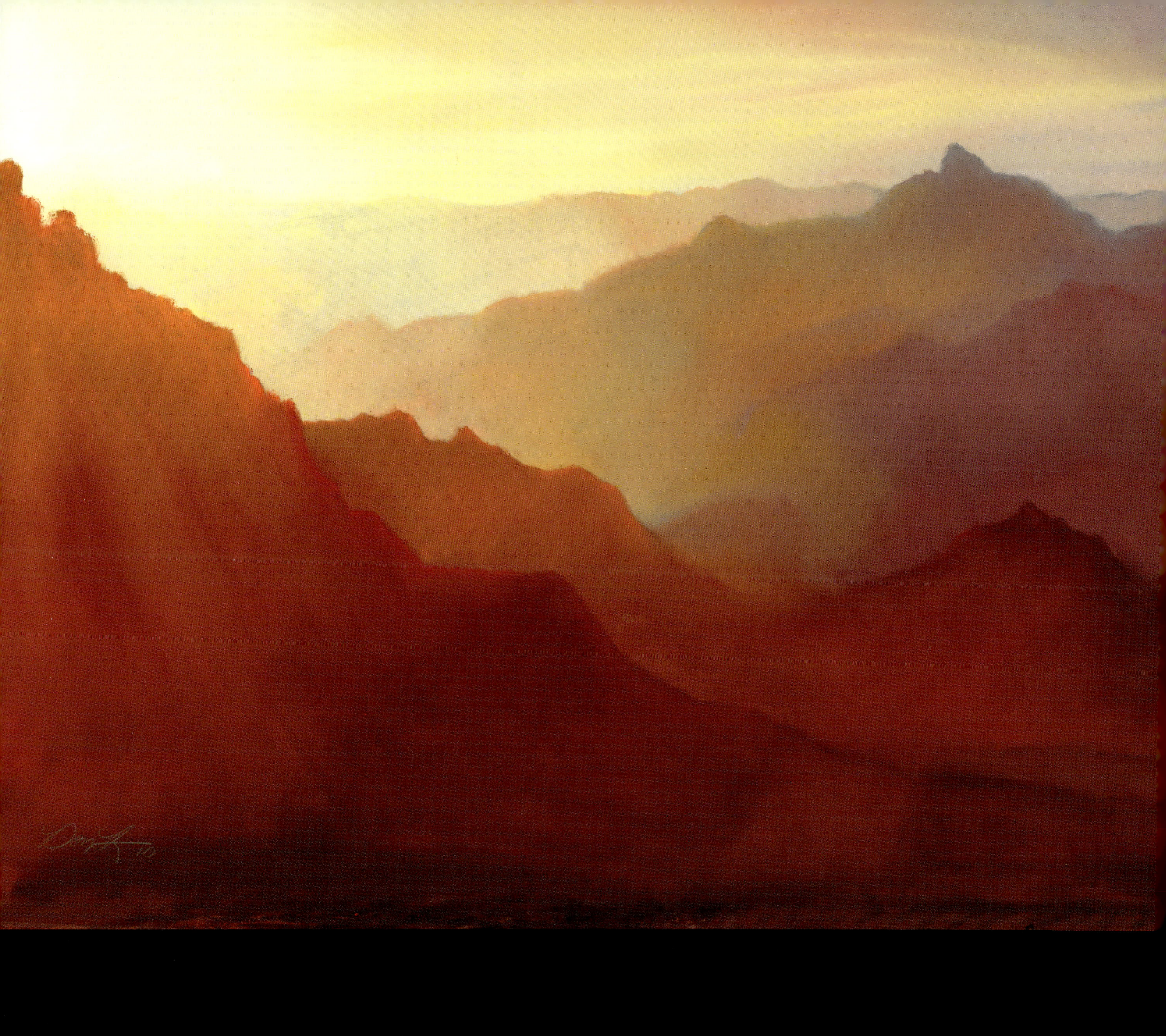

CANYON COLOR Don Rantz Pastel on Wallis paper 18" × 24" (46cm × 61cm) Private collection

DAVID ROTHERMEL

David Rothermel grew up near the Susquehanna River in central Pennsylvania and received much of his art education at the historic Pennsylvania Academy of Fine Arts, home of such luminaries as Mary Cassatt and Thomas Eakins. His own ancestor, Peter Frederick Rothermel, had earlier been a director at the academy, and had painted the enormous *The Battle of Gettysburg* that hangs in the State Museum of Pennsylvania. Even with such a history in his home state, David Rothermel moved to New Mexico in 1981. "For the last twenty-five years as an artist I have been painting and marveling over the true spiritual nature of this land," he says. "The paintings reflect the grace and synchronicity of the western landscape and my relationship to it. The gratitude I have for being able to participate in the phenomenon that happens when light, weather, space and beauty come together is overwhelming."

Q&A

What inspired this painting?

As you approach Santa Fe from the south, you come up a hill and onto a pinnacle, where all of a sudden the lights of Santa Fe appear, with the deep night sky and the stars that look as if they are sprinkled on the desert floor. The image is indelible in my mind's eye.

Is your painting inspired by spirituality? How is that seen in your art?

Spirituality is certainly a driving force in my creations. I notice when I don't paint for a while, I seem to be off-balance. The synchronicity that I experience seems to disappear. I know in my innermost self what my gifts are intended to do—that is to inspire God's feelings of beauty and light, to reveal the sublime.

Do you paint en plein air?

I do occasionally paint on location, mostly if I'm fishing or camping. I usually take along some watercolor materials. When I paint, it's usually some quick "splash and-dash" pieces, more to demarcate a certain place and time than anything else. I totally enjoy the freshness and spontaneity of these unfinished pieces. Sometimes the water I use with my paints will have all sorts of crazy minerals in it and the interactions with the pigments create some very unexpected results.

What mediums do you use and what are your main techniques?

I use mostly acrylics. The painting shown here is acrylic washes with pastel. My main technique is pouring the paint and spreading into layers. I then sand the paint to reveal the previous layers. Sometimes I will coat them with resin to give a magnified finish.

What's your best advice to students on painting landscapes?

Dare to be lousy.

SANTA FE PILLOWS David Rothermel Acrylic and pastel 53" × 39" (135cm × 99cm) Private collection

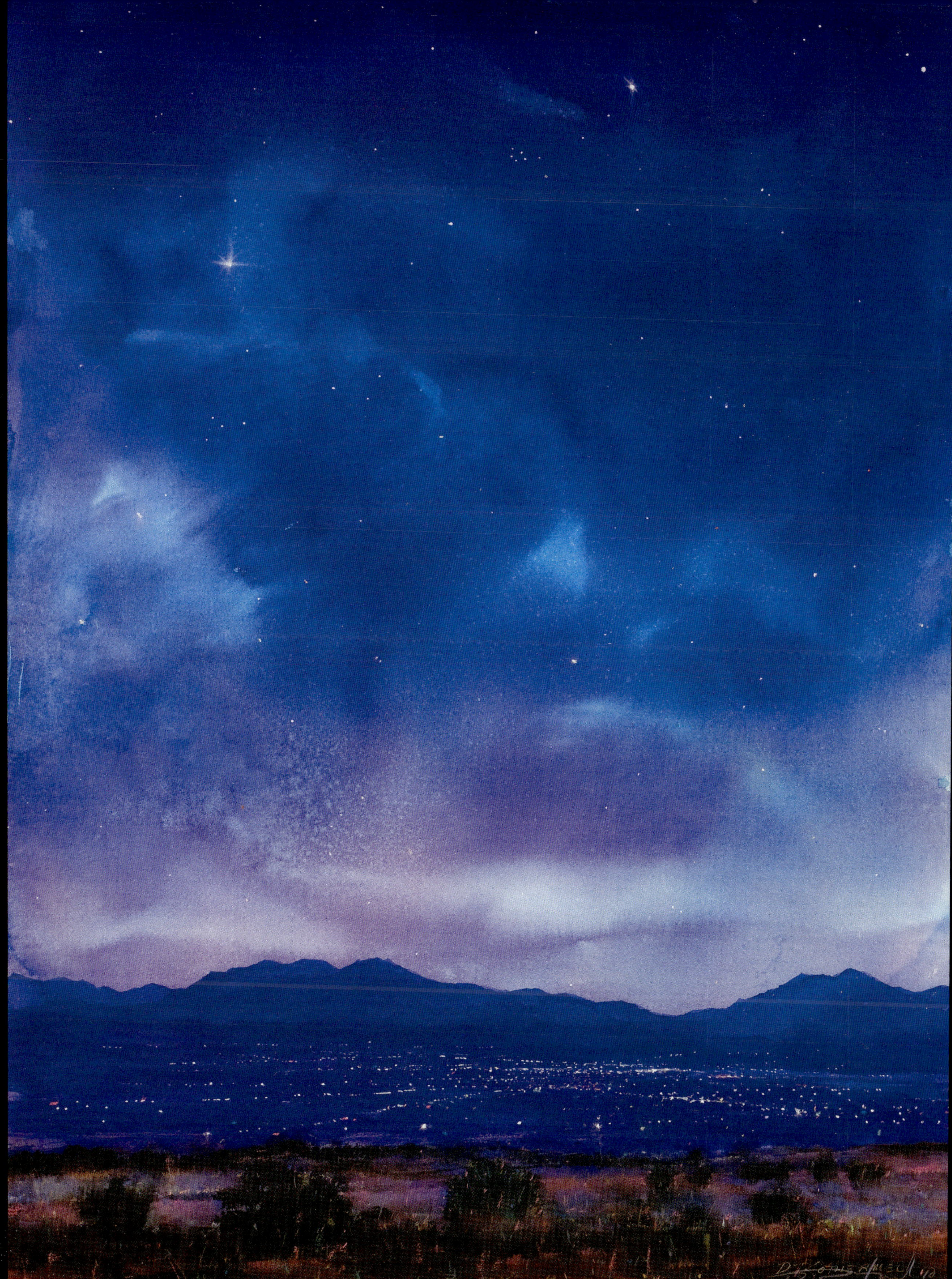

JOHN SALMINEN

Duluth, Minnesota, resident John Salminen's approach to painting city life is distinctive and memorable. Highly atmospheric, almost romantic, his watercolors are alive with movement, light and color. Many celebrate the joyous decorative elements found in the ethnic neighborhoods of big cities in America and abroad. "My favorite painting locations tend to be urban," he says. "The wealth of information found in city streets provides ample opportunity for rich and complex compositions. I'm particularly drawn to the rich subject matter of San Francisco, New York City and Chicago neighborhoods." While perhaps best known for his urban landscapes, Salminen has also gained recognition for his mixed-media abstract paintings, one of which won first place in *The Artist's Magazine*'s art competition in the experimental category judged by Edward Betts. Salminen's work is in many national and international collections, including the permanent collections of both the Asian Museum of Watercolor Art and the Quanhua Watercolor Art Gallery in Zhoujiajiao, China.

What inspired this painting?

One of the things that inspired me to paint *Winter Light* is the fact that the viewer is looking up the hill. This "stacked perspective" is an important part of the composition and it tends to read less as a conventional representation than as an arrangement of abstract shapes. As a painter I'm always drawn to subjects that allow me to experiment with strong underlying abstract qualities.

Do you prefer particular seasons or times of day?

Winter light can yield dramatic value-based paintings, and late or early horizontal light casts dramatic shadows. But what I look for most is that combination of light and humidity that creates interesting atmospheric qualities. I often work from photos that I take on the street—sometimes in bright, midday light—and later, in my studio, I choose whether to reproduce the mood that existed when I took the photograph or to turn the scene into a rainy or foggy day, or even a night scene.

How do you plan your compositions?

I initially plan my compositions through the camera lens, looking for a basic design that interests me as I crop the subjects through my telephoto lens. When I paint, I look for the abstract possibilities of the photo reference. My photo is a starting point from which the painting begins to take shape, but as the piece progresses it develops a life of its own and often dictates its own trajectory. My job is to keep a balance between my original vision as discovered through the camera's viewfinder and my desire to listen to the painting.

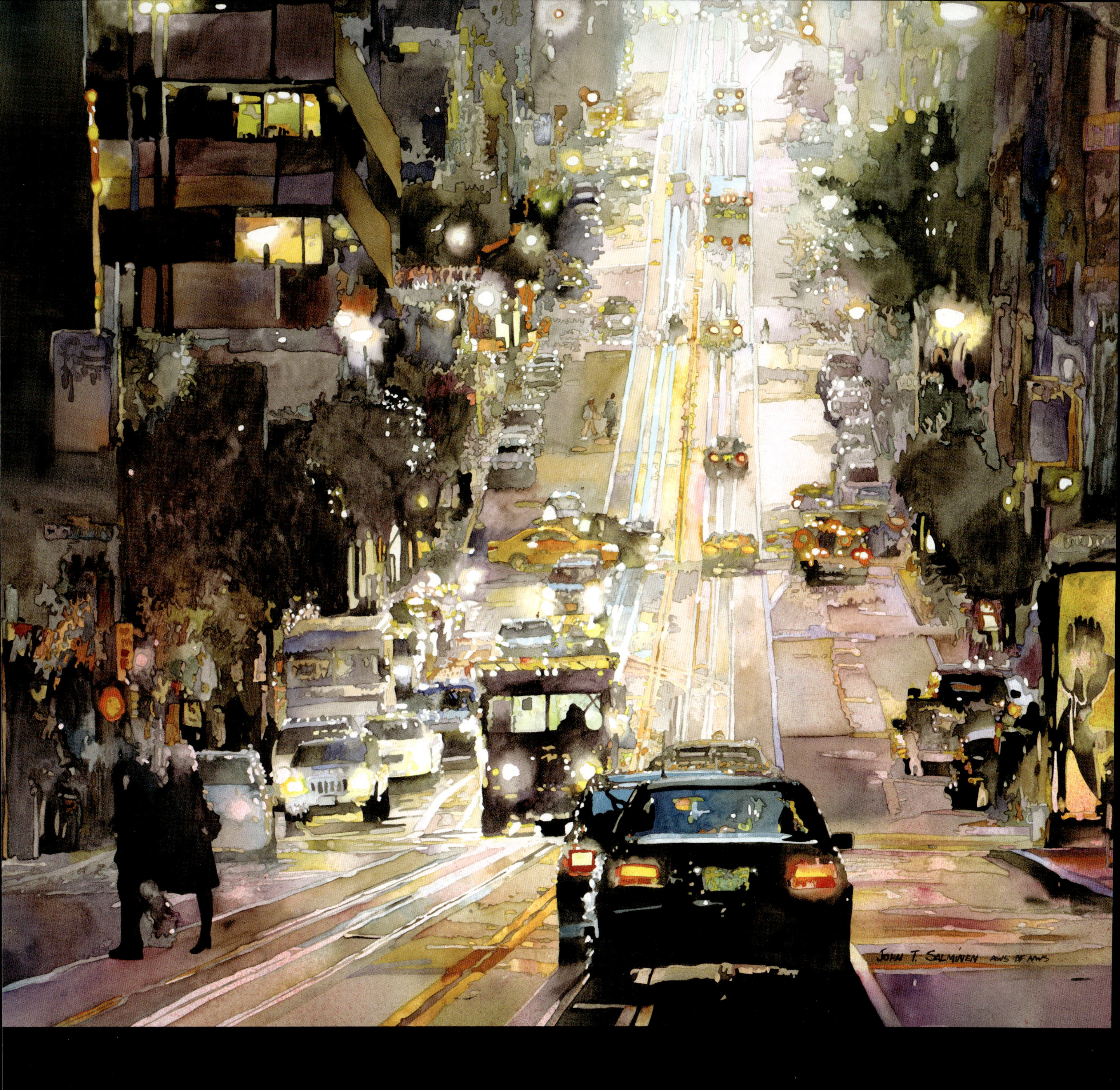

WINTER LIGHT John Salminen Transparent watercolor 33" × 36" (84cm × 91cm)

ED SANDOVAL

Ed Sandoval is one of the most renowned and popular contemporary artists in northern New Mexico. Born in Nambe, he now lives in Taos with his artist wife, Ann Huston. His gallery, Studio de Colores, is tucked away down the winding one-way street of Quesnel. Sandoval's roots in New Mexico inspire him to capture the past life and customs that are the grounding force of the Southwest. The old figures that inhabit his paintings are of the rich and unique heritage that is the soul of this part of the country, with its striking mountains, sweeping vistas and intimate valleys. They are common people caught in a moment, walking down a path or entering a humble adobe home. When he isn't painting, Sandoval is often seen riding his Arabian horse, El Patron, to breakfast or dressed like Zorro riding through the plaza. He is also proud of his turquoise 1951 Chevy pickup that sits just outside of his gallery. President Barack Obama recently chose a Sandoval painting to adorn his official thank-you cards for New Mexico, and is currently considering a painting for the White House.

What inspired this painting?

Moonlight is magical. There is a strong creative and spiritual energy during the quiet night hours when others are asleep. That's when the ghosts of the past can be the most clearly felt. In this scene, we see the old couple walk up near the church. The old man leans on his cane beneath the pale clouds, perhaps reflecting on this special moment. In the winter, I often get up before sunrise to paint because I want to capture that solemn, thoughtful mood. *Moonlight* is set in the dark still of night, but I think the scene glows with life as the old figures move through the elongated shadows of twilight.

In what locations do you paint?

I load up my art supplies into my aging motor home and wind along the northern New Mexico back roads. I'm drawn to Mora Valley, beneath the Sangre de Cristo Mountains near the Santa Fe and Carson national forests and the Pecos Wilderness. Throughout the valley, there are beautiful old churches and casitas. Many are long forgotten and neglected, and they are being reclaimed by the natural landscape. Crumbling earthen walls reveal glimpses of old adobe bricks and timbers, and the once-shiny tin roofs have aged and darkened into a deep red wine color. They have become a physical part of the mountain vistas, and I am compelled to stop and capture the beauty of those scenes.

How would you describe your painting style?

I lean toward expressionism with a sip of romantic influence. I'm known for my northern New Mexico village scenes, which are accentuated by a vibrant red undercoat. I'm not concerned with painting realism. What's important to me is expression, mood and movement. I create commanding landscapes that are unapologetic in their assertiveness, with colors that merge with reckless precision. My intent is to capture movement, sweeping currents of color, light, shadows and texture. You bring all this stuff together and then you throw in your own magic, your own style and feeling, and it comes together with the help of angels.

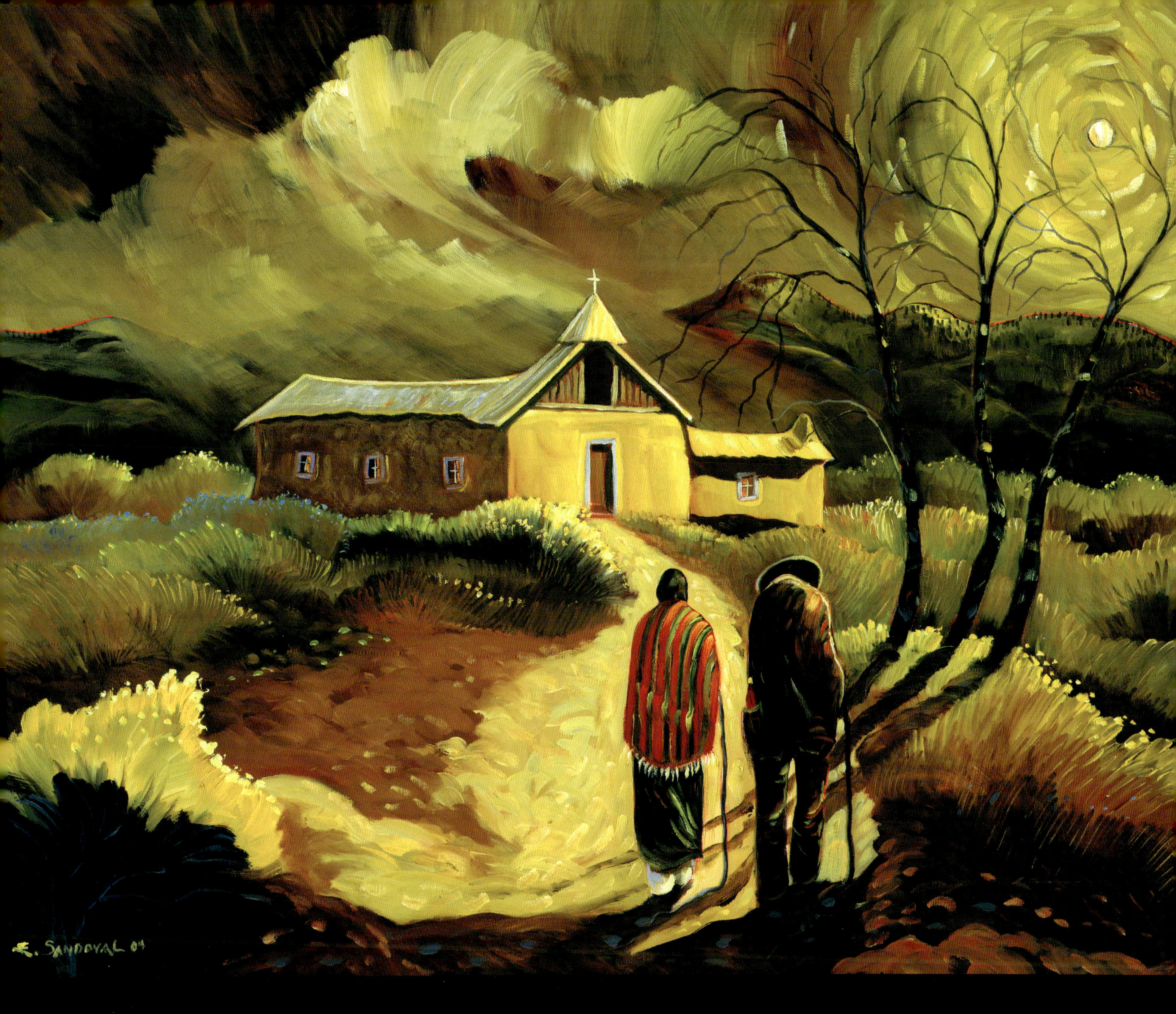

MOONLIGHT Ed Sandoval Oil 22" × 28" (56cm × 71cm)

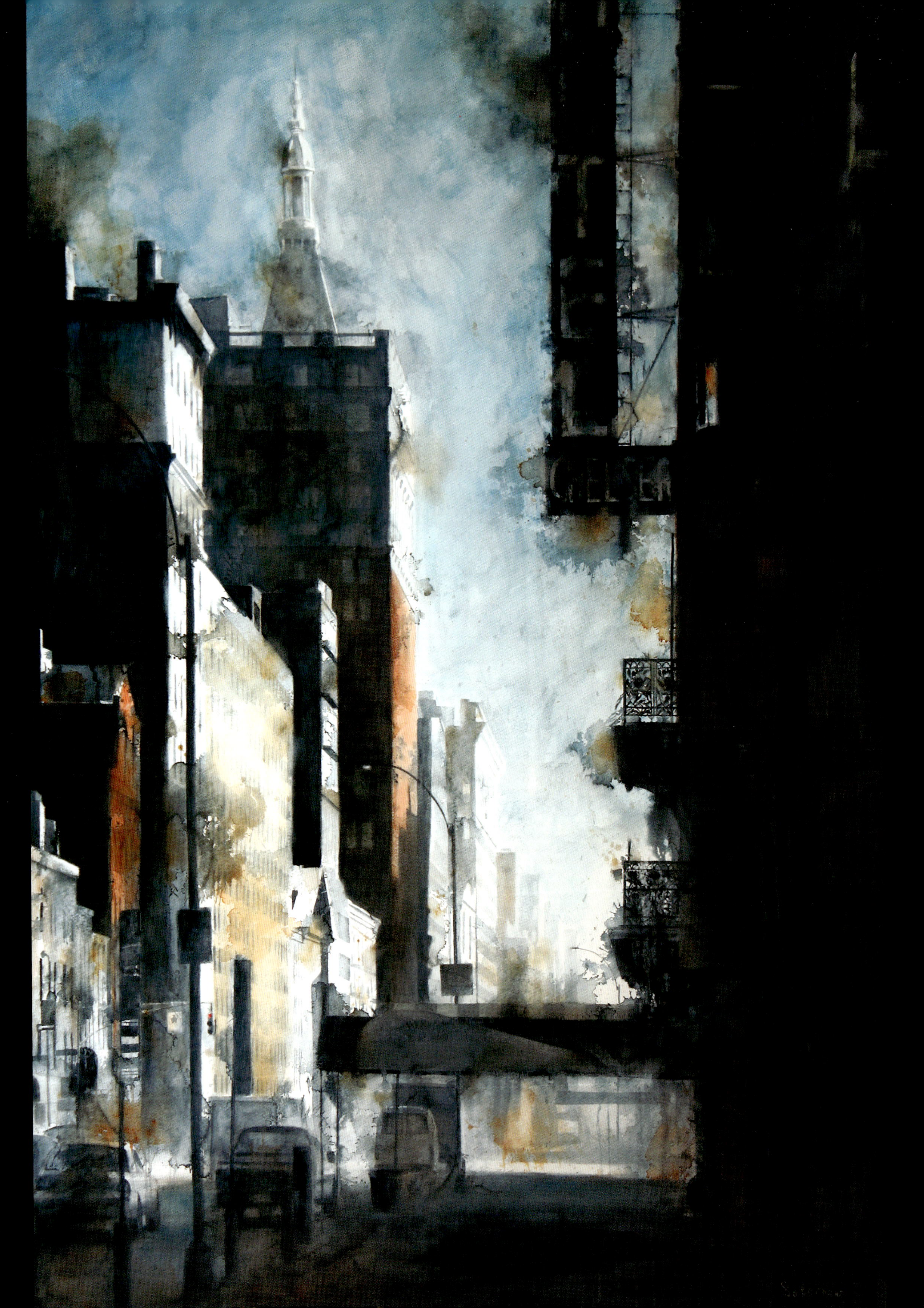

TIM SATERNOW

Although some people may not consider city scenes as true landscape paintings, to many city dwellers the city *is* their landscape, the only one they know. New York artist Tim Saternow knows it too, and finds tremendous beauty, texture and energy in the grit and rust of these ordinary, everyday areas of New York City. "In the 19th century, the American frontier was defined by landscape painters traveling west to show the beauty of America to those back East who would never get to see it," he says. "As a contemporary painter I'm not so interested in directly recording the scene I see before me. I want to infuse my paintings with a sense of drama and emotional energy and communicate these feelings to the viewer. That's much more important, and much more interesting." Saternow is also a theatre set and lighting designer, and has designed on Broadway and in many regional theatres across the country. He was nominated for an Emmy Award for Outstanding Art Direction on a Hallmark Hall of Fame production of *The Piano Lesson* by August Wilson.

What inspired this painting?

I walk the streets of my Chelsea neighborhood every day and watch how the sunlight and shadows define the buildings of New York City. I am drawn to the contrasts in these city scenes: lightness and darkness; hard edges and soft edges; warm and cool colors; the clear and the muddled. This painting is not a portrait of the famous Hotel Chelsea. It's more what the hotel sees through its gorgeous filigree balconies looking across West 23rd Street in the morning light.

How do you plan your compositions?

The city is vertical, so most of my work's emphasis is on that height and the long, tall lines reaching up. But I also look for breaks in that verticality: stoplights arching over the street, business and street signs, wires, street lights. It's that contrast that makes an ordinary street scene powerful. I use the light to play through and around these objects. There must be contrasts and counterpoints, brightness and darkness, to shift the eye and create ambiguity.

What mediums do you use and what are your main techniques?

I draw much of the street with pencil, but I also edit and move around what's before me. I build the lights and darks in a true grisaille technique, using a monochrome of dark blues to build and emphasize the light before any color is added. I then break down this carefully painted layer by laying the paper on the floor and throwing water and paint all over it and letting it puddle. Then I lift the paper to an easel and let it run and drip down the entire length. I repeat the building of the darks using complements of the original blues—sepia and burnt sienna, adding detail, and creating an even denser dark. I'll repeat the "breaking down"' process again and again, pushing and pulling the darks and lights, building the details while obscuring other areas. The very last step is glazing a little local color in some places to build focal areas and interest.

WEST 23RD STREET, HOTEL CHELSEA   Tim Saternow   Watercolor on Arches paper   60" × 40" (152cm × 102cm)   Private collection

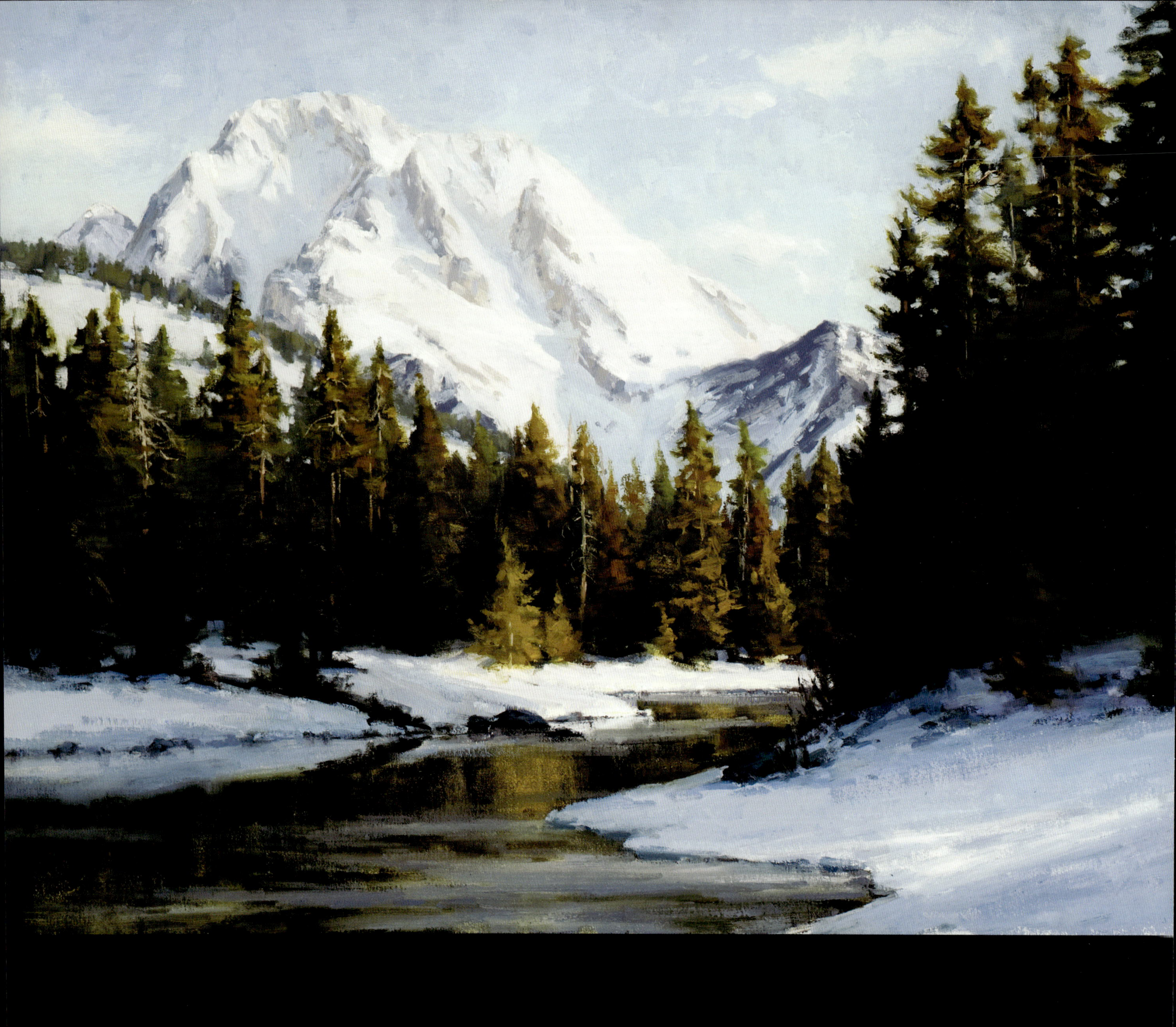

AARON SCHUERR

Aaron Schuerr has the good fortune of painting almost every day, in the studio or in the field, trying to understand and distill the amazing variety of beautiful landscapes in his corner of Montana. Although he takes one or two trips a year to other parts of the West, Schuerr paints mostly within a twenty-mile radius of his home in Livingston, Montana, and also in Yellowstone National Park. "I'm a fan of painting familiar places again and again, so as to get beyond the iconic subjects and into something more personal. I'm not out to impress, but to share," he says. When painting outdoors, Schuerr believes "it's important to relax and have a sense of humor. Don't try for polish and finish. Just get out and respond. Concentrate on the process, on what you are learning. Plein air painting is a place to try out new ideas. You must have room to fail, or you'll atrophy. I'll beat myself up back in the studio, but while I'm out, it's all about the freedom to explore."

What inspired this painting?

I was on what I call a "dirtbag painting adventure" in Grand Teton National Park, basically sleeping in my van, cooking on a camp stove and painting from dawn to dusk. It had been quite a winter, and although it was May, the snow was still waist-deep in places. I was painting in a place that is normally crawling with tourists, but I had it all to myself. Insulated by snow, and with Mt. Moran dominating the view, this was an irresistible subject. As I was about to start painting, a bird landed on the panel, hopped back and forth, and then hopped right onto my hand. I watched it in amazement! As the sun moved overhead it warmed the hard surface of snow, and I sunk to my thighs, like quicksand. Fortunately I was done with the painting, and I packed up.

Is your painting inspired by spirituality? How is that seen in your art?

In the Genesis story, God finishes each day with a statement: "and it was good." He doesn't need to explain why or to justify its need: it is simply good. If I need to deliberately infuse my art with spirituality, then I show that I don't trust the inherent power of art. It is simply good, or it is not. I don't need to justify it or explain it. If I want to explain my spiritual beliefs, then I will use words. If I want to share my intuitive response to the visual world, then I will paint.

How do you plan your compositions?

On location I start with a thumbnail sketch before embarking on a plein air painting. Back in the studio I do a full-sized charcoal drawing, often making significant changes to the composition. I call this my "what if" stage. What if I took out those trees, or moved that ridge, or changed the light? I can make changes quickly in charcoal to see if they work. I can also see the composition better without color. Once I'm satisfied, I either grid out the drawing (if I'm working larger than the drawing) or make a transfer with tracing paper and charcoal. So in a studio painting, I'm referencing both the study and the drawing. I do take photos, but they are a secondary reference.

FRANK SERRANO

Contemporary landscape artist Frank M. Serrano was born in Los Angeles in 1967. He developed an early interest in art and nature, studying throughout his school days, but is largely self-taught. His natural talent eventually gained him a lucrative career as a freelance commercial artist. He has served as plein air painting consultant for Walt Disney Studios, has taught at the Disney Academy in Burbank, California, and has worked with DreamWorks film studio. After his success in the commercial field, Serrano decided to pursue his passion for traditional oil painting and has since developed a strong following. He is recognized for his keen sense of atmospheric observation and his ability to spontaneously interpret his personal connection with nature on canvas, but in his world, that includes the urban landscape as well. Serrano is a long-standing member of the California Art Club, and has written and illustrated an art instruction book, *Plein Air Painting in Oil*, as well as filmed a DVD, *Painting on Location with Frank Serrano*.

What inspired this painting?

This particular river scene is just outside the town of Bishop in the eastern Sierra Nevada mountain range in California. Paintings such as this are a challenge since I'm painting the rhythm and flow of the river. I want the viewer to see and feel its engaging beauty.

In what locations do you paint?

I paint just about anywhere outdoors, but mostly the western United States. There is so much diverse subject matter here, from stunning coastal scenes to majestic mountain scenes and all different seasons of color.

Do you prefer particular seasons or times of day?

Winter and fall to me are the best times. You get much more color and drama in the landscape during these times, which makes for great paintings.

How would you describe your painting style?

I would classify my style as realism. Although I may paint somewhat loosely, my brushwork is decisive.

Do you paint en plein air? What practical advice do you have for those who would like to try it?

I mostly paint plein air because I love being outdoors. For me painting from life is the only way to truly learn to paint. Subtle nuances of color and light and value can only be properly achieved by the experience of painting on location. For those wanting to venture outside to paint, my advice is to keep it simple. Using a limited palette will get you off to a great start. Also, keeping your supplies compact will help on longer jaunts.

OWENS RIVER SPARKLE Frank Serrano Oil on linen mounted to board 10" × 8" (25cm × 20cm)

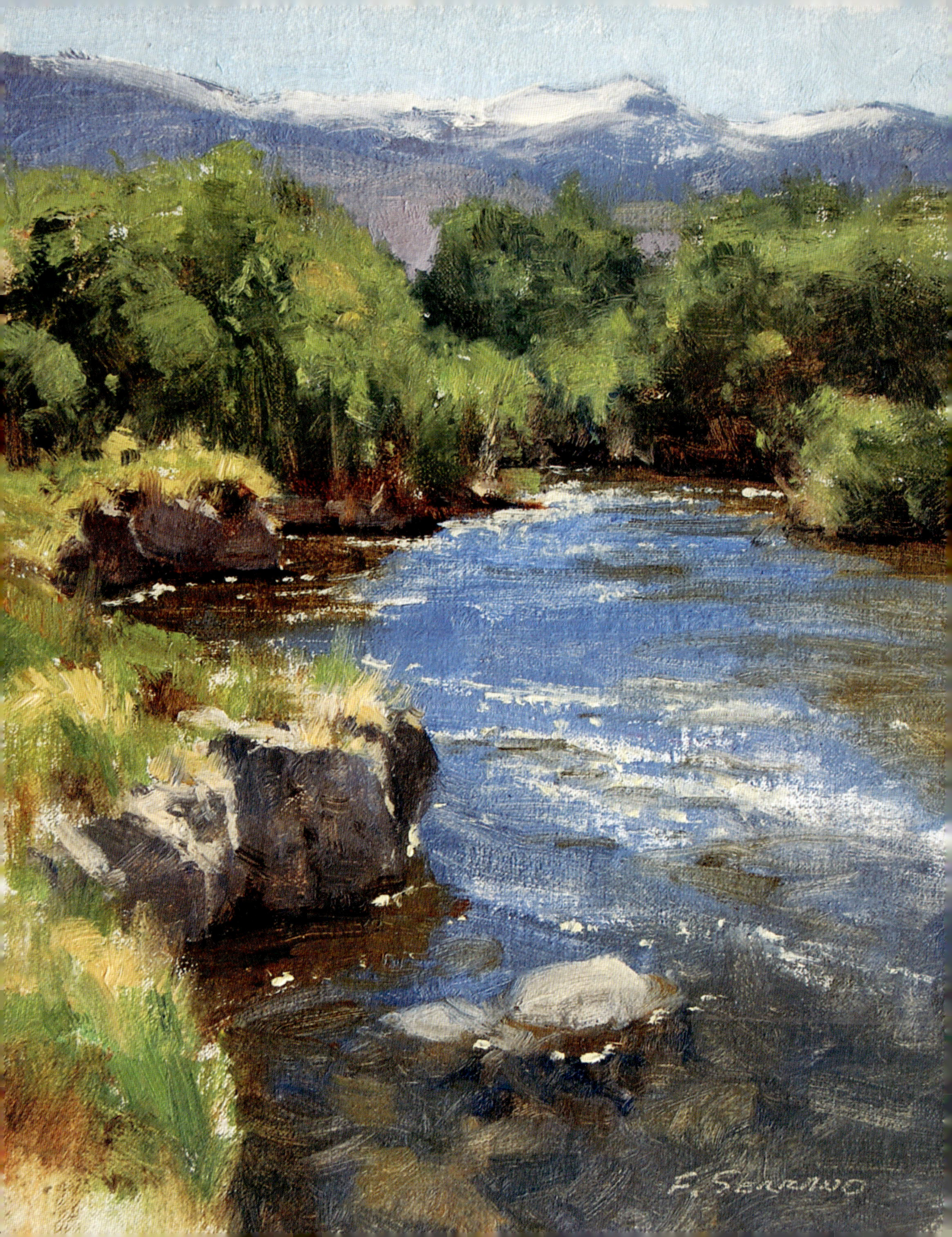
F. Serrano

VALERIE SHESKO

Valerie Shesko grew up in urban Brooklyn, New York. When she was ten, she traveled to the White Mountains of New Hampshire and was completely enthralled by the landscape. Shesko has had the good fortune to live in Ireland and Scotland in addition to having traveled throughout the United States, Europe and Norway. "The unique light and shapes in each type of landscape excite the urge in me to sketch and paint," she says. "The very act of sketching helps imprint a memory of the place that's equally important as referring to the sketch later on." Shesko now makes her home in Cincinnati, Ohio. With advanced degrees in art history, art education and painting, she has built a long and successful career that includes numerous museum and group exhibitions, solo shows, awards and honors, public and private commissions, collections and publications. A former associate editor for *The Artist's Magazine*, she now writes on a diverse array of art topics, including a feature article on "Landscape into Art" published in April 2010. Currently her work is on view at the Cincinnati Art Galleries.

Q&A

What inspired this painting?

I've been inspired by all kinds of landscape painting as diverse as the Hudson River School and Chinese painting. I came of age during the Abstract Expressionism and the Color Field painters and was especially influenced by Morris Louis and Robert Rauschenberg. I was drawn to their innovative use of materials and their use of process to find meaning and subject matter. The composition of *Canyon Dream* was not planned in a step-by-step way. I reassembled existing, unresolved work. The result looks like it was always the way it is, but actually there was a lot of trial and error involved.

What mediums do you use and what are your main techniques?

Over the years I've experimented with many different materials in order to stimulate my imagination. I've painted with blueprint chemicals, sumi ink, encaustic, egg tempera, oil, acrylic and collage. Often the experiments lead nowhere but I'll come back to the work years later. This is what happened with *Canyon Dream*. The main mountain image came from an earlier, much larger work where I had painted with acrylic glazes on heavyweight watercolor paper and used archival tissue paper to create mountain texture. The original piece didn't work; the bright, light sky was lovely but the mountains were stiff and the composition contrived. However, I saved the piece because something intrigued me about it. Years later I thought I'd try painting acrylics on Dura-Lar polyester film that I had around the studio for protecting matted work. I intended to peel off the dried acrylic paint and collage it onto another surface. That didn't work out either but I also saved it. Eventually I discovered that I could combine the two separate experiments for a more dynamic and totally new result.

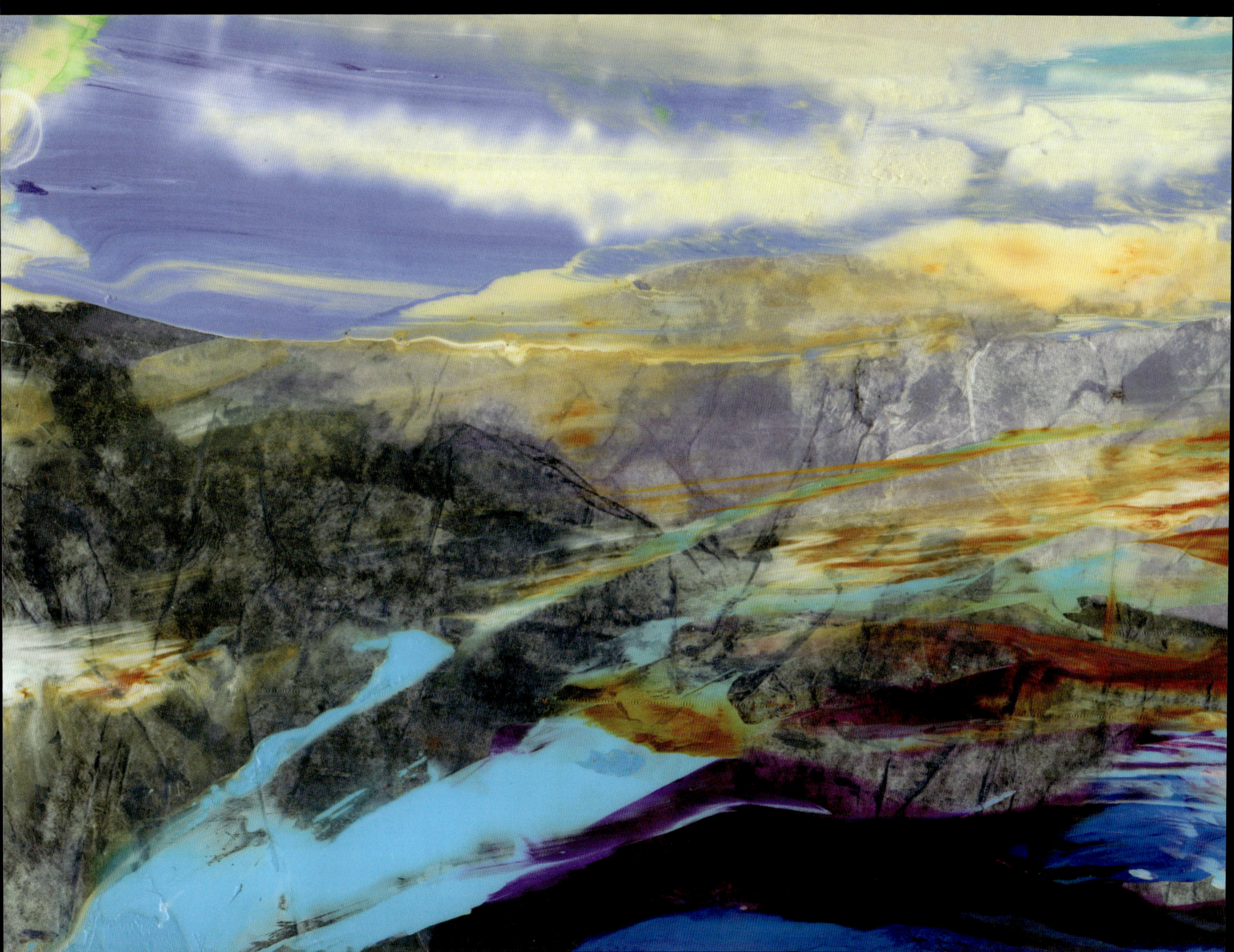

FRED SOMERS

Fred Somers once opened an art class of high school students by standing on his head. The lesson was that to learn something new, one has to work through the "wobbling." This idea has been expressed through a variety of adventures, including a trip to the Canadian wilderness where Somers and several friends capsized a canoe filled with his art materials and gear into a rain-swollen river. Since leaving college teaching in 1975, Somers has been a full-time artist working from his home studio near Northfield, Minnesota. "The land surrounding my farmhouse in Minnesota has beautiful hardwood forests and spring-fed streams," he says. "I look forward to the dramatic seasonal changes and long shadows this latitude affords." Somers is a member of the Oil Painters of America and the Pastel Society of America. He was also honored to have been inducted into the Masters Circle of the International Association of Pastel Societies. His oil and pastel landscapes and portraits are included in more than 400 public, private and museum collections in the U.S. and in Europe, and he continues to teach art workshops.

What inspired this painting?

I am fascinated with the breadth of potential images when it is possible in one moment to see the heights of sky on water at my feet, and stones beneath that once resided under ocean depths. When I found this, I felt a part of an exquisitely ordered creation. St. John's Abby in Minnesota recently commissioned the first illuminated Bible in 500 years. The use of gold in that text inspired me to explore the use of gold leaf in my work.

How do you plan your compositions?

I believe that in all creation, the Word comes before the manifestation—before the art. The flow of words in my mind is a continual conversation as I make a painting, but there are times in the countryside when I can only pause in awe and words are not enough to express the beauty I see. I generally paint from 15 feet away where I speak what I will do at the easel. I want a painting that is strong both from a distance and upon close inspection, like a banquet table where you enjoy the beautiful table setting and then you get to taste the mashed potatoes.

What mediums do you use, and what are your main painting techniques?

I paint in both pastel and oil. Recently I have been exploring the use of 22-karat gold leaf with both media. Using gold allows me to bring the brilliance of reflected sunshine on water into my artwork. Gold itself is a middle-value color that hides among the common hues, but when it is touched by radiant light, it reflects a brilliance that can't be matched by pigment. These circles of gold speak to me of eternity and of the incredible gift that this life is to us.

Do you paint en plein air? What practical advice do you have for those who would like to try it?

Wear a hat.

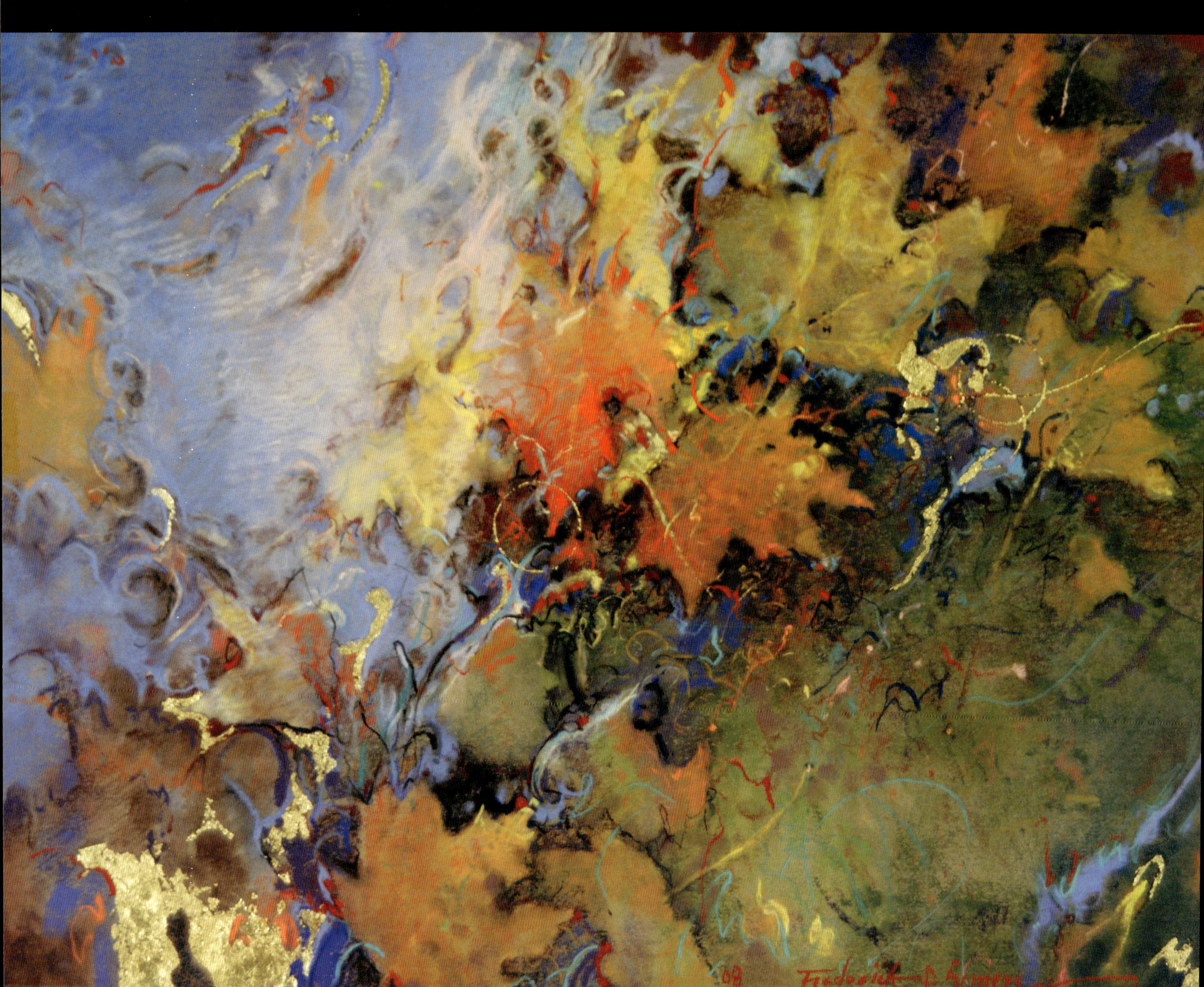
'08
Frederick D. Somers

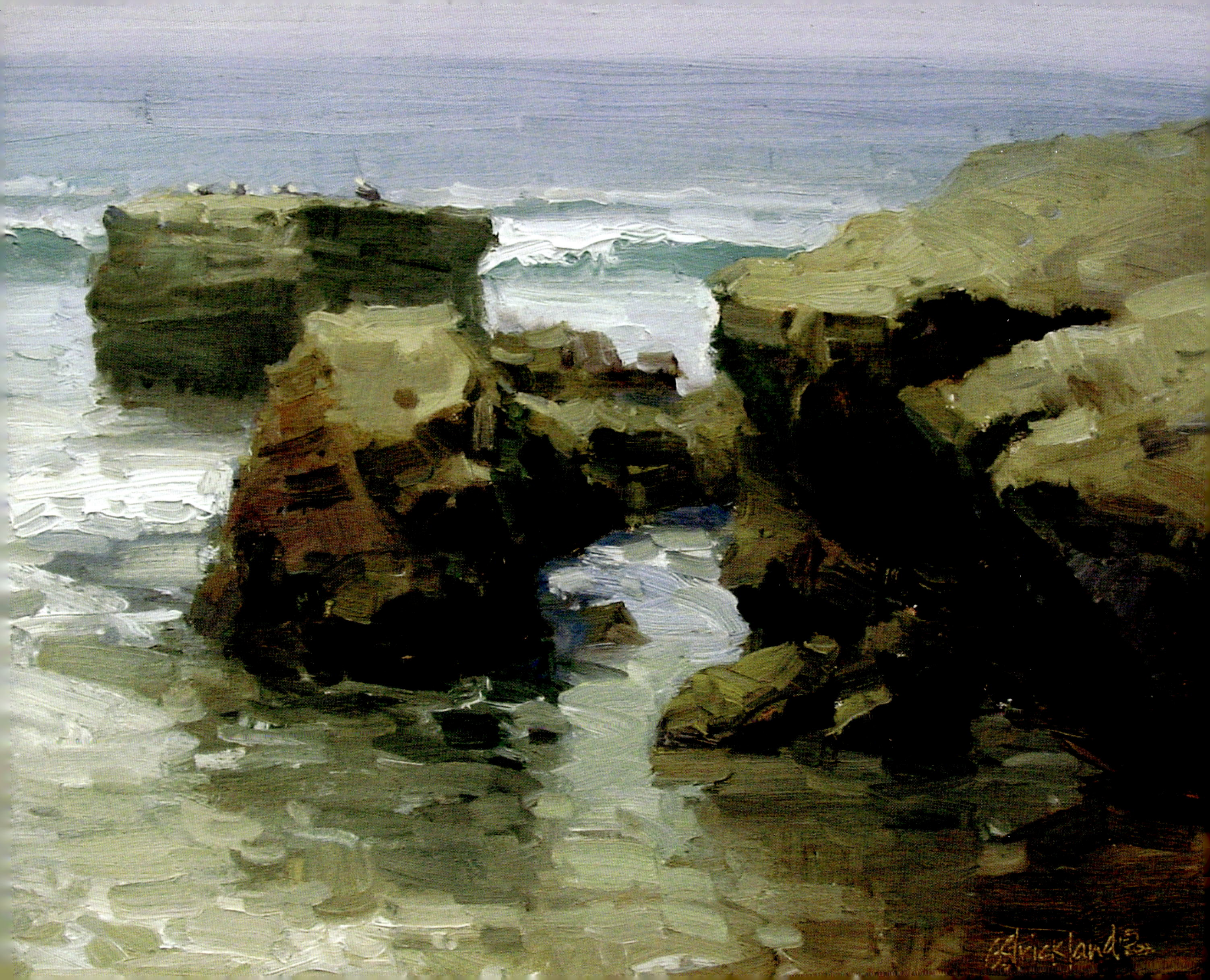
Strickland

GEORGE STRICKLAND

Born and raised in San Antonio, Texas, George Strickland finally settled in Tucson, Arizona, with his wife, Carolita. He started his career as a commercial artist and slowly made the transition to fine art by attending workshops with painters he admired. Howard Terpning, William F. Reese and several others gave him direction and inspiration through several years of transition. His subjects these days include landscapes, seascapes, and rural and urban scenes. "I particularly love painting farms, old nostalgic vehicles and machinery," Strickland says. "Mostly, though, I just look to paint things that speak to me visually. Often, I imagine a scene as if it were already painted; it seems easier to focus on qualities such as colors, patterns, edges, textures and shapes. It seems the overall mood is more important than the individual objects in a painting." Strickland is a member and past president of the Plein Air Painters of America, and a member of Northwest Rendezvous and the California Art Club.

What inspired this painting?

A few years ago I was part of a plein air painting event in Laguna Beach, California. One particularly beautiful morning I decided to paint down on the beach near some great rocks in the water. I took my sandals off and painted on the edge of the water as it lapped at the legs of my easel. This was one of those occasions where I got lost in the painting process and the actual scene and painting melded in my mind. Even now, just looking at the painting, I can relive that experience. The combination of smells, sounds, feel of the breeze and cool sand made a perfect sensory-filled painting experience.

In what locations do you paint?

I paint in all kinds of locations here and abroad, and it seems the more often I paint, the more I appreciate our visual world. The process of discernment raises my sensitivity to color and beauty. If I paint outdoors every day for a few days, I can see prospective paintings everywhere. If I don't paint for a while, I may drive for miles and not find a painting. They are surely there, but I can't see them.

How would you describe your painting style?

My style is somewhere between realistic and impressionistic. Different days, different looks. If I am feeling exuberant, my painting will show some of that. Sometimes my excitement causes me to be a little quick on the draw (sorry for the pun) so I try to stay steady and not get ahead of myself in the painting process.

What's your best advice to students on painting landscapes?

My best advice is to paint miles of canvas on location, en plein air. Doing two or three small paintings every day outdoors will make you a good landscape painter quickly—well, that is, more quickly than painting from photos all day long. Painting directly from life gives you a real sense of what things should look like, and forces you to make quick assessments. That experience will really pay off, both in and out of the studio.

LAUREN TILDEN

Lauren Tilden studied at the University of Delaware and received her MFA from the Pennsylvania Academy of the Fine Arts, where she had the opportunity to study with Sidney Goodman, Vincent Desiderio and Patrick Connors. She was the recent recipient of a grant from the Elizabeth Greenshields Foundation, which seeks to support artists in the early stages of their careers. Tilden lives and works in New Jersey, where, in addition to painting, she enjoys cooking and gardening.

What inspired this painting?

The beauty of the light as it pierced through the trees and clouds inspired me to paint *Dusk at Lightning Bluffs*.

Why is American landscape painting important today, in the 21st century?

The legacy of the 21st century is one of irony and desecration of morality. American landscape painting is a reminder to society of the higher virtues of beauty, truth and goodness, which the landscape symbolizes.

Do any historical movements, periods or artists inspire your painting?

The works of the Hudson River School provide great inspiration for my paintings, as well as the landscapes of George Inness and Andrew Wyeth.

Is your painting inspired by spirituality? How is that seen in your art?

My paintings are inspired by my belief that God is the Creator and His divine nature is evident in the created landscape.

How do you plan your compositions?

I often use the "armature of the rectangle," as named by Charles Bouleau, which is a method of dividing the picture plane based on the Golden Ratio or Golden Mean.

What mediums do you use, and what are your main painting techniques?

I use linseed stand oil and Turner Medium by Sennelier. I paint a series of thinly-glazed layers over an underpainting.

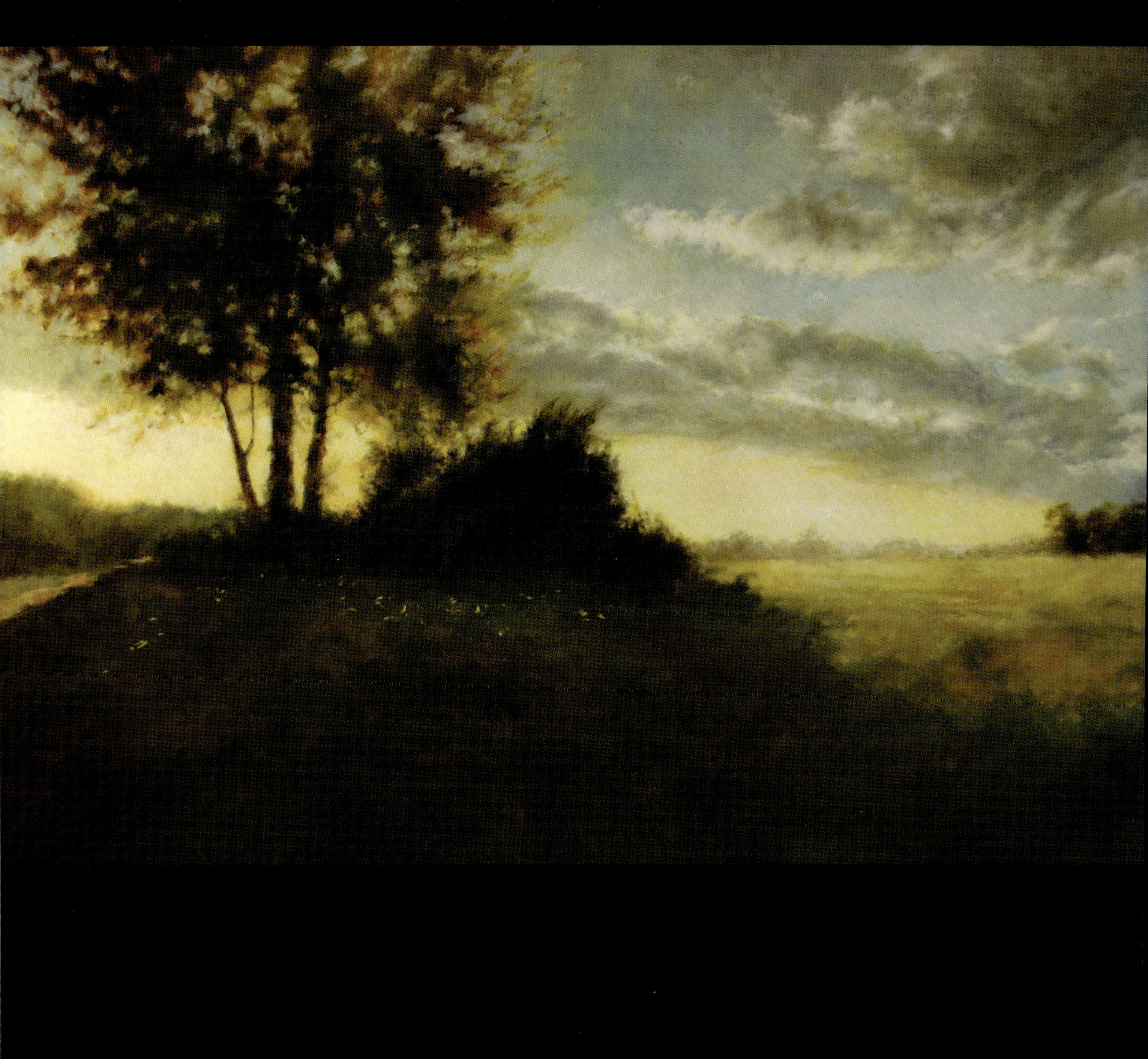

DUSK AT LIGHTNING BLUFFS Lauren Tilden Oil on panel 18" × 24" (46cm × 61cm) Collection of MJ Settelen Construction

JAMES TOOGOOD

Artist, author and teacher James Toogood paints the people, places and things that make up contemporary life, from cities such as New York and Philadelphia, to places like Venice, Bermuda and the United Kingdom. All have their different challenges and all are appealing to him. He is particularly fascinated by cityscapes and has been painting them since his days as a student at the Pennsylvania Academy of the Fine Arts in Philadelphia, where he now teaches. Toogood is a signature member of the American Watercolor Society and the National Watercolor Society, and has won countless awards including the 2010 Allied Artists of America "Gold Medal of Honor" for best of show. He's the author of the book *Incredible Light & Texture in Watercolor*, published by North Light Books, and a contributor to over twenty more.

Q&A

What inspired this painting?

I feel that good representational paintings are also good abstract paintings. The items in the painting—the street, the play of light, the buildings—are all simply shapes first, abstract shapes that need to be arranged in a pleasing and cohesive manner. Then there is the mood. This is 20th and Broadway, New York City, looking south. Manhattan, usually one of the busiest places on earth, is on Sunday morning quiet and still. Shafts of light spill across the otherwise dark, empty street. A series of lines in the street, the sidewalk and the buildings all point toward Union Square in the distance.

How do you plan your compositions?

My compositions are based on studies I have done, often over the course of several days, as was the case here. Knowing that I would find the city empty on Sunday, I went to the general location and started sketching and photographing. I had some sense of what I wanted but I wasn't completely sure. Once I decided on the rough composition, I started taking a number of photographs. I do my finished paintings in my studio, so photos are useful; even so, my paintings are not of photographs. Lots of things are added, and many taken out. Anyone who's familiar with New York City knows that buildings are constantly being covered with scaffolding and netting when being worked on. This was the case with several of the buildings depicted in this painting—most notably the tall, dark building on the corner, in the right center of the painting, across the street from the building with the mansard roof. The bottom floors of both buildings were obscured by scaffolding, which meant I had to just make up large portions of those buildings, but designing buildings in midtown Manhattan can be a lot of fun. I intentionally left the bottom floor of the corner building with the mansard roof empty. It not only provides an interesting opportunity for that diagonal shaft of light and shadow but it also helps to create the quiet, still mood I was looking for.

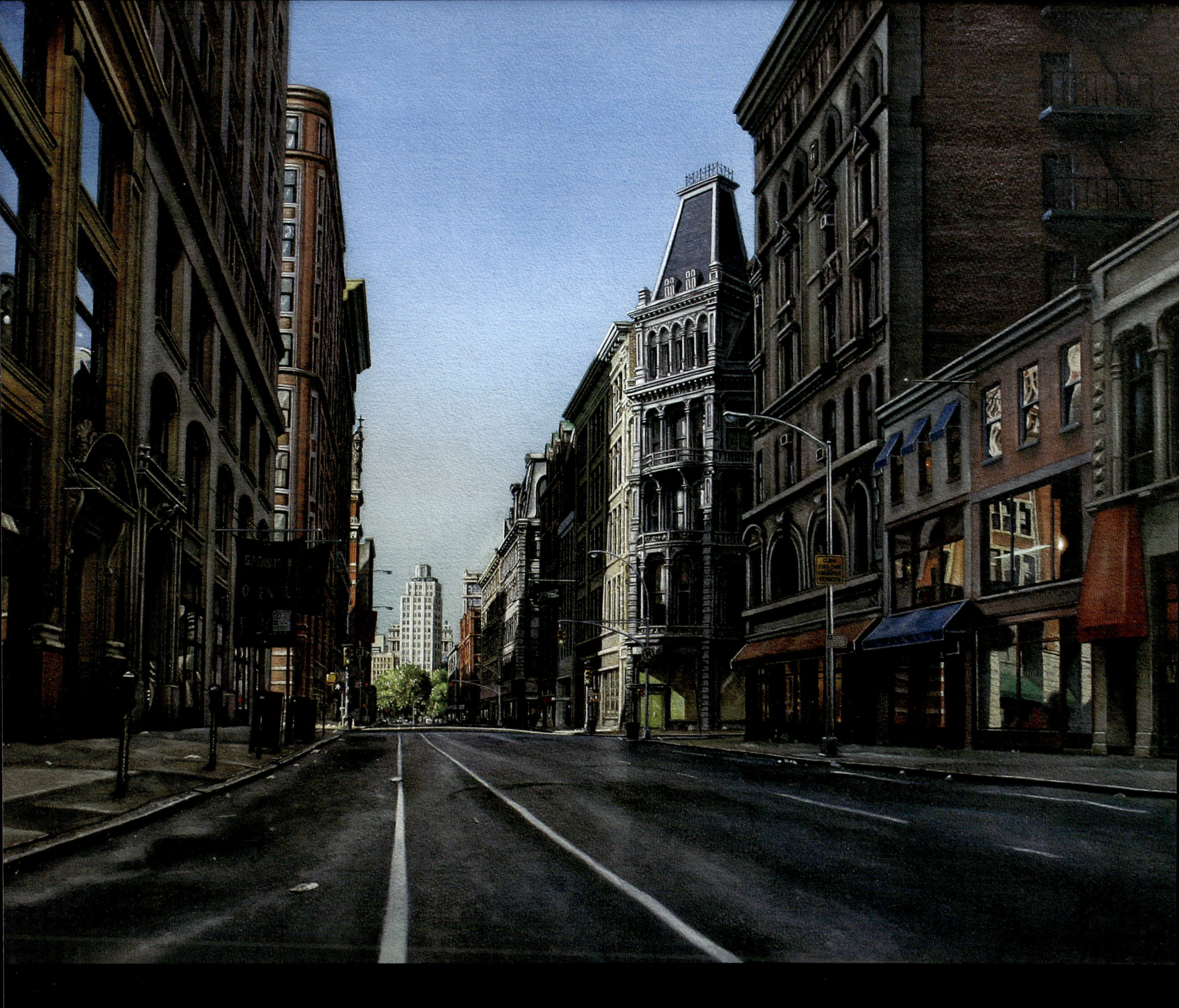

SUNDAY MORNING, THE FLATIRON DISTRICT James Toogood Watercolor 22" × 29" (56cm × 74cm)

CLIVE R. TYLER

Clive Tyler was raised in an encouraging artistic atmosphere. He studied fine art and design at Kent State University in Ohio, and twenty years later, after a successful design career, he is now known as one of the best pastelists on a national level. Tyler has moved quickly into the art scene, enjoying museum invitationals and winning awards and acceptance from collectors. His classical-oil-painting style is unique for pastel painting. As a plein air painter, he has always been inspired by nature and the quiet in the wilderness. "I have been painting in Rocky Mountain National Park in Colorado for ten years," he says. "I travel to Montana and Oregon to paint as well. Rivers, snow scenes, tall aspens, moose, bison and elk are all on the list of subject matter that I enjoy painting." Tyler is a member of the American Impressionist Society and in March 2011 was featured in *Southwest Art* magazine. He also won first place in the pastel category worldwide in the first annual Autumn Arts Painting Challenge on Facebook.

What inspired this painting?

This painting represents an experience I had working en plein air in the aspen forest of Colorado for three days, sitting and staring and getting a sense of what a forest of aspens is all about. I remember sitting there, sketchbook in hand and easel set up for painting, and wondering, "How do I paint a million trees, branches, leaves and trunks and still see through the trees to a view of more trees and mountains beyond?" Well, I discovered, you don't. You paint the experience, the moment, the emotion you feel. Then you paint color and form, and the rest will follow. That one day has taken me on a great journey of painting a series of aspen paintings. It started with summer and has now moved to fall and spring; winter is still on the horizon. What I have learned as an artist is to paint the truth of nature, not the ideal. Trees live, move, talk, die and fall down and then are reborn. The forest is truly a reflection of and a metaphor for life.

How would you describe your painting style?

I paint on many levels. One, on a sense of beauty, peace and hope. Two, I paint my personal experience of place and the spiritual experience that I have with nature. Three, I paint and respect my medium of soft pastel. I let it do what it was designed to do: to be pure color in an impressionistic sense when seen from a distance, and to be pure abstraction when seen up close. So, from a distance my paintings take on a representational look, but up close the viewer will feel the emotion and abstraction of form, shape, line and color.

What mediums do you use and what are your main techniques?

I paint in soft pastels on a sanded paper from Germany. The pastels I use are a French brand called Sennelier, a brand created for Degas and Monet. Some of the colors are even the same. It's a dry form of pigment/paint. Pastel is made of pure pigment or ore and stone, so the colors glow with a luminous feeling.

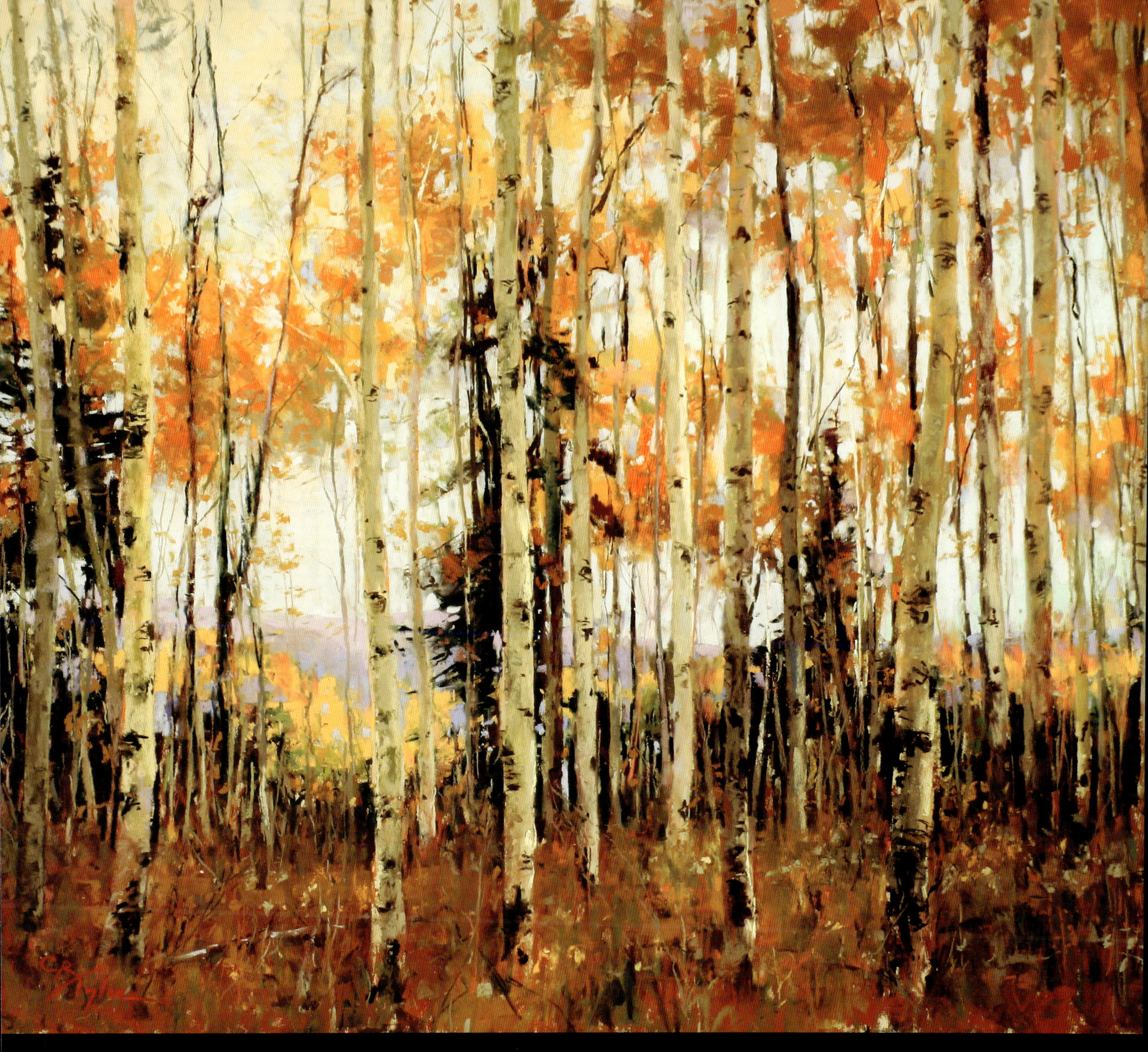

THE ASPENS Clive R. Tyler Soft pastels on sanded paper 21" × 27" (53cm × 69cm)

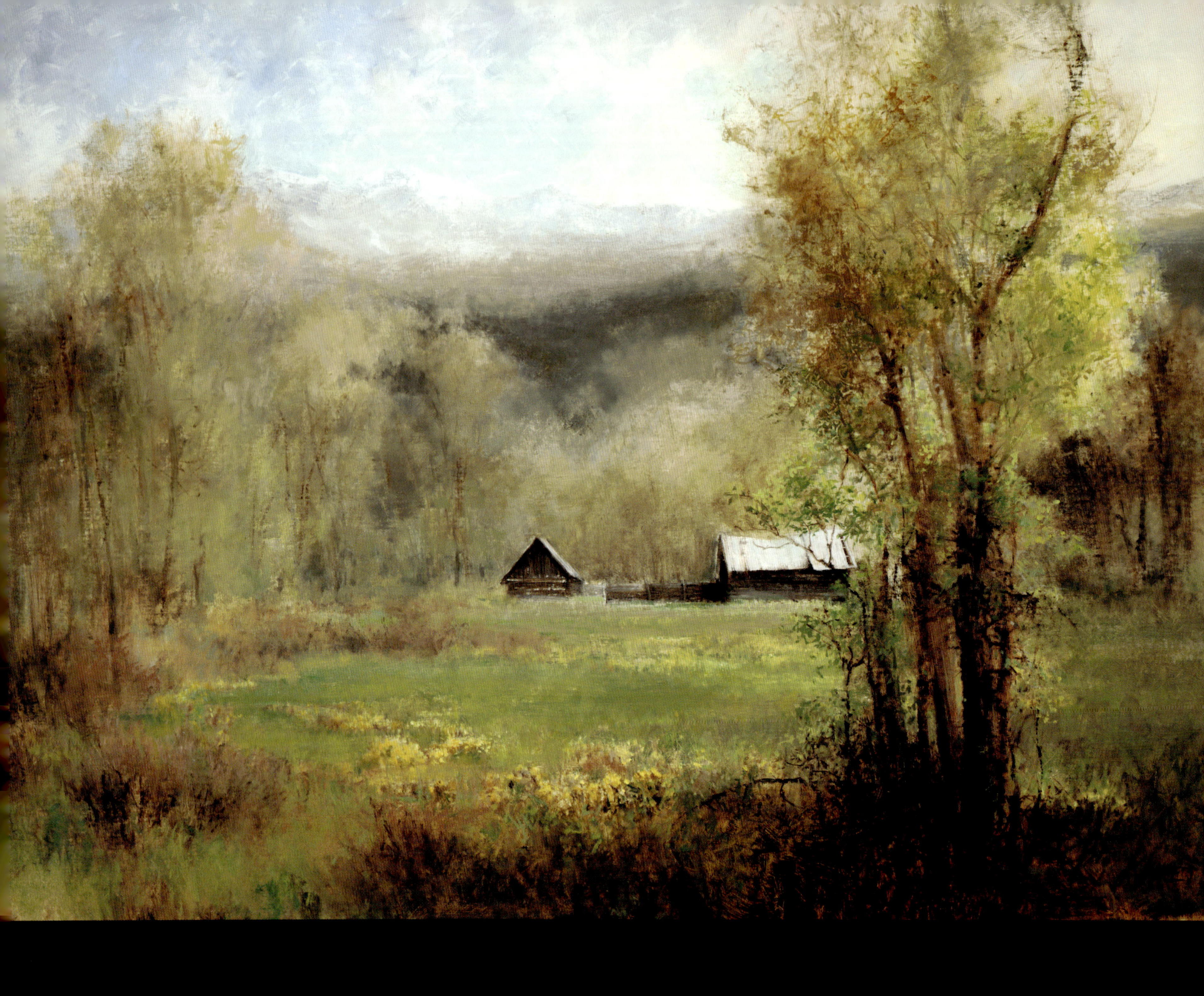

 ANOTHER SPRING Karen Vance Oil on linen 28" × 36" (71cm × 91cm)

KAREN VANCE

Karen Vance was born in Chicago into a family of artists and has been studying and creating art as long as she can remember. Her work has won many local and national awards and hangs in prominent public and private collections, including the permanent collection of the Whitney Gallery of Western Art at the Buffalo Bill Historical Center in Cody, Wyoming, and the collection of Lord and Lady Waterford of Curraghmore, Ireland. Asked how she would describe her painting style, Vance replies, "I've been described as a 'contemporary impressionist' by art writers and critics alike, and I truly embrace that term with honor. I have always loved the Impressionist painters of the late 19th and early 20th centuries. As a child, when I would collect trading cards, I would trade one card of a cute dog for three cards of paintings from this era." Vance's art career includes twelve years as a graphic artist and the past twenty-six years creating fine art professionally. She is a master signature member of American Women Artists.

What inspired this painting?

This is the Murphy Ranch near the confluence of the Colorado and Fraser rivers in Granby, Colorado, at about 8,000 feet above sea level. It's been a working ranch and in the same family for four generations. These two barns are more than one hundred years old and still standing. The winters in this valley are harsh and long, with heavy snow. When I set up my easel to paint, I was moved by the beauty of this setting, with the peaks of the Continental Divide in the distance and the fresh signs of spring—dandelions in the pasture, cottonwoods beginning to leaf out, and the sturdy, well-built barns that made it through to "another spring." It speaks of the quiet and tenacious spirit that settled the American West, and still lives on today in ranching communities everywhere.

Why is American landscape painting important today, in the 21st century?

This ranch, and the people who own it, are "hanging on." America is losing much of its landscape to development, and the history of this beautiful and mighty country is being lost along with it. With paint and brush, landscape painters are able to preserve it and celebrate it for this generation and generations to come.

Do you paint en plein air? What advice do you have for those who would like to try it?

I paint en plein air to capture the emotion of a place, as well as accurate colors and values. It also allows me to capture "sounds and smells" in my painting, unlike painting in the studio. I've had patrons tell me that they can "smell the air" or "hear the trickling stream" when they experience my paintings. To become a good landscape painter, you must paint en plein air. It teaches you to see color, and how the color of the sky affects a hillside as it turns from the sun. It teaches you to see atmospheric perspective and tonal changes as a landscape moves away from the viewer. It teaches you respect for nature. It is an essential exercise and learning experience, and it gives the painter excellent reference material for studio paintings.

CURT WALTERS

Curt Walters, whom *Art of the West* magazine declared the "Greatest Living Grand Canyon Artist" in 1997, and one of "Eight True Masters" in 2007, today makes his home in Sedona, Arizona. Much of Walters' art reflects his environmental concerns with regard to the Grand Canyon. His reverence for the Grand Canyon is not only documented through his body of art, but also in his dedication to preserving Arizona's national treasure. "When I first moved to Sedona," Walters says, "there were great fields of yucca plants, which I would rush out to paint every summer. Those locations are now mostly devoid of yuccas and have been developed with motels and gas stations. Future landscape artists in Sedona will no longer get to see, or paint, the same landscape I did. We are so fortunate in the United States to have the National Park System, which has helped to preserve so many western landscapes, especially the Grand Canyon."

What inspired this painting?

I was raised in the Four Corners region in New Mexico. When I was a child my father explored much of the Navajo Reservation and it was during this time I fell in love with the landscape of the Colorado Plateau. Monument Valley has become the iconic symbol of that landscape. *Monuments to Infinity* was inspired by a plein air painting I had worked on just before this painting. I would watch the monsoon storms roll through in the afternoon, and those sunset moments I could not capture in the plein air painting became part of this studio painting.

Do any historical movements, periods or artists inspire your painting?

For me, the greatest art was created in the period between 1870 and 1935. The artists of that time were well trained in the atelier style of painting, yet availed themselves of new and modern techniques and materials, as well as embracing the cultural freedom to paint a more personal vision. When I see the American and French Impressionists of that time, I still get excited, because, while subject is important, the well-trained artist can paint any subject and impart mood, light and atmosphere. So, the question of who I am as a painter is borne out of my love for this period of art.

How do you plan your compositions?

All my work starts en plein air. I rarely paint canvases in the studio that I have not studied first out on location. I think it is impossible for a landscape artist to convey emotion and the true character of the landscape if they have not first sketched or painted or studied it on location. I have also studied the principles of dynamic symmetry and the Golden Mean, which are always useful compositional tools. I am, for the most part, an alla prima painter. I simply find it easier to control my edges, colors and values with wet-into-wet paint.

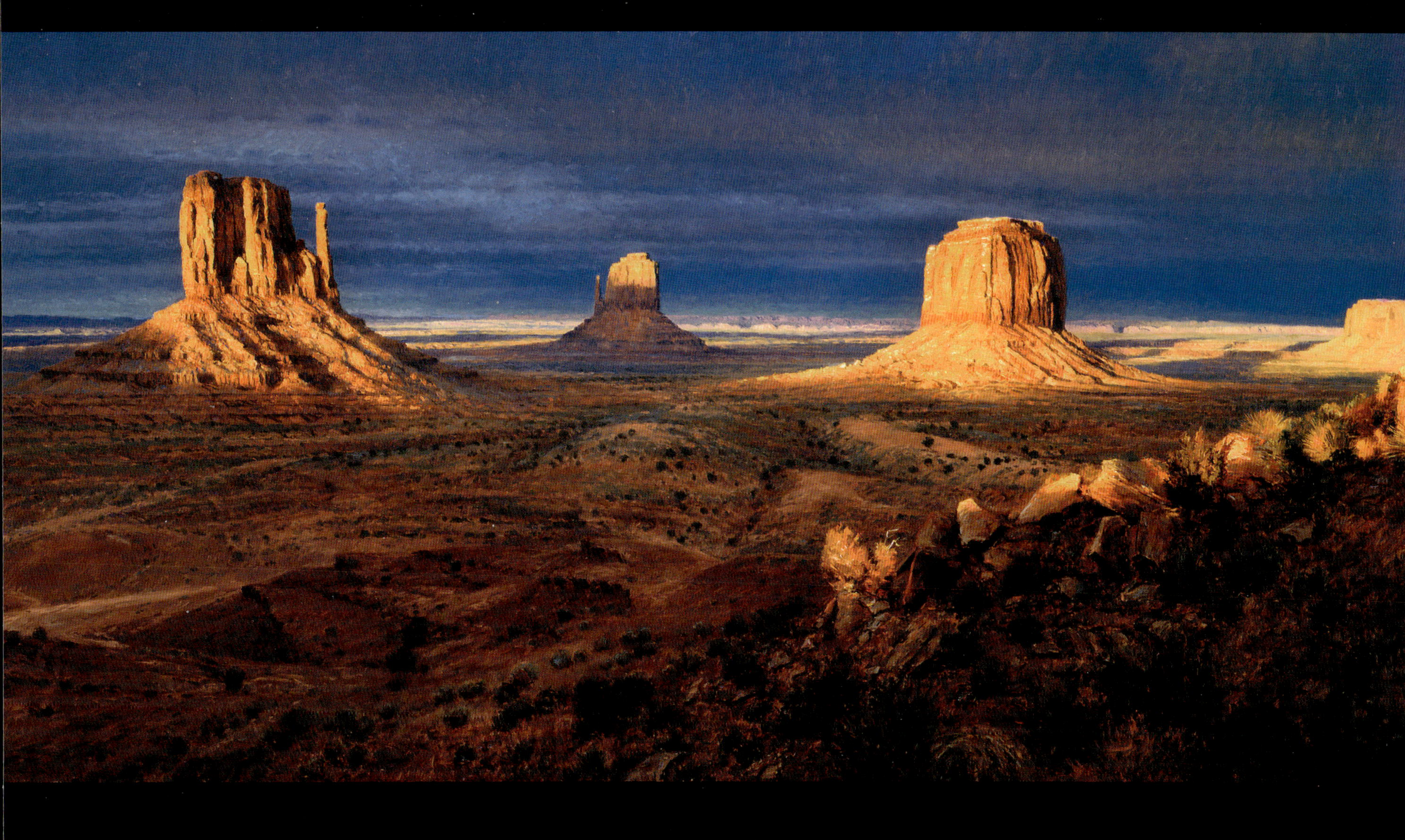

MONUMENTS TO INFINITY Curt Walters Oil on canvas 30" × 80" (76cm × 203cm) Collection of Glen and Carolyn French Photo courtesy of Tom Alexander Photography

ERIC WIEGARDT

After graduating from the American Academy of Art in Chicago, Eric Wiegardt returned to his hometown of Ocean Park, Washington, to live, pursue his art, marry, and raise five delightful children who are the joy of his life. Wiegardt and his family live on an isolated peninsula surrounded by large bodies of water. Their community's livelihood has been traditionally based on the shellfish and fishing industry and this is reflected in much of his painting subject matter. "Having grown up in my father's oyster business, I have many fond memories of working on the water," Wiegardt says. "Marine subject matter comes naturally to me and I have an emotional attachment to it. We paint best what we know best, and having observed reflections and seascapes in my youth to this day, I am very familiar with the patterns water and reflections make." Besides being a signature member of the American Watercolor Society, National Watercolor Society, and others, he is a national juror and a popular workshop instructor. He's also an avid outdoorsman, and can be found hunting ducks and clamdigging in the most inclement of weather.

What inspired this painting?

Storm Surf at Cape Disappointment is part of a once-in-a-lifetime painting collection called *The Life and Times of the Long Beach Peninsula*. This collection is a personal journey for me in which I chronicle one year in the place I was born and still live. Each month, I capture events, places unique to the Peninsula, how people here on this strip of land in the Pacific earn their living, the plant and animal life, and of course, the storms, like the one shown in this painting. *Storm Surf at Cape Disappointment* is from December 2010 in *The Life and Times of the Long Beach Peninsula.*

How do you plan your compositions?

I most often will start a painting with a value study. A value study is very helpful in organizing my thoughts through value placement and, just as importantly, it gets the creative juices flowing. Once I get the big patterns established, then I proceed with a very loose drawing on the paper that takes just minutes. I realize that if I get the big relationships right, then the rest of the painting will take care of itself.

Do you paint en plein air?

I enjoy painting plein air when it is not raining! Because I live in the Pacific Northwest, I have to sometimes catch favorable weather in between rain squalls. However, I have done several paintings under docks, in breezeways and in other protected areas as I escaped from the rain.

What mediums do you use and what are your main painting techniques?

I paint in watercolor as directly as possible. I aim for the first stroke in a passage to be my last. Of course, there's always some adjustment, but I try to get it right in the first stroke. I'm not much for long periods of time involved for successive layering; I don't think I have the patience. I also think watercolor displays its intrinsic edge and color-mixing qualities that no other medium has when done directly.

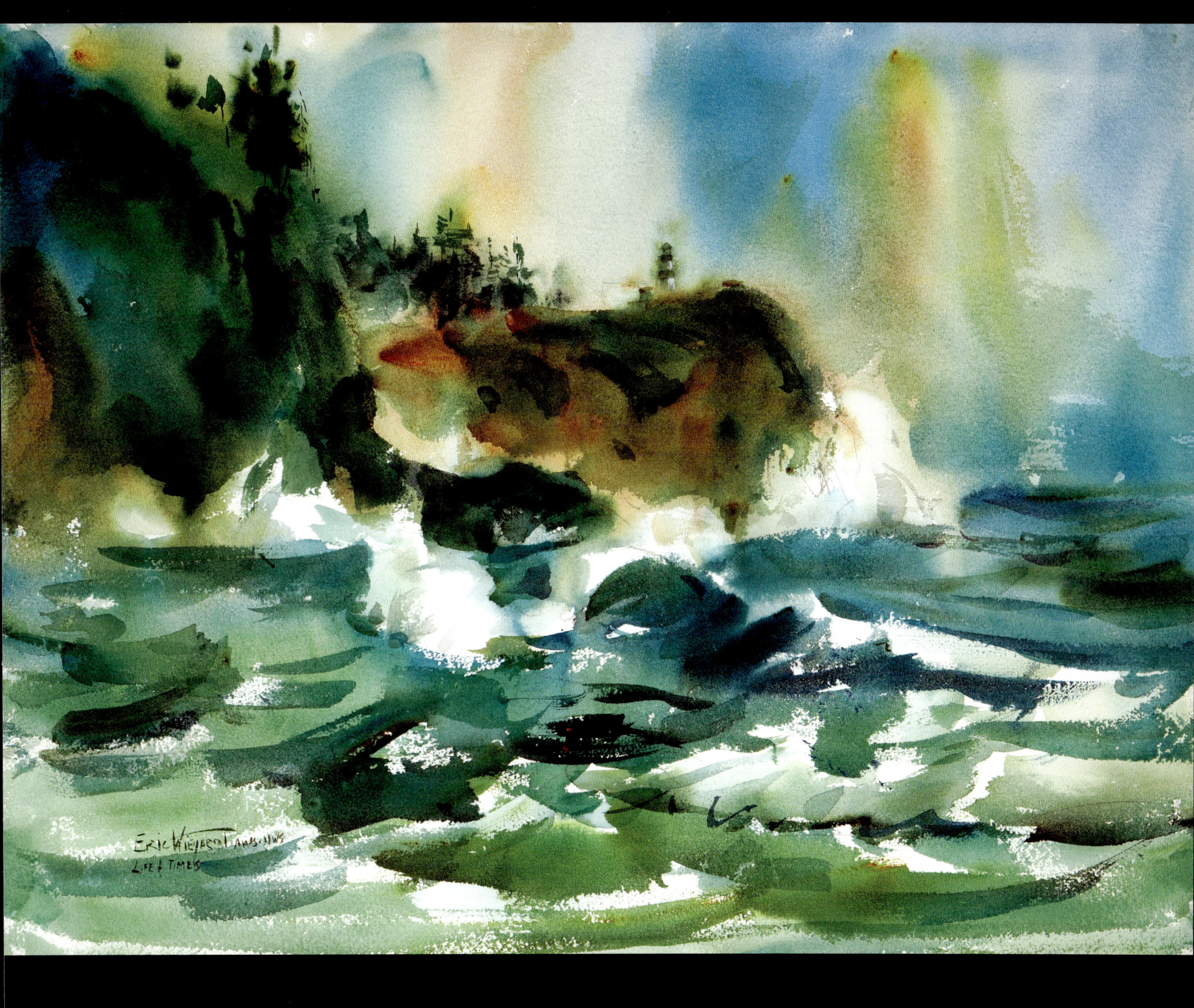

STORM SURF AT CAPE DISAPPOINTMENT Eric Wiegardt Watercolor 22" × 30" (56cm × 76cm) Private collection

TERUKO T. WILDE

Born in Nagoya, Japan, Teruko T. Wilde moved to the United States as a teenager and studied at the University of Cincinnati as well as the Columbus College of Art and Design in Ohio. She first established herself as a pastel and watercolor artist before moving to Taos, New Mexico, in 1986. Inspired by the magnificence of the landscape, she began her "Southwest Series" in oils, painting expansive Southwestern skies, approaching storms, and moody sunsets. Currently, Wilde is combining all of her life experiences into multiple styles and techniques. Her work is the culmination of her Japanese heritage and American experiences as she re-creates emotional as well as physical elements from her surroundings with overlays of color, creating texture and intriguing shapes as past and present merge.

What inspired this painting?

The inspiration for *Sunset Reflections with Clouds* came from a visit to the Seattle, Washington, area. The large number of trees, the fresh vegetation and humid climate reminded me of Japan. After having concentrated on painting the American Southwest landscape for many years, the Northwest landscape proved to be quite an exciting, inspiring experience for me. I've painted my "Tree Series" now for several years, developing a controlled drip technique to indicate the trees rather than using brushwork.

In what locations do you paint?

I love the Southwest. After painting it for more than two decades, I still find it awesome and inspirational. I am fortunate to have a spectacular, almost 360-degree view of the Taos landscape from my studio. My favorite seasons to paint are autumn and winter, in the early morning dawn, sunset, and early evening. I feel grateful and thank God for allowing me to have the marvelous views each morning and each evening from my studio.

Do any historical movements, periods or artists inspire your painting?

I am very much into classical music. The phases in classical music and in art are correlated. It's difficult to pick just one historical movement or period that inspires me the most, but I would choose the mid-1800s to early 1900s for both the music and the visual arts. I love, respect and admire a good number of artists, but have never allowed them to influence my technique.

How would you describe your painting style?

My painting style does not quite fit into any one category. It's a combination of realism, abstraction, and impressionism. I simply call it "contemporary landscape." Like myself, it does not "belong" in any particular place or thing.

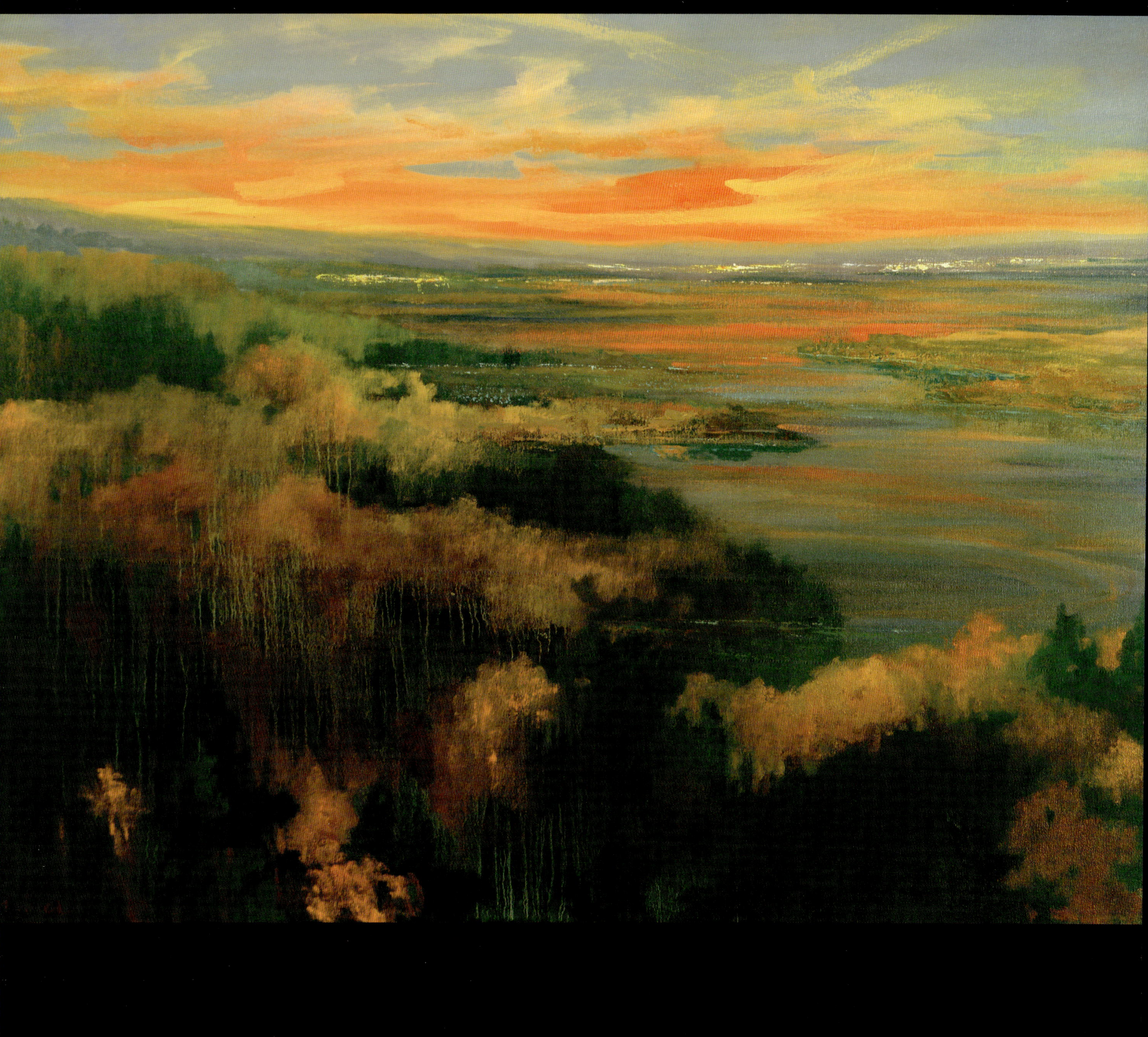

SUNSET REFLECTIONS WITH CLOUDS Teruko T. Wilde Oil on canvas 30" × 40" (76cm × 102cm) Private collection Photo courtesy of Joe Justad

DON WILLIAMS

"I've been interested in night paintings since I was a student at the University of Nebraska and first saw Edward Hopper's painting *Room in New York*," says pastel artist Don Williams. "Night images often have elements of drama and mystery that will draw me into the picture and hold my interest." Williams lived in San Francisco for ten years before moving to Sonoma, California, where he now lives with his wife, Kathleen, a reading teacher. Their son, Cooper, is a commercial fisherman out of Bodega Bay, California. Williams received his MFA from Tulane University in New Orleans. After three years of teaching art at the college level in Louisiana and South Carolina, he moved to San Francisco and began to exhibit in galleries and museums in the Bay Area while supporting himself as a substitute teacher. He's had over thirty-five solo exhibitions, including shows in San Francisco, San Jose, Lincoln, Nebraska, and the Mecene Gallery in Tokyo, Japan.

What inspired this painting?

I came upon the scene in *Country Road in Headlights* while driving the back roads looking for subject matter. It was just after sunset and I was hoping to get some photos of the landscape while there was still some light in the sky. I turned onto a dark road and switched on the high beams. The bright poles against the sky, the road receding into the distant landscape and even the sliver of light at the horizon seemed ready-made for a painting.

What medium do you use and what are your main techniques?

Pastels are very versatile and can produce a wide variety of effects. They blend easily for subtle variations of color and tone and can also create sharply focused detail. I like to work on four-ply museum board. It lies flat, has a texture that will hold the pastel, and is thick enough to withstand lots of rubbing and blending. My working process starts with a light pencil drawing defining the contours of the larger shapes. I then fill in these areas with pastel color, rubbing it into the paper with the palm of my hand. Next, I adjust the relative values and temperatures (light, dark, cool, warm) to get the overall tonality closer to what I want and then redefine the shapes and edges that have been smudged or lost in the process. Working more slowly, I start to add local color and details, gradually bringing the image into focus. I don't use fixative because it darkens colors and can leave a faint, speckled texture. A large painting usually takes three or four weeks. Pastel is a very permanent medium if it's on archival paper and is protected with glass or acrylic.

Do you prefer particular seasons or times of day?

When I'm not looking for night subjects, I prefer the light in the morning or late afternoon when the shadows are longer and add an element of movement and depth to the composition. Sometimes a summer fog will cover the landscape around Sonoma, California, where I live, creating interesting visual effects and giving isolated objects an imposing, almost iconic presence.

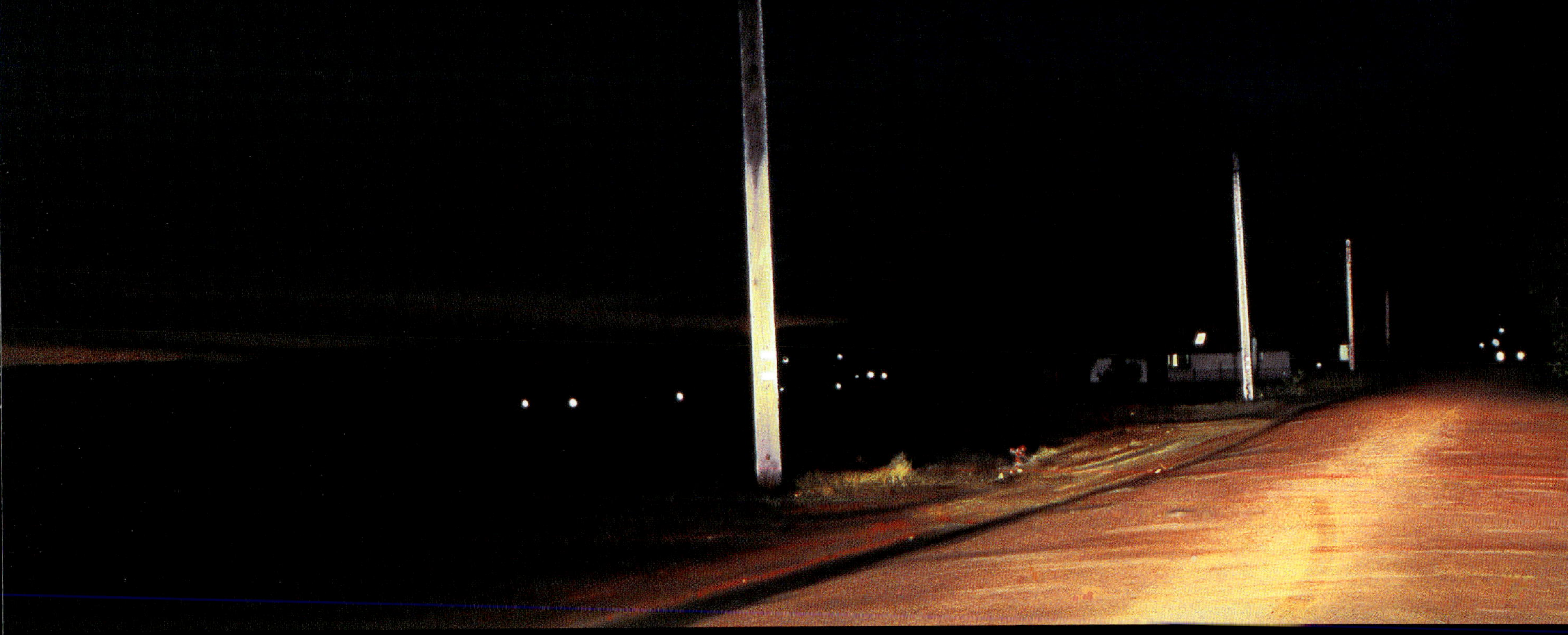

COUNTRY ROAD IN HEADLIGHTS Don Williams Pastel 28" × 50" (71cm × 127cm) Private collection

DOUGLAS WILTRAUT

Douglas Wiltraut is a painter from Pennsylvania who works primarily in egg tempera and watercolor. The president of the National Society of Painters in Casein and Acrylic for over twenty years, he is also a member of the American Watercolor Society and the Philadelphia Watercolor Society, and an honorary member of Allied Artists of America, Audubon Artists and the Salmagundi Club in New York City. Wiltraut's work has received numerous awards, among them the Gold and Silver Medals of Honor from Knickerbocker Artists and the Rouse Gold Medallion from the Adirondacks National Exhibition of American Watercolors, and he is the unprecedented four-time winner of the Ralph Fabri Medal.

What inspired this painting?

I have always been inspired by the artists who have dealt with light and shadow, from Vermeer and Velázquez to the Americans Homer, Hopper and Wyeth. In this painting, the sheer beauty of the scene of the old white headstones standing amidst the beautiful carpet of mountain pinks was striking. With the added symbolism of the tattered flag reminding us of those who have sacrificed to preserve our landscape, the two elements joined together to create a "Heaven on Earth."

Why is American landscape painting important today, in the 21st century?

As artists, we are continually inspired and challenged by the landscape on an almost daily basis. As time passes, the landscape slowly changes due to both the forces of nature and the development of mankind so that today's landscape bears little resemblance to that of our forefathers. It's therefore important that artists provide us with a visual record of the ever-changing landscape.

How do you plan your compositions?

Having always relied on instinctual composition, I find that here the perspective of the rows of headstones lead the eye to the sun-bleached flag whose faded colors once again remind us of the passage of time, something I love to depict in my paintings. My love of the outdoors and all of the activities associated with nature—whether it be birdwatching, blueberry picking, or the collecting of wild mushrooms or seashells—keeps me walking across and in touch with the landscape. There is nothing like walking through a plowed field for hours on end in search of a long-lost arrowhead to serve as a "think tank" and spark my next painting.

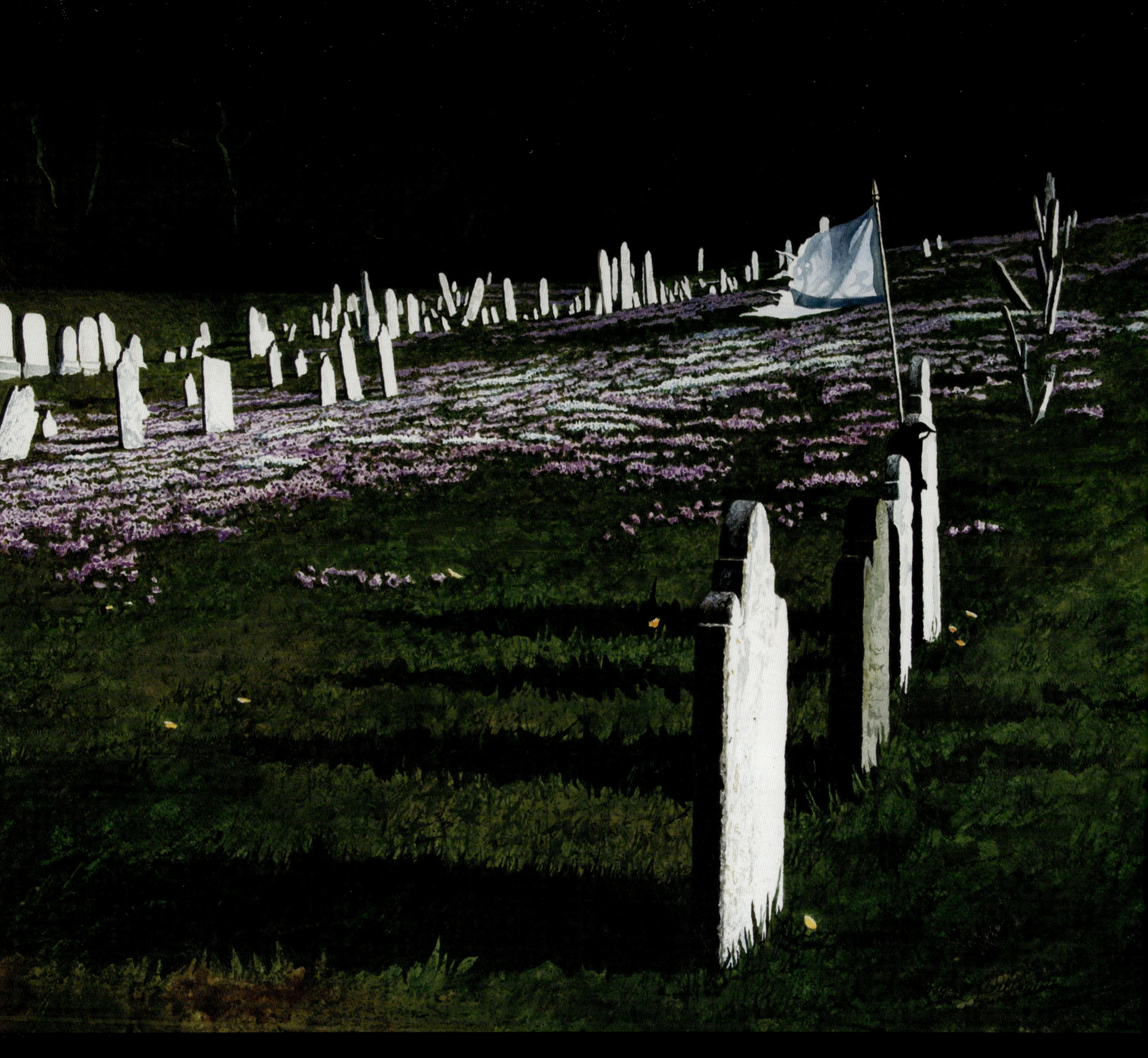

HEAVEN ON EARTH Douglas Wiltraut Watercolor 21" × 29" (53cm × 74cm) Collection of Elaine Diamond

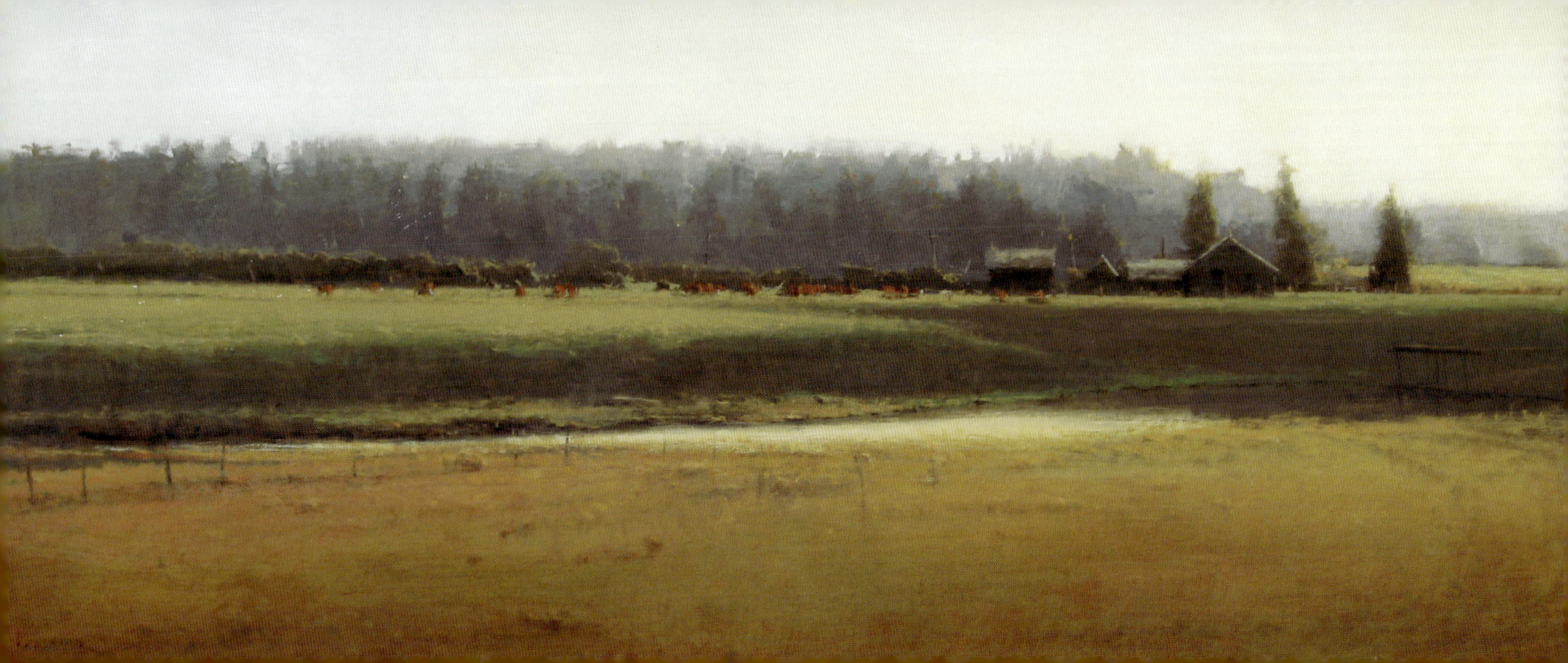

MICHAEL WORKMAN

Born and raised in Highland, Utah, on his family's small farm, Michael Workman developed a deep and abiding love of the great outdoors and rural life that inspires his artwork to this day. He majored in drawing and painting at Brigham Young University, eventually earning a Master of Fine Arts degree, and while there, his work was discovered by a representative of the Meyer Gallery in Santa Fe, New Mexico. Workman continues to make his living as a gallery artist, and now lives in the historic town of Spring City, Utah, on his own small farm with his wife and five children. Of the significance of American landscape painting today, Workman says, "The American landscape as we know it is disappearing, especially the pastoral/domesticated landscape that I'm most fond of. The pastoral landscape is full of metaphor, symbolism and poetry, which is what I am interested in. Most of my work is pretty much in my own back yard."

Do you prefer painting in any particular seasons or times of day?

Late evening, early morning, and rainy days suit me well, as there is drama and a softness that lends to the mystery and poetry that I am seeking. I'm also interested in tonalism. These times of day are suited to the understated subtlety that I'm after.

Do any historical movements, periods or artists inspire your painting?

I'm probably most inspired by the 19th-century landscape painters, pre-Impressionism, especially the Barbizon School. As I mentioned earlier, I feel a connection with American tonalism. The "golden years" of George Inness still inspire me. Although I never consciously set out to be a tonalist, it just seems to come out of me when I paint. There are also some post-Impressionist and modern painters that I am fond of: I like the flat space and design of Vuillard and Bonnard and also Klimt. I also like the subtle but powerful color field paintings of Rothko.

Is your painting inspired by spirituality? How is that seen in your art?

I think or at least hope that my spiritual beliefs are *felt* more than *seen* in my paintings. I have a strong sense that there is a grand design to this existence and I hope there is a feeling of that in my work.

How do you plan your compositions?

The answer to this question is tied to the previous one in that an artist can express personal yet universal truths or ideas through composition as well as other "tools." I'm thankful to have had teachers who helped me understand the power and importance of composition in painting and directed me toward some old techniques of dynamic symmetry that I use in my work. In my opinion, art of any kind is manipulation. The trick is to use the tools in such a way that the viewer or listener is not aware of the manipulation. Most of us love a movie that makes us feel things. But who doesn't feel frustrated when the manipulation is obvious and you feel jerked around against your will?

DINAH K. WORMAN

Dinah Worman's landscape paintings are instantly recognizable for their clarity and depth. Light is everywhere. It filters through the trees and streams, between the clouds. She is able to retain this vitality because she is continually renewing her vision. "I work to press beyond method and into a flow of creative instinct, using pastel, oil, acrylic or printmaking to express myself with unusual compositions and expanding vision." Her work ranges from representational to imaginative variations taken from a creative viewpoint of man and his relationship to the landscape. Worman found her way to Taos, New Mexico, through her art and started showing in Act l Gallery almost twenty years ago. She kept returning to paint and photograph, each time wanting to stay longer. She finally made the move and has not regretted a minute of it. Worman was named a Master Pastelist by the Pastel Society of America, and is also a member of the International Association of Pastel Societies and the Pastel Society of New Mexico. She enjoys teaching workshops, traveling, dogs, friends and gardening.

What inspired this painting?

The most compelling aspect was the stepped landscape that provided layers and diagonals.

In what locations do you paint and why?

I am looking for two things: I want to see the "bones" of the landscape found in the openess of an arid climate or the stacked fields of cultivated land. I also love the compositional elements of a cluttered, close scene that allows me to treat the landscape much like a still life. This is especially true of my aerial views and large foreground pieces. I'm looking for the compositional elements of both of these types of landscape paintings rather than the beauty of individual objects.

How do you plan your compositions?

I look for patterns created by the planes of the landscape. I want a blueprint of the landscape with the forms adjusted or reconstructed to create a dynamic composition.

Do you paint en plein air?

I do paint en plein air. I rarely finish on location. I start with a compositional underpainting and advance to color and contrast notes. I finish in the studio with inside lighting to match the light that the painting will be displayed in. Most of all, I keep it simple and have a planned selection of pastels or oils to avoid being burdened with too much "stuff." My main medium is pastel with an underpainting of pastel dissolved in alcohol.

COWS ON THE EDGE Dinah K. Worman Pastel 12" × 12" (30cm × 30cm) Photo courtesy of Barry Norris Photography

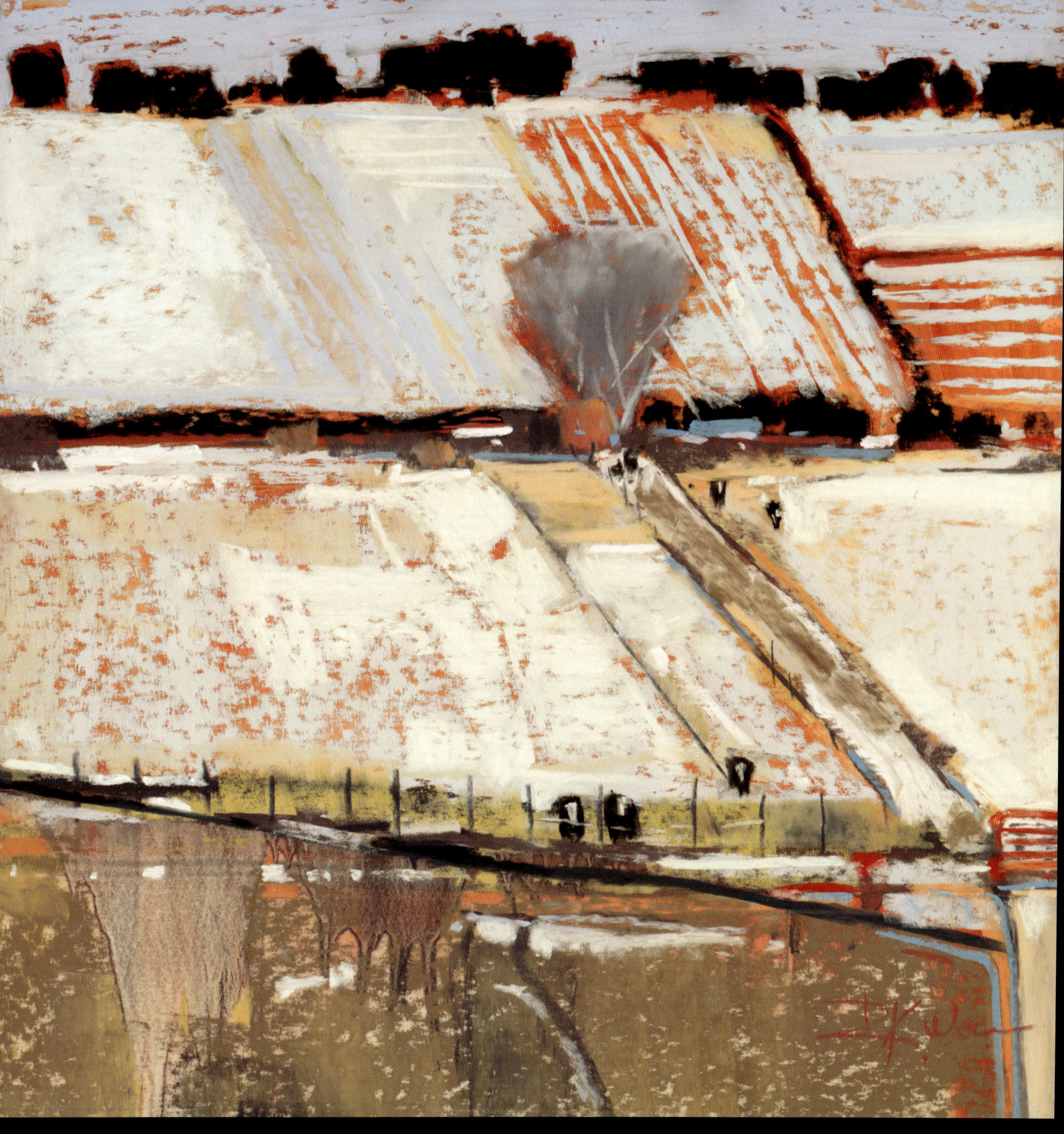

KEIKO YASUOKA & DUNCAN SIMMONS

Keiko Yasuoka was born and raised in Japan. From the age of six, her primary artistic pursuit was calligraphy. After moving to the United States in 1991 with her husband, Yasuoka discovered watercolor in a class at the Glassell School of Art in Houston. In 2002, she met Duncan Simmons there. Simmons did not pursue art until he was 31, and at age 58 finally became a full-time artist. Having met in art class, Yasuoka and Simmons realized that they both not only wanted to paint realism but were drawn to the same or similar motifs. Their professional collaboration began when Simmons, now 75, finding it a bit difficult to paint large commissions, asked Yasuoka if she would become his partner and collaborate with him on painting the large commissions. She agreed and they now work on the same canvas simultaneously, with a certain understanding: during the creative process, they may choose to paint over each other's work. This is done in the spirit of opening each other's eyes to different possibilities. In 2012, Yasuoka and Simmons will mark their tenth anniversary of being painting partners and will celebrate by having two gallery exhibitions.

What inspired this painting?

We were inspired to paint this particular subject because of the beautiful spring colors. The flowers are Texas bluebonnets and Indian paintbrush. We usually find inspiration in the Texas hill country and toward the Gulf Coast.

What mediums do you use and what are your main techniques?

We both paint in acrylic and watercolor. We collaborate on our large acrylic canvas paintings. Our technique is considered unique because when we work on large paintings, we paint them together, at the same time, from start to finish. We decide on the motif and the size of the stretcher. We make the stretcher, stretch the canvas and gesso it. We both draw the motif onto the canvas and block the shapes in. Then we each start painting on the part of the painting that attracts us. We have two basic rules: 1) We may paint over the other person's work and they are not to say anything or indicate in any way that they are displeased. They may paint back over the work and are entitled to the same courtesy from the other partner; 2) Each of us is to want, and to encourage, the other person to be the best artist they possibly can.

What's your best advice to students on painting landscapes?

You will want people to enjoy your paintings for a long time. You'll want the viewers to feel like they are walking into and through your painting. Do not try to shock the viewer with wild colors and/or unusual subject matter. This may initially attract the viewers, but they are more likely to tire of the painting over a long period of time.

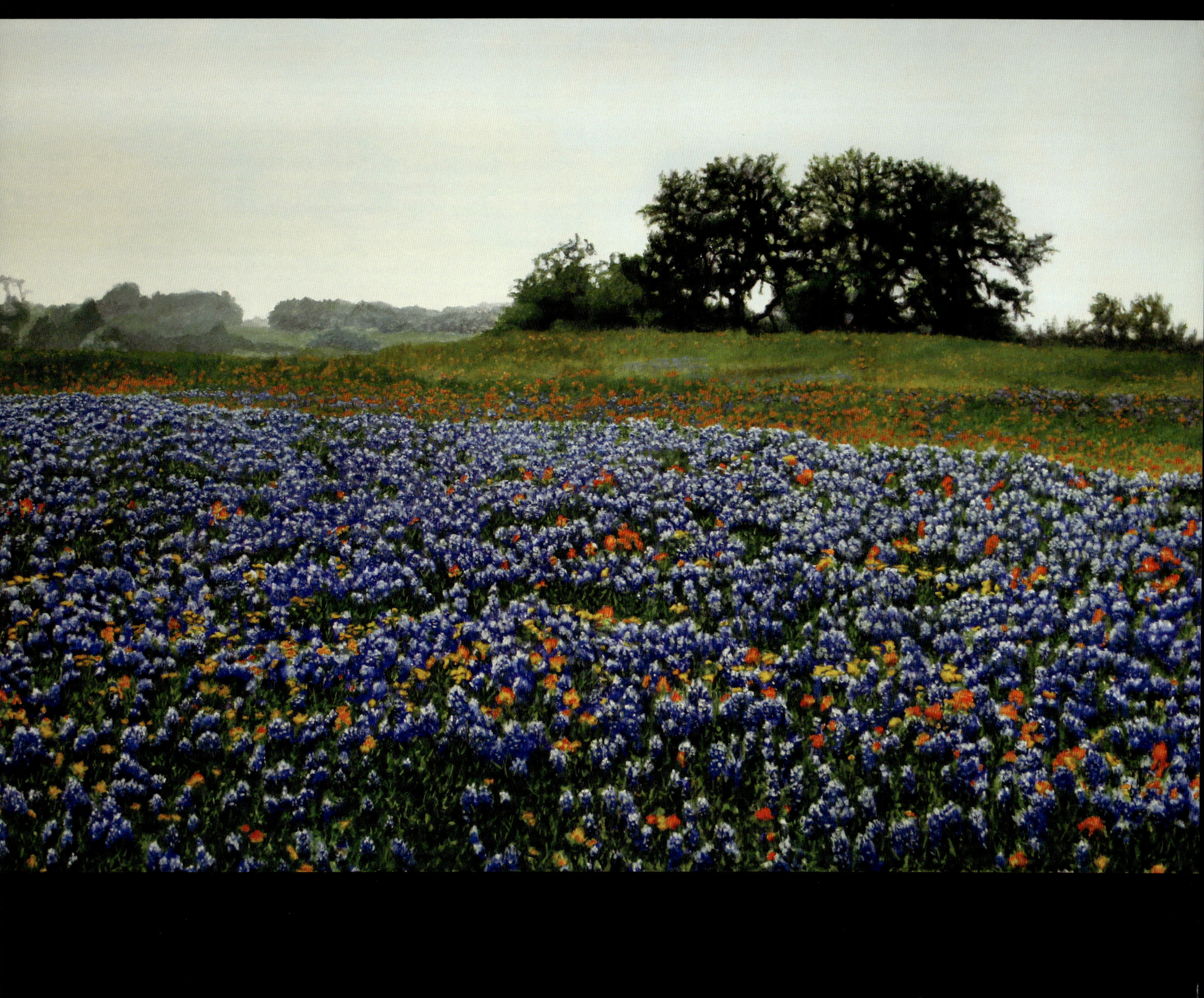

SPRING COLORS Keiko Yasuoka & Duncan Simmons Acrylic 32" × 48" (81cm × 122cm) Collection of David DeMartini

THE ARTISTS

Scott Lloyd Anderson
Gallery MAR
Greenhouse Gallery of Fine Art
Kelley Galleries
McBride Gallery
New Gallery
www.scottlloydanderson.com

Douglas Atwill
The Meyer East Gallery
www.dougatwillstudio.com

Robert L. Barnum
RL Barnum Studios
www.rlbarnumstudios.com

William Berra
Galleria Silecchia
Gallery Elite
Greenhouse Gallery of Fine Art
Nedra Matteucci Galleries
Saks Galleries
The Sylvan Gallery

Gordon Brown
Keating Fine Art
gordon@keatinggallery.com

Nancy Bush
Astoria Fine Art
Beals & Abbate Fine Art
Dawson Cole Fine Art
InSight Gallery
M Gallery of Fine Art
Watts Fine Art
www.nancybush.com

Cole Carothers
studio@fuse.net

Arthur Chartow
Ann Nathan Gallery
www.artchartow.com

Arturo Chávez
Gerald Peters Gallery
Mountain Trails Galleries
www.arturochavez.com

Lorenzo Chavez
Betsy Swartz Fine Art
Grapevine Gallery
Mockingbird Gallery
www.lorenzochavez.com

Len Chmiel
Claggett/Rey Gallery
Simpson Gallagher Gallery
Stremmel Gallery
www.lenchmiel.com

Brian Cobble
Valley House Gallery
cobblebk@aol.com

Gil Dellinger
Carmel Fine Art
Knowlton Gallery
Roger's Gardens
Vertical Peaks Fine Art
www.gildellinger.com

Dennis Doheny
William A. Karges Fine Art
www.dennisdoheny.com

David Drummond
Brazos Fine Art
Weems Galleries
Wilcox Gallery
www.drummondart.com

Joellyn Duesberry
Joellyn Duesberry Studios
www.joellynduesberry.com

Kathleen Dunphy
Argosy Gallery
Knowlton Gallery
Morris & Whiteside Galleries
www.kathleendunphy.com

Sterling Edwards
16 Patton Fine Art
Germanton Art & Winery
Sunset River Marketplace Gallery
www.sterlingedwards.com

Sy Ellens
Ann Arbor Art Center
Ariana Gallery
Synchronicity Gallery
www.syellens.com

Josh Elliott
Claggett/Rey Gallery
Medicine Man Gallery
Simpson Gallagher Gallery
www.joshelliottart.com

Max Ferguson
Gallery Henoch
www.maxferguson.com

Peter Fiore
The Banks Gallery
Cavalier Galleries
Scottsdale Fine Art
Travis Gallery
www.peterfiore.com

Alan Flattmann
Nunnery's at Gallery 119
Windsor Fine Art
www.alanflattmann.com

Terri Ford
Knowlton Gallery
Los Gatos Museums Gallery
Viewpoints Gallery
www.terrifordart.com

Alyce Frank
Fenix Gallery
The Meyer East Gallery
famousa@newmex.com

Jonathan Frank
Framed Image Fine Art Gallery
Navarro Gallery
www.jonathanfrankstudio.com

Guido Frick
Evergreen Fine Art
New Masters Gallery
Sunset Art Gallery of Amarillo
www.guidofrick.com

Jon R. Friedman
Alan Klotz Gallery
www.jonrfriedman.com

Grant Fuller
Ethel Curry Gallery
Peninsula Gallery
Western Canadian Fine Art
www.grantfuller.ca

Catherine Gill
www.catherinegill.com

Michael Godfrey
Huey's Fine Art
McBride Gallery
New Masters Gallery
Trailside Gallery
www.michaelgodfrey.com

Walt Gonske
Claggett/Rey Gallery
InSight Gallery
Nedra Matteucci Galleries
Parsons Gallery of the West
Saks Galleries
www.waltgonske.com

Mark Gould
Giacobbe-Fritz Fine Art
Lanning Gallery
Pierson Gallery
RARE Gallery of Fine Art
www.markgouldart.com

Hugh Greer
American Legacy Gallery
Courtyard Gallery
Wadle Galleries Ltd.
www.hughgreer.com

Lisa Grossman
Dolphin Gallery
Marty Walker Gallery
Strecker-Nelson Gallery
www.lisagrossmanart.com

Albert Handell
Howard Portnoy Gallery
Third Canyon Gallery
Ventana Fine Art
www.alberthandell.com

Liz Haywood-Sullivan
Montana Trails Gallery
Vose Galleries
www.haywood-sullivan.com

Joyce Hicks
www.jhicksfineart.com

Robert Highsmith
Glenn Cutter Gallery
Marigold Arts
www.rhighsmith.com

William Hook
Meyer Gallery
www.williamhook.net

William Hosner
Suttons Bay Galleries
www.williamhosner.com

Cindy House
Cooley Gallery
Edgartown Art Gallery
Haley & Steele
Marine Arts Gallery
www.cindyhouse.com

Colleen Howe
Bingham Gallery
Buffalo Trail Gallery
Village Gallery
www.colleenhowe.com

Rod S. Hubble
www.rodhubble.com
www.TraditionsFineArt.com

M. Katherine Hurley
Art Access Gallery
Bonfoey Gallery
5th Street Gallery
Greenwich House Gallery
North Water Gallery
River Street Studio
www.mkatherinehurley.com

Ann Huston
Studio de Colores Gallery
www.decoloresgallery.com

Margie Kuhn
Anderson O'Brien Fine Art
Rehs Galleries
Strecker-Nelson Gallery
Wynne/Falconer Gallery
www.margiekuhn.com

Donna Levinstone
Jeffrey Leder Gallery
www.donnalevinstone.com

Dennis Liberty
DSG Fine Art
www.dennisliberty.com

Kim Lordier
Debra Huse Gallery
The Fairmont Gallery
James J. Rieser Fine Art
Knowlton Gallery
Sekula's Fine Art & Antiques
Windrush Gallery
www.kimfancherlordier.com

Kevin Macpherson
Coleman Fine Art
Redfern Gallery
Studio Escondido
www.kevinmacpherson.com

Stanley Maltzman
www.gallerydir.com/stanley-maltzman

Richard McDaniel
www.richardmcdaniel.com

Richard McKinley
Artful Deposit Galleries
Mockingbird Gallery
www.mckinleystudio.com

Mark Mehaffey
Bright Rain Gallery
Francesca Anderson Fine Art
Lansing Art Gallery
www.mehaffeygallery.com

Jay Moore
InSight Gallery
Keating Fine Art
Legacy Gallery
Saks Galleries
Sanders Galleries
www.jaymoorestudio.com

Elizabeth Mowry
www.elizabethmowry.com

Paul Murray
Weems Galleries
www.murrayfineart.com

P. A. Nisbet
Medicine Man Gallery
The Meyer East Gallery
Watts Fine Art
www.panisbet.com

Bruce Peil
Grapevine Gallery
www.brucepeilart.com

Tom Perkinson
The Howell Gallery
Manitou Galleries
www.tomperkinson.com

Andrew Peters
Altermann Galleries
Anderson O'Brien Fine Art
The Howell Gallery
Trailside Galleries
www.andrewpetersart.com

Julie Gilbert Pollard
Esprit Decor Gallery
Windrush Gallery
www.juliegilbertpollard.com

John Pototschnik
American Legacy Gallery
Cherry's Art Gallery
G. Stanton Gallery
Greenhouse Gallery of Fine Art
Rutledge Street Gallery
Southwest Gallery
www.pototschnik.com

Maggie Price
www.maggiepriceart.com

Stephen Quiller
Mission Gallery
Quiller Gallery
www.quillergallery.com

Don Rantz
Collector's Room
Ian Russell Gallery of Fine Art
www.donrantzfineart.com

David Rothermel
DR Fine Art
www.drfa-sf.com

John Salminen
American Legacy Gallery
San Marino Gallery
www.johnsalminen.com

Ed Sandoval
Studio de Colores Gallery
www.decoloresgallery.com

Tim Saternow
www.timsaternow.com

Aaron Schuerr
Betsy Swartz Fine Art
Legacy Gallery
Montana Trails Gallery
www.aaronschuerr.com

Frank Serrano
New Gallery
Waterhouse Gallery
www.pleinairgallery.com

Valerie Shesko
Ann Tower Gallery
Greenwich House Gallery
vshesko@fuse.net

Fred Somers
Edgewood Orchard Galleries
Somers Studio and Gallery
SpiritOne Arts Center
www.fredericksomers.com

George Strickland
Trailside Galleries
www.georgestricklandstudio.com
www.p-a-p-a.com

Lauren Tilden
Artists' House Gallery
www.laurentilden.com

James Toogood
www.jamestoogood.com

Clive R. Tyler
Adelante! Gallery
Elk Horn Art Gallery
Evergreen Fine Art
Mary Williams Fine Arts
Saks Galleries
Settlers West Galleries
www.clivetyler.com

Karen Vance
Astoria Fine Art
Bozeman Trail Gallery
Elk Horn Art Gallery
Highlands Art Gallery
Saks Galleries
www.karenvanceart.com

Curt Walters
Nedra Matteucci Galleries
Trailside Galleries
www.curtwalters.com

Eric Wiegardt
Scott Milo Gallery
Wiegardt Studio Gallery
www.ericwiegardt.com

Teruko T. Wilde
Art Forte
Total Arts Gallery
www.terukowilde.com

Don Williams
Modern Arts Midwest
www.artistdonwilliams.com

Douglas Wiltraut
Cavalier Galleries
www.douglaswiltraut.com

Michael Workman
The Meyer East Gallery
www.meyereastgallery.com

Dinah K. Worman
Act I Gallery
Ann Korologos Gallery
M. A. Doran Gallery
www.dinahworman.com

Keiko Yasuoka & Duncan Simmons
Ambleside Gallery
Harris Gallery
National Art Services
www.2collaboratingartists.com

Bonus Materials

Enjoy more beautiful landscape paintings by several of these artists at ArtistsNetwork.com/Art-Journey-America

GALLERY LISTINGS

Act I Gallery
Taos, NM
www.actonegallery.com

Adelante! Gallery
Ashland, OR
Oklahoma City, OK
www.adelantegallery.com

Alan Klotz Gallery
New York, NY
www.klotzgallery.com

Altermann Galleries
Santa Fe, NM
www.altermann.com

Ambleside Gallery
Greensboro, NC
www.amblesidearts.com

American Legacy Gallery
Kansas City, MO
www.americanlegacygallery.com

Anderson O'Brien Fine Art
Omaha, NE
www.aobfineart.com

Ann Korologos Gallery
Basalt, CO
www.korologosgallery.com

Ann Nathan Gallery
Chicago, IL
www.annnathangallery.com

Ann Tower Gallery
Lexington, KY
www.anntowergallery.com

Argosy Gallery
Bar Harbor, ME
www.argosygallery.com

Ariana Gallery
Royal Oak, MI
www.arianagallery.com

Art Access Gallery
Bexley, OH
www.artaccessgallery.com

Art Forte
Seattle, WA
www.artforte.com

Artful Deposit Galleries
Bordentown City, NJ
www.theartfuldeposit.com

Artists' House Gallery
Philadelphia, PA
www.artistshouse.com

Astoria Fine Art
Jackson Hole, WY
www.astoriafineart.com

The Banks Gallery
New London, NH
www.thebanksgallerynewlondon.com

Beals & Abbate Fine Art
Santa Fe, NM
www.bealsandabbate.com

Betsy Swartz Fine Art
www.betsyswartzfineart.com

Bingham Gallery
Mt. Carmel, UT
www.binggallery.com

Bonfoey Gallery
Cleveland, OH
www.bonfoey.com

Bozeman Trail Gallery
Sheridan, WY
www.bozemantrailgallery.com

Brazos Fine Art
Taos, NM
www.brazosfineart.com

Bright Rain Gallery
Albuquerque, NM
www.brightraingallery.com

Buffalo Trail Gallery
Jackson Hole, WY
www.buffalotrailgallery.com

Carmel Fine Art
Carmel, CA
www.carmelfineart.biz

Cavalier Galleries
Greenwich, CT
Nantucket, MA
www.cavaliergalleries.com

Cherry's Art Gallery
Carthage, MO
www.cherrysartgallery.com

Claggett/Rey Gallery
Vail, CO
www.claggettrey.com

Coleman Fine Art
Charleston, SC
www.colemanfineart.com

Collector's Room
Arizona-Sonora Desert Museum
Tucson, AZ
www.desertmuseumgiftshop.com

Cooley Gallery
Old Lyme, CT
www.cooleygallery.com

Courtyard Gallery
Lindsborg, KS
www.courtyardgallery.com

Dawson Cole Fine Art
Laguna Beach, CA
www.dawsoncolefineart.com

Debra Huse Gallery
Balboa Island, CA
www.debrahusegallery.com

Dolphin Gallery
Kansas City, MO
www.thedolphingallery.com

DR Fine Art
Santa Fe, NM
www.drfa-sf.com

DSG Fine Art
Albuquerque, NM
www.dsg-art.com

Edgartown Art Gallery
Edgartown, MA
508.627.6227

Edgewood Orchard Galleries
Fish Creek, WI
www.edgewoodorchard.com

Elk Horn Art Gallery
Winter Park, CO
www.elkhorngallery.com

Esprit Decor Gallery
Phoenix, AZ
www.espritdecor.com

The Ethel Curry Gallery
Haliburton, Ontario Canada
www.theethelcurrygallery.com

Evergreen Fine Art
Evergreen, CO
www.evergreenfineart.com

The Fairmont Gallery
Sonoma, CA
www.fairmontgallery.com

Fenix Gallery
www.fenixgallery.com

The 5th Street Gallery
Cincinnati, OH
www.5thstreetgallery.com

Framed Image Fine Art
Moab, UT
www.framedimagemoab.com

Francesca Anderson Fine Art
Lexington, MA
781.862.0660

G. Stanton Gallery
Dallas, TX
214.361.9611

Galleria Silecchia
Sarasota, FL
www.galleriasilecchia.com

Gallery Elite
Carmel, CA
www.galleryelite.net

Gallery Henoch
New York, NY
www.galleryhenoch.com

Gallery MAR
Park City, UT
www.gallerymar.com

Gerald Peters Gallery
Santa Fe, NM
www.gpgallery.com

Germanton Art & Winery
Germanton, NC
www.germantongallery.com

Giacobbe-Fritz Fine Art
Santa Fe, NM
www.giacobbefritz.com

Glenn Cutter Gallery
Las Cruces, NM
www.glenncutterjewelers.com/gallery

Grapevine Gallery
Oklahoma City, OK
www.grapevinegalleryokc.com

Greenhouse Gallery of Fine Art
San Antonio, TX
www.greenhousegallery.com

Greenwich House Gallery
Cincinnati, OH
www.greenwichhousegallery.com

Haley & Steele
Boston, MA
www.haleyandsteele.com

Harris Gallery
Houston, TX
www.harrisgalleryhouston.com

Highlands Art Gallery
Chester, NJ
www.highlandsartgallery.com

Howard Portnoy Gallery
Carmel, CA
www.portnoygalleries.com

The Howell Gallery
Oklahoma City, OK
www.howellgallery.com

Huey's Fine Art
Santa Fe, NM

Ian Russell Gallery
Prescott, AZ
www.ianrussellart.com

InSight Gallery
Fredericksburg, TX
www.insightgallery.com

Jeffrey Leder Gallery
Long Island City, NY
www.jeffreyledergallery.com

Joellyn Duesberry Studios
Greenwood Village, CO
www.joellynduesberry.com

Keating Fine Art
Aspen, CO
www.keatinggallery.com

Kelley Galleries
Woodbury, MN
www.kelleygalleries.com

Knowlton Gallery
Lodi, CA
www.knowltongallery.com

Lanning Gallery
Sedona, AZ
www.lanninggallery.com

Lansing Art Gallery
Lansing, MI
www.lansingartgallery.org

Legacy Gallery
Scottsdale, AZ
www.legacygallery.com

Los Gatos Museums Gallery
Los Gatos, CA
www.museumsoflosgatos.org

M Gallery of Fine Art
Charleston, SC
www.mgalleryoffineart.com

M. A. Doran Gallery
Tulsa, OK
www.madorangallery.com

Manitou Galleries
Santa Fe, NM
www.manitougalleries.com

Marigold Arts
Santa Fe, NM
www.marigoldarts.com

Marine Arts Gallery
Salem, MA
www.marineartsgallery.com

Marty Walker Gallery
Dallas, TX
www.martywalkergallery.com

Mary Williams Fine Arts
Boulder, CO
www.marywilliamsfinearts.com

McBride Gallery
Annapolis, MD
www.mcbridegallery.com

Medicine Man Gallery
Tucson, AZ
www.medicinemangallery.com

The Meyer East Gallery
Santa Fe, NM
www.meyereastgallery.com

Meyer Gallery
Santa Fe, NM
www.meyergalleries.com

Mission Gallery
Taos, NM
575.758.2861

Mockingbird Gallery
Bend, OR
www.mockingbird-gallery.com

Modern Arts Midwest
Lincoln, NE
www.modernartsmidwest.com

Montana Trails Gallery
Bozeman, MT
www.montanatrails.com

Morris & Whiteside Gallery
Hilton Head Island, SC
www.morriswhiteside.com

Mountain Trails Galleries
Sedona, AZ
www.mountaintrails.com

National Art Services
Houston, TX
www.nationalartservices.net

Navarro Gallery
Sedona, AZ
www.navarrogallerysedona.com

Nedra Matteucci Galleries
Santa Fe, NM
www.matteucci.com

New Gallery
Dallas, TX
www.newgallerydallas.com

New Masters Gallery
Carmel, CA
www.newmastersgallery.com

North Water Gallery
Edgartown, MA
www.northwatergallery.com

Nunnery's at Gallery 119
Jackson, MS
www.gallery119.net

Parsons Gallery of the West
Taos, NM
www.parsonswest.com

Peninsula Gallery
Sidney, BC Canada
www.pengal.com

Pierson Gallery
Tulsa, OK
www.bostonavenueframetheavenuestudio.com

Quiller Gallery
Creede, CO
www.quillergallery.com

RARE Gallery of Fine Art
Jackson Hole, WY
www.raregalleryjacksonhole.com

Redfern Gallery
Laguna Beach, CA
www.redferngallery.com

Rehs Galleries
New York, NY
www.rehs.com

James J. Rieser Fine Art
Carmel, CA
www.rieserfineart.com

River Street Studio
Sandwich Village, MA
www.3riverstreetstudio.com

Roger's Gardens
Corona del Mar, CA
www.rogersgardens.com

Rutledge Street Gallery
Camden, SC
www.rutledgestreetgallery.com

16 Patton Fine Art
Asheville, NC
www.16patton.com

Saks Galleries
Denver, CO
www.saksgalleries.com

San Marino Gallery
Pasadena, CA
www.sanmarinogallery.com

Sanders Galleries
Tucson, AZ
www.sandersgalleries.com

Scott Milo Gallery
Anacortes, WA
www.scottmilo.com

Scottsdale Fine Art
Scottsdale, AZ
www.scottsdalefineart.com

Sekula's Fine Art & Antiques
Sacramento, CA
www.sekulas.com

Settlers West Galleries
Tucson, AZ
www.settlerswest.com

Simpson Gallagher Gallery
Cody, WY
www.simpsongallaghergallery.com

Somers Studio and Gallery
Northfield, MN
www.fredericksomers.com

Southwest Gallery
Dallas, TX
www.swgallery.com

SpiritOne Arts Center
Wayzata, MN
www.spiritonearts.com

Strecker-Nelson Gallery
Manhattan, KS
www.strecker-nelsongallery.com

Stremmel Gallery
Reno, NV
www.stremmelgallery.com

Studio de Colores Gallery
Taos, NM
www.decoloresgallery.com

Studio Escondido
Taos, NM
www.kevinmacpherson.com

Sunset Art Gallery
Amarillo, TX
www.sunsetartgalleryofamarillo.com

Sunset River Marketplace Gallery
Calabash, NC
www.sunsetrivermarketplace.com

Suttons Bay Galleries
Suttons Bay, MI
www.suttonsbaygalleries.com

Sylvan Gallery
Charleston, SC
www.thesylvangallery.com

Synchronicity Gallery
Glen Arbor, MI
www.synchronicitygallery.com

Third Canyon Gallery
Denver, CO
www.thirdcanyongallery.com

Traditions Fine Art
www.traditionsfineart.com

Trailside Galleries
Jackson Hole, WY
www.trailsidegalleries.com

Travis Gallery
New Hope, PA
www.travisgallery.com

Total Arts Gallery
Taos, NM
www.totalartsgallery.com

Valley House Gallery
Dallas, TX
www.valleyhouse.com

Ventana Fine Art
Santa Fe, NM
www.ventanafineart.com

Vertical Peaks Fine Art
Jackson, WY
www.verticalpeaksfineart.com

Viewpoints Gallery
Los Altos, CA
www.viewpointsgallery.com

Village Gallery
Lahaina, Maui, HI
www.villagegalleriesmaui.com

Vose Galleries
Boston, MA
www.vosegalleries.com

Wadle Galleries Ltd.
Santa Fe, NM
www.wadlegalleries.com

Waterhouse Gallery
Santa Barbara, CA
www.waterhousegallery.com

Watts Fine Art
Zionsville, IN
www.wattsfineart.com

Weems Galleries
Albuquerque, NM
www.weemsgallery.com

Western Canadian Fine Art
Prince George, BC Canada
www.greenwichworkshop.com

Wiegardt Studio Gallery
Ocean Park, WA
www.ericwiegardt.com

Wilcox Gallery
Jackson, WY
www.wilcoxgallery.com

William A. Karges Fine Art
Beverly Hills, CA
Carmel, CA
www.kargesfineart.com

Windrush Gallery
Sedona, AZ
www.windrushgallery.com

Windsor Fine Art
New Orleans, LA
www.windsorfineart.com

Wynne/Falconer Gallery
Chatham, MA
www.wynne-falconergallery.com

Art Journey America: Landscapes. Copyright © 2011 by F+W Media, Inc. Manufactured in China. All rights reserved. No part of this book may be reproduced in any form or by any electronic or mechanical means including information storage and retrieval systems without permission in writing from the publisher, except by a reviewer who may quote brief passages in a review. Published by North Light Books, an imprint of F+W Media, Inc., 10150 Carver Rd., Blue Ash, Ohio, 45242. (800) 289-0963. First edition.

NOTE: The copyrights to the paintings in this book are held by the individual artists. No painting may be reproduced in any form without prior written permission from the artist.

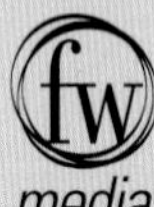

Other fine North Light Books are available from your favorite bookstore, art supply store or online supplier. Visit our website at www.fwmedia.com.

15 14 13 12 11 5 4 3 2 1

DISTRIBUTED IN CANADA BY FRASER DIRECT
100 Armstrong Avenue
Georgetown, ON, Canada L7G 5S4
Tel: (905) 877-4411

DISTRIBUTED IN THE U.K. AND EUROPE BY
F&W MEDIA INTERNATIONAL, LTD
Brunel House, Forde Close, Newton Abbot, TQ12 4PU, UK
Tel: (+44) 1626 323200, Fax: (+44) 1626 323319
Email: enquiries@fwmedia.com

DISTRIBUTED IN AUSTRALIA BY CAPRICORN LINK
P.O. Box 704, S. Windsor NSW, 2756 Australia
Tel: (02) 4577-3555

Edited by Kathryn Kipp
Cover design and interior layout by Clare Finney
Interior designed by Wendy Dunning
Production coordinated by Mark Griffin

About The Editor

Kathryn Kipp is an Acquisitions, Development and Content Editor for North Light Books and has enjoyed a career in publishing spanning 25 years. Formerly the Manager and Acquisitions Editor for North Light's Creative and Decorative Painting books, Kathryn has edited over 200 titles ranging in subject matter from home décor to classical portraiture, including many books on painting landscapes in watercolor, oil, acrylic, pen & ink, and pastel. Some of her previous titles include *Decorative Painting: A Classic Collection* and *The Best of Flower Painting*. A graduate of the University of Cincinnati, she lived in Los Angeles, California, for fifteen years where she worked in the entertainment and aerospace industries as a technical editor. Kathryn now resides in Cincinnati, Ohio.

Dedication

With love to Bill, Una, Tom, Betsy, Bob, Pat, Amy, Steve, David, Megan, Michael, Lauren and Isaac.

Acknowledgments

First and foremost, a huge round of applause for all the gifted artists who submitted their work for this book! Immensely talented and wonderfully creative, these artists have opened our eyes to the beauty and strength of the American landscape and made us even more grateful for the privilege of living here. Thank you!

I am also indebted to the editors of the following publications for their help and guidance, especially to Maureen Bloomfield for writing the exemplary Foreword to this book:

- Maureen Bloomfield, *The Artist's Magazine*
- Anne Hevener, *The Pastel Journal*
- Kelly Kane, *Watercolor Artist*
- Kristin Hoerth, *Southwest Art*
- Jill Johns, former publisher, *The Collector's Guide*

Special thanks to Colleen Franco, editor of *The Collector's Guide*, who kindly and patiently gave extra time and assistance to help bring this book to fruition.

Thanks also to freelance editor, Stefanie Laufersweiler, who has been through it all before and so graciously shared her knowledge and experience.

METRIC CONVERSION CHART

to convert	to	multiply by
inches	centimeters	2.54
centimeters	inches	0.4
feet	centimeters	30.5
centimeters	feet	0.03
yards	meters	0.9
meters	yards	1.1

INDEX

Abstract style, 112-113
 "contemporary landscape" and, 172-173
Acrylic paintings, 10-11, 32-33, 44-45, 72-73, 74-75, 86-87, 100-101, 116-117, 182-183
 and pastel, 142-143
Autumn scenes, 110-111, 136-137

Boats, 66-67, 108-109
Bridge, 112-113
Buildings, 52-53
 adobe, 70-71
 barns, 54-55, 64-65, 82-83, 166-167
 churches, 26-27, 146-147
 city, 144-145, 148-149, 162-163
 farm, 30-31
 farmhouse, 13
 Floridian, 42-43
 houses, 74-75, 134-135
 industrial, 22-23, 112-113
Bushes, 58-59

Canvas. *See* Painting surfaces
Canyon, 84-85, 140-141, 154-155
Cars, 134-135, 144-145, 148-149
Cemetery, 26-27, 176-177
City scenes, 148-149
 French Quarter, 52-53
 industrial, 20-21, 22-23
 streetscape, 144-145, 162-163
Clouds, 52-53, 102-103, 124-125, 160-161, 172-173
Cows, 180-181

Desert, 122-123, 124-125
Dock, 66-67

Expressionism, 146-147
 Taos, 56-57

Farms, 30-31, 64-65, 82-83, 180-181
 coastal, 178-179
Fields, 50-51, 74-75, 82-83, 96-97, 98-99, 104-105
 See also Meadows
Flowers, 74-75, 114-115
 hollyhocks, 70-71
 meadow, 104-105, 182-183
 mountain pinks, 176-177
Forest, 164-165
 wildflowers, 92–93

Glaciers, 130-131
Goats, mountain, 118-119
Gold leaf, 156-157
Grasses, 27, 30-31, 34-35, 50-51, 72-73, 76-77, 86-87, 112-113, 114-115
 See also Marsh, Rushes

Hills, 106-107
 coastal, 86-87
 and marsh, 38-39
 red rock, 58-59
Horse, 56-57
Human figures, 126-127, 134-135, 146-147

Impressionistic style, 18-19, 26-27, 66-67, 82-83, 168-169
 "contemporary landscape" and, 172-173
 and photorealism, 102-103
 and realism, 158-159
India ink, 58-59

Landscape, 18-19
 See also Autumn scenes, City scenes, Fields, Grasses, Hills, Meadows, Mesa, Mountains, Pasture, Roadway, Rocks, Trees, Valley, Waterscapes, Winter scenes
Leaves, 100-101
Light
 and humidity, 144-145
 and shadow, 138-139
Linen. *See* painting surfaces

Marsh, 38-39
 See also Rushes
Meadows, 72-73, 114-115, 182-183
Mesa, 122-123, 128-129
Mixed media, 154-155
Monument Valley, 168-169
Moonlight, 146 147
Mountains, 92-93, 104-105, 118-119, 120-121, 130-131, 150-151, 152-153
 distant, 112-113, 136-137, 142-143
 red rock, 24-25
 and valley, 14-15
 See also Glaciers, Hills, Rocks

Night scene, 142-143, 146-147
 headlights, 174-175

Ocean. *See* Waterscapes
Oil paintings, 8-9, 12-13, 14-15, 16-17, 18-19, 20-21, 22-23, 24-25, 28-29, 34-35, 38-39, 40-41, 46-47, 48-49, 50-51, 56-57, 60-61, 62-63, 68-69, 70-71, 76-77, 78-79, 94-95, 96-97, 104-105, 108-109, 112-113, 118-119, 120-121, 122-123, 124-125, 126-127, 130-131, 134-135, 146-147, 150-151, 152-153, 158-159, 160-161, 166-167, 168-169, 172-173, 178-179
Orchards, vineyard, 32-33

Painterly style, loose, 70-71

Painting surfaces
 Arches paper, 82-83, 148-149
 archival board, 106-107
 artist's sanded paper, 80-81
 Canson paper, 156-157
 canvas, 12-13, 20-21, 22-23, 46-47, 48-49, 60-61, 62-63, 68-69, 86-87, 94-95, 96-97, 104-105, 116-117, 124-125, 132-133, 168-169, 172-173
 coarse linen mounted on board, 122-123
 linen, 14-15, 18-19, 24-25, 34-35, 38-39, 40-41, 56-57, 152-153, 166-167
 linen mounted to panel, 50-51, 178-179
 museum board, 110-111
 panel, 8-9, 16-17, 28-29, 100-101, 160-161
 paper, 42-43
 rag paper, 64-65
 sanded paper, 90-91, 98-99, 164-165
 Wallis paper, 140-141
 watercolor paper, 44-45
Panel. *See* Painting surfaces
Park, 48-49
Pastels, 26-27, 30-31, 88-89, 52-53, 54-55, 92-93, 106-107, 110-111, 114-115, 136-137, 140-141, 174-175, 180-181
 and acrylics, 142-143
 black and white, 102-103
 soft, 80-81, 90-91, 98-99, 164-165
 with 22-karat gold leaf, 156-157
Pasture, 166-167
Photorealism, and impressionism, 102-103
Plateau, 168-169
Poetic style, 120-121
Power station, 22-23
Prairie, 76-77

Rain, 128-129
 See also Storm, Virga
Realism, 34-35, 44-45, 62-63, 80-81, 84-85, 92-93, 152-153
 "contemporary landscape" and, 172-173
 and impressionism, 158-159
 loose, 60-61
 trompe l'oeil, 100-101
Representational style, 12-13, 58-59, 104-105, 140-141
 abstract, 42-43
 impressionistic, 54-55
River. *See* Waterscapes
Roadway, 46-47, 136-137, 174-175
Rocks, 120-121, 132-133
 coastal, 36-37, 90-91, 158-159
 red, 24-25, 58-59
 sandstone walls, 84-85
 and waterfall, 78-79
 See also Hills; Mountains; Waterscapes, rocky shore
Rushes, 62-63

Shadow, 138-139, 148-149
Snow, 8-9, 12-13, 24-25, 28-29, 46-47, 48-49, 68-69, 88-89, 138-139, 150-151
Spring scene, 166-167, 182-183
Stars, 142-143
Storm, 51-52, 170-171
Surrealism, 22-23

Tonalism, 178-179
Trees, 34-35, 44-45, 48-49, 50-51, 56-57, 64-65, 68-69, 72-73, 74-75, 80-81, 88-89, 94-95, 106-107, 110-111, 114-115, 118-119, 126-127, 130-131, 132-133, 134-135, 136-137, 150-151, 160-161, 166-167, 172-173, 182-183
 aspen, 138-139, 164-165
 cottonwood, 92-93
 palm, 42-43
 poplar, 92-93
 willow, 98-99
 See also Bushes, Forest

Valley
 industrial, 20-21
 and mountains, 14-15
Vineyard, 32-33
Virga, 122-123

Water, 42-43
Watercolor paintings, 36-37, 58-59, 64-65, 66-67, 84-85, 132-133, 148-149, 162-163, 170-171, 176-177
 and mixed media, 128-129
 transparent, 42-43, 82-83, 144-145
Watermedia, 138-139
Waterscapes
 alpine lake, 130-131
 bay, 66-67, 108-109
 creek, 68-69, 132-133
 lake scene, 8-9
 lily pond, 56-57
 ocean, 86-87, 90-91, 158-159
 river, 28-29, 34-35, 44-45, 58-59, 88-89, 102-103, 112-113, 152-153
 rocky shore, 16-17, 36-37, 40-41
 stream, 150-151
 surf, 170-171
 waterfall, 10-11, 78-79, 126-127
Winter scenes, 8-9, 12-13, 24-25, 28-29, 46-47, 68-69, 88-89, 138-139
 city, 144-145
 field, 50-51

IDEAS. INSTRUCTION. INSPIRATION

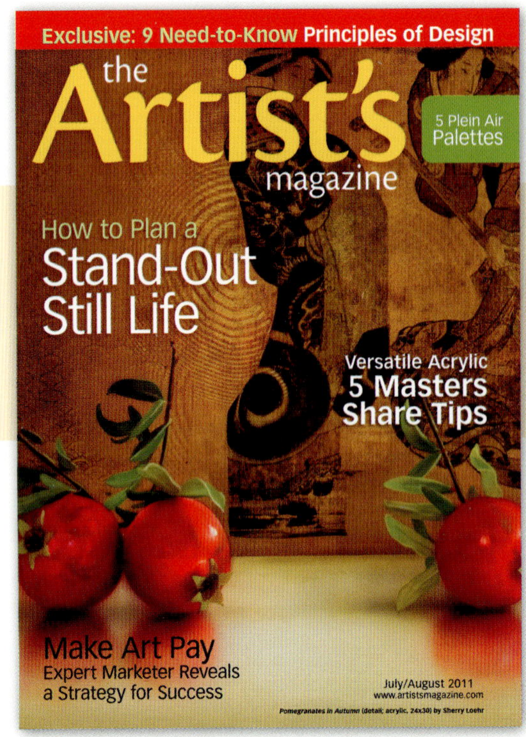

Receive **FREE** downloadable ***bonus materials*** when you sign up for our free newsletter at artistsnetwork.com/Newsletter_Thanks.

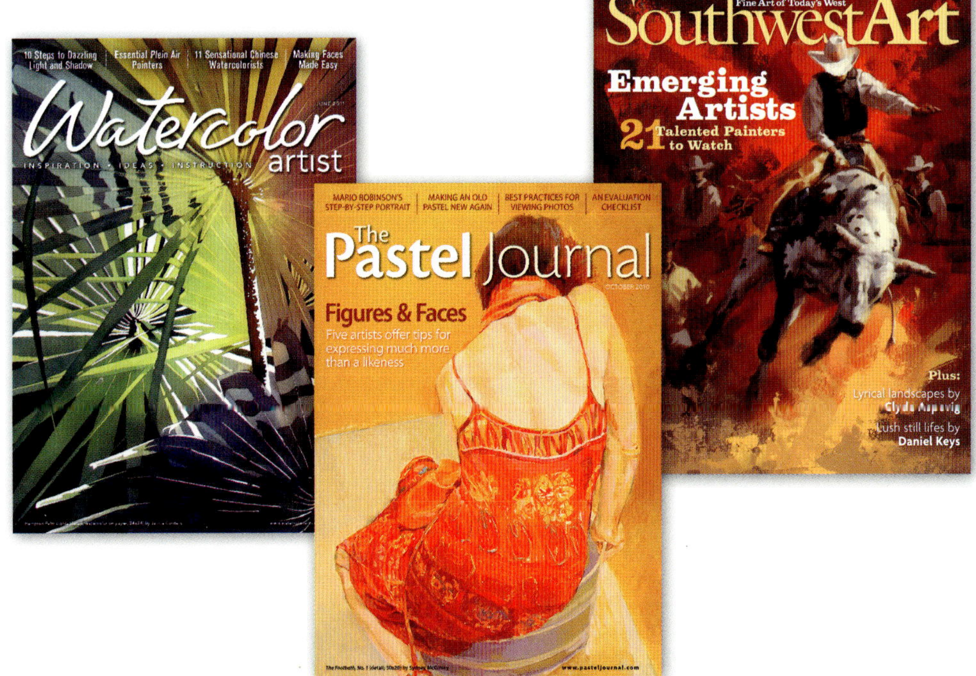

These and other fine F+W Media products are available at your local art & craft retailer, bookstore or online supplier. Visit our websites at artistsnetwork.com and artistsnetwork.tv.

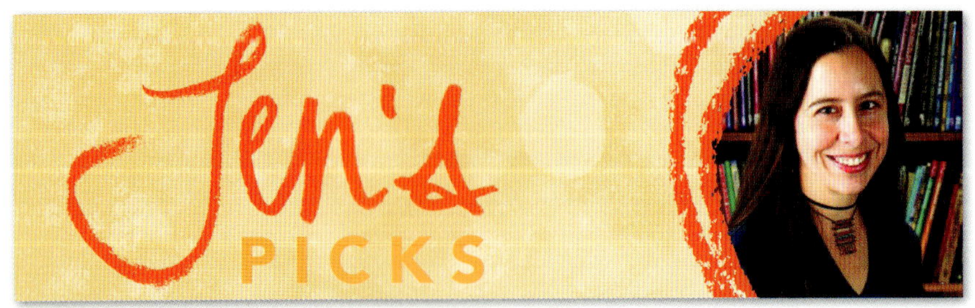

Visit artistsnetwork.com and get Jen's North Light Picks!

Get free step-by-step demonstrations along with reviews of the latest books, videos and downloads from Jennifer Lepore, Senior Editor and Online Education Manager at North Light Books.